RE/USES

RE/USES

2133 Ways to RECYCLE and REUSE the Things You Ordinarily Throw Away

CAROLYN JABS

Line drawings by Robert Duffek

CROWN PUBLISHERS, INC. ★ NEW YORK

ILLUSTRATION CREDITS

Page vii, National Center of Appropriate Technology; page viii, from United States War Production Board pamphlet "Scrap and How to Collect It," ca. 1943; page 5, photo: Documerica; page 6, *top and bottom*, reprinted from *The Lamps and Lighting Book* by Thelma Newman, by permission of Crown Publishers, Inc.; page 10, reprinted from *Pedal Power* by James McCullough, by permission of Rodale Press, Inc.; page 14, *left and right*, courtesy Clivus Multrum; page 15, reprinted from *Art from Found Materials* by Mary L. Stribling, by permission of Crown Publishers, Inc.; page 18, courtesy American Paper Institute; page 19, *top and center*, reprinted from *Nomadic Furniture* by James Hennessey and Victor Papanell, by permission of Pantheon Books, Inc.; page 21, courtesy American Paper Institute; page 24, photo: Wayne McCall; page 25, photo: Larry Pacilio; page 28, courtesy Weed Eater; page 29, *top and bottom*, courtesy Pierce Products; page 30, courtesy Campbell's Soup; page 32, courtesy The Recycler, Inc.; page 33, courtesy Can Manufacturers Institute; page 34, courtesy Buckminster Fuller Archives; page 37, reprinted from *Creations with Rug Remnants* by Betty Rayside, by permission of Crown Publishers, Inc.; page 38, *top*, photo: G. Murrell; page 38, *bottom*, courtesy National Association of Recycling Industries; page 39, *top*, courtesy Oak Ridge National Laboratory; page 39, *center and bottom*, courtesy SITE; page 46, courtesy Perma-Brew; page 52, courtesy City of Los Angeles; page 57, drawings by Carolyn Jabs; page 60, reprinted from *Rags* by Linda and Stella Allison, by permission of Crown Publishers, Inc.; page 62, reprinted from *Pantyhose Craft Book* by Jean Ray Laury and Joyce Aiken, by permission of Taplinger Publishing Company, Inc.; page 63, *top and bottom*, reprinted from *Styroflyers* by Platt Montfort, by permission of Random House, Inc.; page 66, photo: Carolyn Jabs; page 71, photo: Carolyn Jabs; page 75, reprinted from *Rags* by Linda and Stella Allison, by permission of Crown Publishers, Inc.; page 76, photo: courtesy Hazel Pearson Handicrafts © 1974; page 80, United States Department of Health and Human Services; page 82, courtesy Justin Kramer, Inc.; page 84, *top and center*, photos: Clara Wheldon, used by permission of the Institute of Scrap Iron and Steel, Inc.; page 84, *bottom*, courtesy Glass Container Manufacturers Institute; page 85, National Center of Appropriate Technology; page 87, courtesy Glass Container Manufacturers Institute; page 91, courtesy L'Eggs Products, Inc.; page 92, courtesy Mount Vernon Museum of Incandescent Lighting; page 96, courtesy Institute of Scrap Iron and Steel, Inc.; page 97, photo: Neal Chisolm, used by permission of Pelham Journal; page 98, courtesy Playper Corporation; page 101, reprinted from *Art from Found Materials* by Mary L. Stribling, by permission of Crown Publishers, Inc.; page 102, *top*, reprinted from *Oldies But Goodies* by Donna Lawson, by permission of Butterick Publishing Co.; page 102, *bottom*, courtesy NASCO; page 103, reprinted from *Woman's Day* by permission of CBS Publications, Inc.; page 104, courtesy National Association of Recycling Industries; page 106, courtesy Transition Graphics; page 107, *left and right*, photo: John Habraken; page 108, photos: Documerica; page 109, courtesy American Paper Institute; page 110, courtesy American Paper Institute; page 120, reprinted from *Art from Found Materials* by Mary L. Stribling, by permission of Crown Publishers, Inc.; page 121, reprinted from *Clothing Liberation* by Laura Torbet, by permission of Ballantine Books, Inc.; page 125, courtesy Oak Ridge Laboratories; page 128, reprinted from *Woman's Day*, by permission of CBS Publications, Inc.; page 130, courtesy Toobee Toys, Inc.; page 131, *top right*, photo courtesy Hazel Pearson Handicrafts © 1975; page 131, *bottom left*, courtesy Reynolds Aluminum; page 132, photo: Documerica; page 134, photo courtesy Hazel Pearson Handicraft © 1977; page 135, reprinted from *The Pantyhose Craft Book* by Jean Ray Laury and Joyce Aiken, by permission of Taplinger Publishing Company, Inc.; page 136, photo: Ellen-Weber from *The Passionate Collector*, by permission of Simon and Schuster; page 139, *top and bottom*, courtesy Playground Clearinghouse, Inc.; page 140, photo: Richard Gray; page 141, courtesy Goodyear Tire and Rubber Company; page 145, reprinted from *Oldies But Goodies* by Donna Lawson, by permission of Butterick Publishing Co.; page 155, cartoon by Alan Pratt, by permission of *Seattle Times*; page 161, courtesy Recycling & Conservation, Inc.; page 162, Transition Graphics; page 164, courtesy United States Bureau of Mines; page 167, United States Environmental Protection Agency; page 168, United States Bureau of Mines; page 169, United States Bureau of Mines; page 174, courtesy Institute of Scrap Iron and Steel, Inc.

Copyright © 1982 by Carolyn Jabs
Line drawings copyright © 1982 by Robert Duffek

All rights reserved. No part of this book may be reproduced or transmitted in any form or by any means electronic or mechanical, including photocopying, recording, or by any information storage and retrieval system, without permission in writing from the publisher.

Published by Crown Publishers, Inc., One Park Avenue, New York, New York 10016 and simultaneously in Canada by General Publishing Company Limited

Manufactured in the United States of America

Library of Congress Cataloging in Publication Data

Jabs, Carolyn.
Re/Uses: 2133 ways to reuse and recycle the things you ordinarily throw away.

1. Home economics.
2. Recycling (Waste, etc.)
I. Title.
TX147.J3 1982   640   81-17378
ISBN: 0-517-546639   AACR2
   0-517-54363X (paper)
Book design by Camilla Filancia
10 9 8 7 6 5 4 3 2 1
First Edition

Contents

Acknowledgments

Ideas that go into a book like this come from so many sources that the thanks due everyone concerned could require a short book. In addition to those mentioned in the text, I'm grateful to all the organizations, corporations, and individuals who contributed suggestions and source materials. I'm also indebted to countless anonymous tinkerers who invented those many reuses that are now established classics.

Thanks also go to many behind-the-scenes people who made it possible for me to convert files bulging with ideas into a book. Among them, I include my parents, who instilled in me the thrifty values in which this book is grounded; DZ, who's always been able to make me believe I can do what I want to do; my agent, Bobbe Siegel, who rescued this project at the eleventh hour; Naomi Kleinberg, who helped with innumerable details; Rosemary Baer, who steered the book through the complex production process; and designer Camilla Filancia, who brought the pages to life. But the greatest thanks is due Nach Waxman, my editor, who contributed the original idea as well as the insight and stamina to see it through to completion.

Introduction

How much did you throw away today? If you're like most people, you'll have to think for a moment before you answer that question. Most of us are so casual about throwing things away that we aren't even aware of the Styrofoam cup from the morning coffee, the ballpoint pen that stopped writing, or the sock with the hole in the toe.

If we did try to record what goes into the wastebasket each and every day, the list would be shocking. Though Americans represent only 5 percent of the world's population, they produce over half its waste. In one day we generate enough trash to fill the New Orleans Superdome—twice. And you, if you're average, throw away in that one day almost four pounds of stuff, ranging from lawn clippings to the envelopes in the day's mail.

The idea of being wasteful makes many of us uncomfortable. Yet most of us continue to waste because we can't think of anything better to do with last year's

GROWTH OF GARBAGE

AVERAGE AMOUNT OF PAPER USED IN ☆ U.S. ☆ BY 1 (ONE) PERSON ANNUALLY

1900
58
lbs.

1973
639
lbs.

920 lbs. PAPER

140 lbs. FOOD & YARD WASTES

200 lbs. GLASS

160 lbs. METALS

140 lbs. WOOD

140 lbs. CLOTH, RUBBER PLASTIC, LEATHER

= 1 TON GARBAGE

★ MAKING ★ GARBAGE

An analysis of the American garbage can is sobering. In a study of residential garbage, University of Arizona students learned that in one year the average household in Tucson throws away 500 bottles, 1,800 plastic items, 850 steel cans, 500 aluminum cans, and more than 13,000 individual items of paper and cardboard. Even more startling, 8 percent of the garbage in most households was edible food.

> When an article is worn out, obsolete or otherwise useless—it is still far from worthless. Then it becomes "Scrap" and scrap is one of America's most vital needs today.
>
> For this "Scrap"—the miscellaneous junk that clutters basements and lies around farms and factories—is actually a raw material. And it is necessary in the forging of Victory.
>
> —Government pamphlet published during World War II

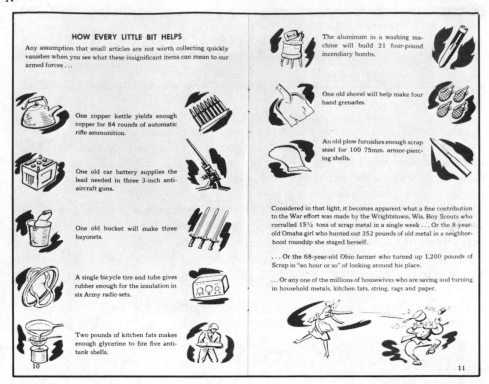

phone book, a bunch of empty soda cans, or a sweater with holes in the sleeves. We're conditioned to think of things that are old, empty, worn, or broken as useless, so we throw them away without much thought.

RE/USES tries to help you break through that conditioning. It starts with the assumption that the used material that flows through our lives could be a resource instead of a nuisance. Waste, after all, is in the eye of the beholder. So if we look, really look, at the things we've been throwing away, we can learn to see them as raw materials that can be reused to solve everyday problems and satisfy everyday needs.

RE/USES is part of a thrifty American tradition. During the Revolution, the patriots of Bowling Green, New York, recycled a statue of George III into bullets. One hundred years ago housewives looked forward to an annual visit from the itinerant scrap peddlar who bought up old pots and pans. During World War II children were mobilized to carry out scrap drives, collecting everything from newspapers and tin cans to animal fat and metal foil to help the nation's war effort.

Though recognition of scrap materials as a national resource declined after the war, many people have continued to use waste materials as a private resource. Some are string savers who simply can't bear to throw anything away. Others are putterers who like to spend their spare time making something out of nothing. Still others are incurable accumulators who believe everything will prove useful sooner or later. Almost everyone has something that they can't throw away, even though it's outlived its original usefulness.

Most of us, however, haven't even begun to exploit the resources in our trash, and the consequences of our waste are beginning to catch up with us. Landfills are overflowing, making trash disposal a critical, and costly, problem in most communities. Careless disposal of hazardous wastes over the past decades is now polluting ground water and contaminating land. Ever higher prices are being paid to import virgin raw materials while the same resources lie neglected in our dumps. This last problem in particular has awakened us to the fact that waste itself may be a resource. Now we must adjust our public policies and personal habits to reflect these facts.

The adjustment need not be painful. Once we have abandoned the idea that trash is something to be put out of sight as quickly as possible, then we're free to experiment with RE/USES. There are three big rewards:

First, RE/USES save money. Instead of spending money on the things you want and need, spend imagination. Do you want a tote bag, a camping stove, a terrarium? Make them from a pair of pants, a coffee can, a liter soda bottle. When you have a household problem, solve it with resources you already have rather than rushing out to buy still more goods. On a larger scale, communities can save and even make money by recycling waste materials or converting them into energy. And many consumer products would cost less if the nation as a whole treated trash as a native resource rather than paying premium prices to import raw materials.

Second, RE/USES conserve resources. Given that our planet is a closed system with finite supplies of oil, metal, and other vital substances, conservation is the only rational policy. Instead of debating about whether our supplies of one or another natural resource will last ten or one hundred years, it makes more sense to use—and reuse—everything as wisely as we can. Much as we need to initiate large-scale efforts to recover wasted resources, each of us can contribute by developing a reuse reflex and getting into the habit of asking ourselves, "What else can I do with that broken chair, that old appliance, that worn jacket?" By inventing RE/USES we learn to appreciate basic materials such as wood, metal, and fabric. This appreciation, in turn, makes us more respectful of the complex processes that make those materials available to us.

Third, RE/USES satisfy the human urge to make things. Creating what you want from what you have is an unusually rewarding form of self-reliance. Even if you have never been much of a tinkerer, the fact that discarded materials are "free" liberates you to experiment until you find the RE/USES that work for you.

RE/USES is based on the assumption that people can and should take responsibility for the waste they create. This doesn't mean an obsessive preoccupation with every can you throw away. It does mean considering each discard as a potential resource, rather than automatically dismissing it as mere trash. This book is part of that process, a brainstorming collection of tips and hints, projects and possibilities. It includes both do-it-now ideas for individuals and reuses that call for community-wide cooperation. It poses the basic question about trash, "Is that all there is?" and answers it with a decisive "No!"

Part I.
HOUSEHOLD RESOURCES:

What to Do with Everything You Ordinarily Throw Away

Moment of Truth at the Trash Can

It happens every day. You stand beside the garbage can holding something that has outlived its original purpose and weighing its value. Is it trash? Or is it a household resource? The Recycler's Encyclopedia that follows should tip more objects into the resource category. It includes more than one hundred fifty common throwaways, selected either because they are ubiquitous (cans and bottles) or because throwing them away seems to be especially traumatic (eyeglasses and shoes). The entries are organized alphabetically so you can look up the object whose fate is in your hands.

The entries also suggest an alternate way of looking at the Things that flow through our lives. Instead of dismissing a possible throwaway because it's outlived its original purpose, *Re/Uses* concentrates on its underlying qualities and invents new purposes. Rather than buying more and more, we can uncover new ways to build what we need out of what we have. We can replace contempt for trash with appreciation for it as a household resource.

Of course, virtually none of us can use all the resources that pass through our lives, and Part II of this book suggests ways in which we, as citizens, can help our communities cope more creatively with trash. As with many social movements, however, a new approach to trash begins at home. If you start looking—really looking—at the things you throw away, chances are you'll be surprised by the many uses for objects you once dismissed as useless.

Some reuses are classics, and they are described once at the outset in the Recycler's Hall of Fame. The rest of the encyclopedia contains hundreds of ideas gleaned from people, publications, and personal experience. Although the emphasis is on practical ideas that solve household problems, no one will find all of them equally useful. An idea that's good for one reader may strike another as outlandish, tacky, or just too much trouble. Nonetheless, most of these suggestions save time and/or money.

Far from being the final word, our suggestions should stimulate your own ideas about the objects you find around you. The best reuses are often highly personal, responding to circumstances and situations that no one can anticipate. If this book fulfills its purpose, you will seize upon specific ideas and shape them to the needs of the moment and the materials at hand.

> *The true economy of housekeeping is gathering up the fragments so nothing is lost. . . . Nothing should be thrown away as long as it is possible to make any use of it, however trifling that use may be.*
> —Mrs. Lydia Childs,
> *The American Frugal Housewife*

Keeping Trash Out of the House

Anyone who makes a conscientious effort to recycle what he or she used to throw away will at first be staggered by the sheer volume. The average person produces three to five pounds of trash per day. If you're serious about *Re/Uses,* you'll also want to cut down on the amount of waste you produce by becoming a waste-conscious consumer. Even before you buy a product, think about the speed with which it will become waste. It would be paralyzing to consider the disposability of every purchase, but these guidelines will help.

Take a hard look at what you buy. Ask yourself, do I need it? Will I use it? Could I make it out of materials I already have?

Buy products with a long life span. Look for appliances that can be repaired. Shop for "classic" well-made clothes. When possible, select packages that can be reused.

Buy large packages. Things cost less that way and you'll have only one package to recycle instead of several. Obviously, the rule backfires if you buy more than you can use and part spoils.

Look for alternatives to paper products. Try using cloth napkins instead of paper, regular dishes instead of paper cups and plates, rags made from outworn clothing instead of paper towels, handkerchiefs instead of tissues, and so on.

Avoid excess packaging. Some manufacturers think consumers are impressed by bottles packaged in boxes that are wrapped in cellophane. Prove them wrong. Buy another brand whenever possible.

Buy refillable containers whenever possible. Find a supermarket that sells returnable bottles for beer, soda, and/or milk. When purchasing other containers, buy bottles and cans that can be recycled instead of plastic that can't.

Encourage stores to sell unpackaged merchandise. Buy clothes off the rack, fruits and vegetables loose, and ballpoint pens without packaging. Tell store managers you like unpackaged merchandise because you can examine it more closely.

Don't buy disposable products. Instead of disposable pens, lighters, razors, and other small objects, purchase their refillable relatives.

Buy recycled products whenever you can. Many recycled products—motor oil, fabric, paper products—mention their origins on the label. By purchasing such products you help create a market for scrap materials.

Make your preferences known. Consumers do influence product trends by "voting with their dollars," but direct communication often gets quicker results. If you want your favorite supermarket to identify products packaged in recycled materials, ask the manager. If you'd like to see returnable bottles made mandatory in your state, write to your legislators. If you find a product or package wasteful, write to the company and get your friends and neighbors to do the same.

Waste is simply some useful substance we do not have the wit to use.
—Athelstan Spilhaus

America is simply running out of room for its trash.

★ RECYCLER'S HALL OF FAME: ★ SIX WORKS-EVERY-TIME IDEAS FOR RECYCLING ALMOST ANYTHING

The six objects that follow are practical, necessary items that can be made from almost anything. In short, they are a recycler's dream, an excuse for keeping, and even accenting, any favorite thing that is just too cute, old, remarkable, or outrageous to throw away.

Lamps. People have made track lights out of soup cans, reading lamps out of stovepipe elbows, table lamps out of wine bottles, and lamp shades out of plastic cups. Two rules: A lamp base should be heavy enough so it won't tip over; a lamp shade should be large enough so it doesn't touch the light bulb and start a fire. All the parts and directions for wiring a standard lamp are available in kits sold in hardware stores. For ideas about designing and wiring lamps, see *The Lamp and Lighting Book* by Thelma R. Newman (Crown Publishers, 1976).

Planters. Anything with a cavity in it can be a planter. That includes old shoes, toy wagons, tea tins, beer balls, and Styrofoam cups. If the object you want to use isn't leakproof, line it with a plastic container cut to the proper size (*see* PLASTIC CONTAINERS). Be sure there are drainage holes at the bottom of the planter, and add a few fragments of chipped crockery (*see* DISHES) to keep the dirt from falling out of the holes.

Bird Feeders. A bird feeder must be strong enough to support a bird and light enough to be suspended from a tree branch. Plenty of things fill the bill; ever-popular materials include frozen food containers, milk cartons, and fast food containers. If you don't know the preferences of your local birds, get expert advice in a free pamphlet called "Recycle for the Birds," available from the National Wildlife Federation, Dept. 60, 1412 16th Street NW, Washington, DC 20036.

Candleholder. A candleholder is nothing more than a pedestal for a candle, so you can make one out of anything that has a pleasing shape and enough weight so it won't topple over. Appealing possibilities include bottles, piano legs, and ham cans. If you need an anchor for a tall, thin taper, glue on a screw-on bottle cap. For a fat candle, drive a nail through the holder and press the candle onto its point.

Bank. A bank is a container with a hole in the top. Sometimes the hole is already there and sometimes you have to cut it. All empty containers are candidates, from pickle jars to bleach bottles. You'll probably have to break the bank to get the money out, so don't start putting your pennies in an heirloom.

Ashtray. Shallow containers seem to make the best ashtrays, but there aren't any firm rules. You can collect your ashes in a pot lid on a pedestal as well as in an empty aspirin tin. Just avoid wood and plastic.

Polystyrene cups, glued together, make a luminous lampshade.

RECYCLER'S ENCYCLOPEDIA:
What to Do with A—Z

A

ALUMINUM FOIL

See FOIL, ALUMINUM

APPLIANCES

See ELECTRICAL APPLIANCES

ASHES

The renaissance of wood heat means more people are facing the grimy task of taking out the ashes. But more than a few of us have also relearned old-time ways to reuse this byproduct of burning. To save your ashes, scoop them into a container—metal is best, in case there are hidden embers—and store them in a dry place. If you've been burning wood with nails in it, sift the ashes through loosely woven screen before trying projects like these:

GOOD THING FOR THE GARDEN. Ashes are 50 to 75 percent lime, which is used to control the pH level in soil. If you sprinkle your ashes evenly over the garden in the winter, you probably won't have to lime in the spring. As a bonus, your soil will get phosphorous, potash, and other trace elements.

PEST REPELLENT. Low ridges of ashes will repel slugs and snails in the garden. Circle individual plants and build embankments between the row crops.

ASH CAN TRACTION. Carry a box of ashes in the trunk of the car during the winter. The weight provides extra traction for the back tires, and if you get stuck, a shovel or two of ashes under the tires often gives the grip you need to get free.

STOVE CEMENT. Ashes can be the basis of a tough cement that's especially good for patching the lining of a wood stove or sealing joints between stovepipe and chimney. Mix 1 quart of fine ashes with a handful of salt and enough water to make a thick paste. Spread with a trowel.

★ SOOTABLE USES ★

Soot, the fine black dust that accumulates in chimneys and stovepipes, was called lampblack by our ancestors and has a number of uses. Mixed with soapy water, it makes perfectly serviceable black ink. Soot can also be used as pigment in other materials, such as paint, stove polish, and cement.

WHY LYE? Lye, an alkali so strong that it is caustic, was one of Grandmother's basic household supplies. It still has plenty of uses and can be made from leftover wood ashes. To make lye, drill holes in the bottom of a wooden or metal bucket or barrel—don't use plastic or aluminum. Fill the container about two thirds full of ashes and suspend it over a second container a little larger than the first. Fill the first container with water and let it leach through the ashes. When all the water has drained out of

the top bucket, pour it through a second time to strengthen the lye.

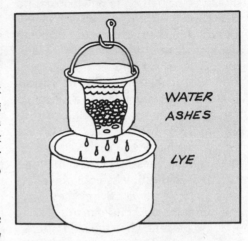

Lye is a very strong chemical that will eat through cloth, bristle brushes, rubber gloves, and skin. Keep it out of reach of children. If you do come in contact with lye, flush the skin immediately with lots of cold water. Homemade lye can be a component in soap (*see* FATS AND GREASE). It can also be used to clean toilet bowls (pour in a small amount and swab the sides of the bowl with a brush), open clogged drains (pour a tablespoonful into the drain and add a cup of hot water, wait five minutes, and run hot water to flush out the lye), and strip away old paint and varnish (apply diluted liquid lye to the furniture with a cotton dish mop, taking care that it doesn't splash on your skin. Allow it to sit for a few minutes until the paint softens. Then hose down the object. This operation should be done on a concrete floor with a drain.). The strength of homemade lye will vary depending upon the type of ashes you use, so always start by using less lye than you think you need and adding more if necessary.

AUTOMOBILES

See CARS

BABY THINGS

As long as baby things are usable, they should be passed on to new babies and their parents. This rule applies to everything from potty chairs to receiving blankets. If you don't know expectant parents who will buy or borrow your stuff, search them out. Put up notices describing what you have at Planned Parenthood, hospital obstetrics clinics, and the local Lamaze class. If you are lucky enough to live in a city with a shop that buys and resells baby items (and maternity clothes!), take your paraphernalia there. Most will take clothes, toys, and furniture on consignment, paying 40 to 50 percent when the item is sold.

BAGS

See PAPER BAGS; PLASTIC BAGS

BATTERIES

Americans own about 480 million battery-operated appliances, so we throw out millions of batteries every year. Unfortunately, there aren't many alternatives to that waste. The most commonly available batteries—carbon zinc—are designed to be discarded after discharging their current, and even gadgets that are supposed to recharge them can't extend their lives for long.

One promising alternative is nickel cadmium batteries, called NiCD, which can be recharged up to a thousand times. You have to make an initial investment in the charger—$10 to $20—and the batteries themselves are more expensive—about $2.50 for a standard C. On the other hand, you should recover that outlay after a few rechargings. Rechargeable batteries come in AA, C, D, and 9-volt sizes. Both batteries and rechargers are available at hardware stores or electronic equipment stores like Radio Shack.

And what do you do with the stash of dead batteries already in your dresser drawer? Here are a few suggestions:

DRAWING STICK. At the center of every carbon zinc battery there's a carbon rod. Carbon, of course, is the material of artist's charcoal and writing implements, so if you can liberate the stick of carbon, you have a free carbon crayon. Peel away the paper on the outside of the battery until you come to a metal canister. Pry the flat disc off the top of the canister and you'll see the tip of the carbon stick. Use pliers to pull the stick out of the battery, and remove the metal end.

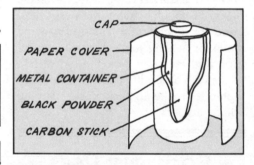

SOOT REMOVER. The canister at the core of small household batteries contains a black powder that is a mixture of manganese dioxide, carbon powder, ammonium chloride, and zinc chloride. These chemicals are similar to those in commercial powders designed to get rid of soot in chimneys. To get at the powder, put the unwrapped canister in a heavy bag and whack it with a hammer. Remove the bits of metal from the bag. Next time you're burning a hot fire in the wood stove or fireplace, toss in the bag. As the powder burns, it will create a chemical compound that reacts with and dissolves the creosote in the chimney. Two notes of caution: First, do not throw an unsmashed battery into the fire, because it will explode. Second, check your chimney for creosote after using this method, because its reliability depends upon the intensity of the fire, the kind of wood you burn, the direction of your chimney pipe, and other variables.

SECOND CHANCE. Sometimes "dead" batteries can be resurrected with this trick: Punch a small hole through the wall of the battery, using a nail and a hammer. Soak the battery for an hour in vinegar, dry it off, and close the hole with electrical tape. The battery should function for a few extra hours.

★ CALLING ★ ALL CARS

No one collects small household batteries for recycling because the materials in them are worth so little. Automobile batteries are another matter. Fifty percent of the lead used annually in the United States comes from old vehicle batteries. That may sound pretty good, but the industry estimates that the lead which is still being discarded could be converted into 60 million new batteries annually.

The moral of this story is recycle your car batteries. The average battery lasts three years and can be recycled over and over, since lead does not lose its essential properties. Often the dealer who sells you a new battery will offer to trade in the old one. If he doesn't, sell the battery directly to an auto parts supply dealer or a scrap dealer for $3 to $5.

BEER CANS

See SODA AND BEER CANS

BELTS

A good leather belt can often recover its rightful place in your wardrobe if you clean it with saddle soap and soften it with lanolin. A belt that can't go out in public anymore can be converted into a tool belt for puttering around the house—punch pairs of holes in the leather with a hammer and a nail and loop thick elastic through them. Tie the elastic in the back of the belt and slip hammers, trowels, clippers, screwdrivers, and other tools through the loops.

If the belt no longer works as a belt, think of it as a long strip of leather or vinyl that can be used to hang, support, or encircle other things. Use a utility knife to cut the leather into smaller sections and a thick nail to punch extra holes, as needed. Then try projects like these:

HANDLE IT. The strap on a shoulder bag always wears out before the bag. Happily, a strap can be replaced with an old belt. Cut the belt to the proper length and punch two holes at each end, one 3 inches and the other 1 inch from the end. Buy two aluminum screw

posts from a stationery supply store—they cost about a quarter apiece. Insert the ends of the belt through the rings that supported the original strap, line up the holes, and secure with the screw posts.

COLLARED. An old belt makes a serviceable collar for your pet. Cut the belt to the right length and punch holes in the end by laying the leather over a scrap of wood and pounding a thick nail through it.

IT'S A CINCH. Keep an old belt near the pantry for opening stubborn jars. Wrap the belt once around the jar lid as shown. Put a ruler beside the doubled strap, grip the belt and ruler tightly, and twist. The leverage loosens the top in a moment.

GUTTER TOOL. To make a simple nonscratch gutter cleaner, cut an 8-inch

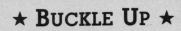
piece of leather from an old belt. Tack one end to a short wooden handle, perhaps a piece of broomstick. Curve the leather back to form a loose loop and tack the other end to the handle. Pull the leather loop through the gutter to loosen leaves and debris.

BAGGAGE BELT. Some suitcases pop open if they are handled roughly. To prevent this, pull an old belt around the luggage and through the handle. Buckle it tightly. If the suitcase is too large for one belt, buckle two together.

HOLD IT. Use old belts as organizers. Nail one to the wall, leaving loops for tools or kitchen utensils. Nail another to the inner wall of a drawer and use the loops to keep prescription bottles and other small objects in order.

See also LEATHER.

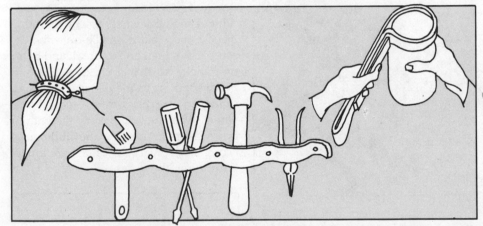

BERRY BASKETS

If you buy berries and cherry tomatoes in the supermarket, you'll probably have to buy the little plastic baskets with them. Fortunately, berry baskets have plenty of reuses. You can use them as lightweight containers (for cotton balls in the bathroom), coarse sifters (for kitchen-made compost), or geometric stencils (for kids on a rainy day—just cut apart the panels). Think about berry baskets when you need a ventilated container, a large-holed strainer, or an impromptu cage for a praying mantis.

You might also try ideas like these:

REFILL. The most delightful thing to do with berry baskets is to refill them with plump fresh berries you pick yourself—either at local U-Pick farms or in wild roadside patches.

QUICK COLANDER. A plastic mesh berry basket makes a sink strainer for kitchen peelings or a colander for draining a single serving of pasta or rinsing the berries you bought in it.

STRING ALONG. Cage that elusive ball of string once and for all in a berry basket. Pound a nail into the wall at an angle. Hang the berry basket on it and

put the ball of string inside, with its tail hanging through a hole. Tack down the opposite side of the basket with another nail.

DRYING HIGH. Use berry baskets to dry herbs for tea or seasoning and flowers for winter arrangements and sachets. Fill the baskets loosely with plants. Tie strings to the four corners of the basket and knot the strings together at the ends. Hang the basket in a sunny, airy spot.

BERRY NICE. Berry baskets lined with florist's moss and filled with a light mixture of potting soil and vermiculite make charming hanging planters for miniature flowers.

A FROG IN YOUR FLOWERS. When arranging a large bouquet, use a berry basket as a frog. Invert the basket at the bottom of the vase and anchor the flower stems in its holes.

BOW BASKET. Have you ever wanted to send a fancy gift without crushing the bow? Now you can. Just invert a berry basket over bow and pack newspaper or Styrofoam around it.

See also PLASTIC CONTAINERS.

BICYCLES

You want to get rid of a bicycle. If it's still in running condition, trade it in on a newer model or wait until spring and put a notice on the local bulletin board: "Bike for Sale. Cheap." If the bicycle doesn't work, fix it. *Glenn's Complete Bicycle Repair Manual* by Harold Glenn and Clarence Coles (Crown Publishers, 1973) is one of the best manuals on the subject. If you can't fix it, make the best use you can of its parts. Here are a few ideas:

BICYCLE BUILT FROM TWO. Buy a new bicycle just like the old one and keep the original around for spare parts.

SHORT SEAT. The seat on a bicycle is mounted on three or four pieces of metal tubing. Cut off the crossbar on a boy's bicycle with a hacksaw, then shorten the other three pieces of tubing so they are 18 inches long. Bend the two parallel pieces outward a little and prop your three-legged seat on the ground. Carry it in the car so you can sit on it when you go fishing, auction hopping, or picnicking.

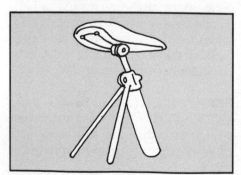

★ PEDAL POWER ★

If your bicycle is in good shape but you don't need it for transportation, convert it into an Energy Cycle. This homemade device is based on an ordinary bicycle and provides power to drive everything from a cherry pitter to a water pump to a lathe to a household generator. Detailed plans for this wonderful invention are explained in *Pedal Power*, edited by James McCullagh (Rodale Press, 1977).

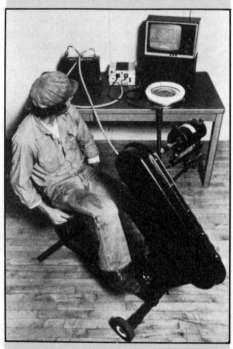

This Energy Cycle built from old bicycle parts generates enough electricity to power a television set—as long as the rider keeps pedaling.

WHEELIES. The wheel in a bicycle is mounted on an axle that's held in place by a simple nut and bolt assembly. If you remove the nuts and bolts, you can take off the wheel and the axle. The axle has threads on one end, so you can remount the wheel sideways by drilling a hole through a piece of wood, poking the axle through the hole, and securing it with a nut. Remove the rubber tire and attach the wheel to the axle so it spins freely. This assembly has uses throughout the house. Bolt it to a floor pole in an inaccessible corner of a closet and hang scarves or ties on the spokes.

Hang it in the bathroom and use it as a drying rack for hand washables. Or clip out the spokes with a wire cutter, suspend the metal rim from the kitchen ceiling by attaching wires at 90-degree intervals, and hang utensils from the rim with S-hooks.

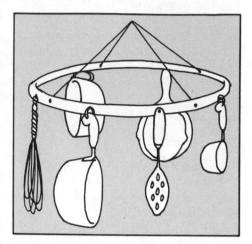

MADE TO MEASURE. To make a simple device for measuring distances, remove the front wheel assembly from a bicycle and weld a handle onto the assembly at a right angle. Break and bend one spoke so that it clicks against the metal supports as the wheel turns. Now measure the circumference of the wheel. Walk the wheel along the path to be measured, counting the number of clicks. Multiply clicks times circumference to get the distance.

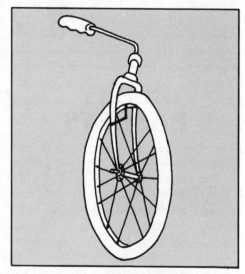

PEDAL YOURSELF THIN. If you can't ride your bicycle outdoors, rig up a stationary indoor exerciser. Remove the wheels of the bicycle and build a wooden frame like the one pictured. To provide resistance when you pedal, weld the rear-wheel sprocket to the handle of something that needs to be turned, perhaps a flour mill or a rock tumbler. Hook a chain between the bicycle and the sprocket and pedal yourself thin. For ideas about doing useful work with such a pedaler, see box.

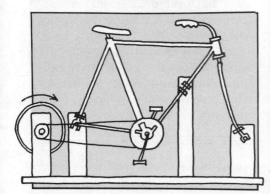

BITS AND PIECES. If you have to dismantle your bicycle, be sure to save the ball bearings from the front fork and wheels, the inner tubes, and the brake cables, as well as the usual nuts, bolts, and gears.

See also INNER TUBES; METAL SCRAP.

BLANKETS AND OLD QUILTS

An old blanket is a treasure, a source of heavy, seamless fabric that would cost plenty if you had to buy it from the usual sources. But before you cut a blanket up, take a good look at it. If it seems shabby because the edging is worn or loose, replace the stuff with blanket binding, available in any fabric store. Simply rip the old binding off and stitch on the new with a zigzag sewing attachment. If the blanket has more serious problems, like holes and thin spots, try adapting it to other situations where warmth and durability are prerequisites. Here are some ideas:

BLANKET COOKER. To make an energy-saving slow cooker, prepare a one-pot meal like stew in a heavy pot and heat it to a high temperature on the stove. Find a cardboard box somewhat larger than the pot and make a nest out

of old blankets. Put the pot in the nest, cover it, and leave it alone for about eight hours. When you come back, dinner should be done!

★ BLANKET ★ PROTECTION

Without any alteration at all, you can use an old blanket for cushioning furniture when you move, as a drop cloth for covering the floor when you paint, a dustcover for protecting things stored in the attic, a liner for a homemade quilt, or a frost blanket for tucking in tomatoes on nippy autumn evenings.

SNUG AS A BUG. People who are always cold need snug sacks, a sort of human cocoon. You can buy one for $30, or you can make one out of an old blanket. Here's how: Lay a single blanket on the floor, right side up. Fold the two long edges into the center, allowing a 4-inch overlap. Stitch across the bottom of the blanket, leaving foot holes if you like. At the top of the blanket, sew one half a heavy snap on each corner. Sew the other half 30 inches down each edge of the opening. Snap the sides together to make rough sleeves. Turn the blanket right side out and sew on more snaps to hold the overlap in place. Get yourself a cup of cocoa and crawl inside your sack.

BEDROLL. A bedroll made out of old blankets is a quick and inexpensive alternative to a sleeping bag. Start with two twin blankets. Lay half of one blanket over half of the other. Fold the two single-layer halves, one over the other, and fold the bottom under. Stitch across the bottom and halfway up both sides, or use large safety pins to hold the blankets in place. To carry the bag, fold it in half lengthwise, roll it up, and fasten with an old belt. This bedroll is suitable for warm-weather camping. Spread a ground cover—perhaps an old shower curtain—under the bedroll before sleeping in it.

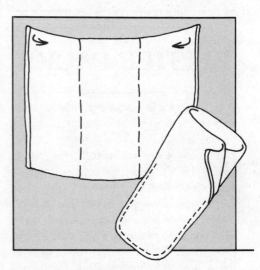

ALL-PURPOSE PONCHO. Turning a blanket into a poncho is amazingly simple. Cut out a square of good fabric 5 feet on each side. Cut a hole in the center of the square for your head. Sew binding or trim to all the raw edges, or unravel the threads for a fringe. If your blanket is too threadbare to go out by itself, use the blanket poncho as a warm lining for a poncho made of better fabric.

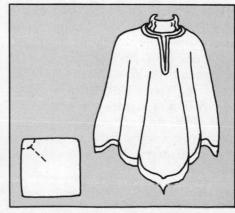

LAP BLANKET. If your blanket is damaged, cut out the largest possible rectangle of good fabric, hem it at the edges, and toss it in the back of the car. Use your lap blanket at football games, on ski weekends, or next time the car breaks down.

See also FABRIC SCRAPS.

BLEACH BOTTLES

See MILK CONTAINERS

BLISTER PACKS

A blister pack is a skin-tight film of plastic surrounding small consumables. For some reason, possibly to make the packaging more pilferproof, the edges of the blister pack are sealed together and sandwiched between slices of cardboard. Opening blister packs is always an ordeal. People have been known to rip at them, slash them, poke them with sharp objects, even tear at them with their teeth. Both cardboard and plastic must be sacrificed to free the product.

There appears to be no way that blister packs can be reused, but they do make a point. Americans consume about 700 pounds of packaging per person per year. Part of that can be reclaimed (*see* BOXES, CARDBOARD; CANS; JARS AND BOTTLES), but far too much of it is designed to be mutilated, so there is no choice but to discard it.

No-choice packaging is a bad choice. Manufacturers could just as well sell combs, screwdrivers, and pencil sharpeners without encasing them in plastic and cardboard. So next time you are confronted by an unnecessary blister pack, stuff its remains into an envelope and mail it to the manufacturer with a brief but pointed note explaining that although you wanted the product, you object to its wasteful and annoying package.

See also PACKAGING.

BLUE JEANS

Blue jeans have been part of the national uniform for so long that almost everyone has a grubby pair hanging at the back of the closet. There's nothing wrong with that. Ancient jeans are the best possible clothes to wear when weeding the garden, refinishing old furniture, or giving the dog a bath.

Sooner or later, however, every pair of jeans develops gaping holes in inconvenient places. That's a cue for you to stop thinking of them as derelict duds and start thinking of them as a source of denim, zippers, and grippers. Denim is one of the toughest fabrics around, and you can usually salvage several good swatches of it even from jeans that have worn seats and knees. Obviously, that fabric can be used to patch other jeans. Or try using it for projects like these:

BLUE TOTE. To make a tough tote bag, cut a 1-foot section off the bottom of both legs. Turn one leg inside out, stitch the unhemmed edge closed, and turn it back. Open one seam on the other piece of denim and cut it into four equal pieces. Right sides together, sew the ends of the pieces together to form one long strip. Fold the strip in half, right side in, and stitch up the long side. Attach a big safety pin to one end of the strip and work it through the tube to turn the strap inside out. Sew the strap to the tote bag with heavy-duty thread.

To make a larger tote, cut 1-foot sections from the bottom of the legs and open the seam in each section. Match up the two sections, right sides facing, and stitch around the unhemmed edges. Make a strap as described above and stitch it to the tote.

DUFFLE BAG. Denim is an ideal fabric for a duffle bag. To make one from a pair of blue jeans, cut a 3-foot section from both legs (you may need to patch or piece the fabric to get a 3-foot length). Open up one side seam on each piece and square off the pieces if the pants are flared. Place the two pieces of denim right sides together and stitch up one long edge, allowing a generous seam. Stitch up the other long edge, leaving a 2-foot gap in the center. Sew a heavy-duty zipper into the gap. Now measure the open end of the jeans and divide the measurement in half. Use that number plus 2 inches as the radius for two circles to be cut from the remaining fabric. Insert one circular piece into one end of the tube, placing right sides

★ THE OVERALL ★ APPROACH

A pair of overalls can be treated as a blue jeans mutation, or you can take advantage of their special design by turning them into a spacious knapsack. Cut off the legs of the overalls just below the seat. Turn the garment inside out and stitch across the holes at the bottom. Now turn it right side out, fill the pack, and slip your arms through the shoulder straps.

together, and stitch it in place, using sturdy thread. Repeat the procedure on the other end of the bag. Sew rings onto each end of the bag and attach a strap (perhaps an old belt). Your bag is now ready to be filled with duffle.

OLD FAVORITES. Everyone knows that blue jeans with worn knees can become cutoffs with two snips of a scissors. Turning a pair of jeans into a skirt is a little more difficult. Start by tearing out the inside seam on both legs. Press the fabric flat. Then cut two triangles of material to fit into the V's between the two legs. With right sides together, stitch one side of the V to one leg, then stitch the other side of the V to the other leg. Repeat on the other side of the skirt and even up the hemline.

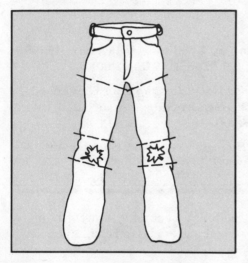

NO SEW PILLOW. To make a fat bolster pillow, cut one leg out of a pair of jeans. Hem the raw edge. Bunch the fabric at one end and tie tightly with a piece of decorative cord. Stuff the left with old stockings or some other filler. When the pillow is filled, tie a second cord around the other end.

HANDYPERSON'S APRON. An old pair of jeans converts neatly into a handy apron with pockets for nails and loops for tools. Cut off the legs of the blue jeans just below the seat. Now cut up the side seams until you come to the waistband. Don't cut the waistband! Instead, cut along it and remove the front half of the jeans. Remove the belt loops from the front of the waistband and sew them onto the seat of the jeans. Add extra pockets if you wish. When you

want to wear the apron, put the pockets in front and snap the waistband in back.

See also CLOTHES; FABRIC SCRAPS; PANTS.

BOBBY PINS

Bobby pins get bent out of shape and lose the little plastic blobs that keep them from digging into your scalp. Still, no one actually throws them away. They just accumulate in a drawer someplace. Bring out those retired pins! Think of them as short pieces of flat wire that can be reshaped for dozens of new purposes. Here are a few examples:

HELPFUL HOOK. Use bobby pins to make almost invisible hooks for lightweight objects. Open the pin into a right angle. Make a small hole in the object to be hung. Squeeze the ends of the pin together and insert them into the hole. When you release the pressure, the ends will spread. Slip a bit of string or wire through the loop of the pin to keep it from disappearing into the hole. These hooks are ideal for mobile parts, Christmas ornaments, paper lanterns, and so on.

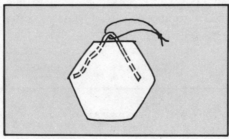

#?&*¢$%&)*! Instead of swearing because you hammered your finger, use a bobby pin to hold nails in place while you pound.

PINS AND NEEDLES. A bobby pin makes an adequate needle for lacing up leather and other craft projects. Tape the tips together with one layer of clear tape and thread your lace through the bulb at the other end.

FEATHERWEIGHT HARD-WARE. Bobby pins are made out of such lightweight metal that they can easily be bent into useful clips and hooks. Use a needlenose pliers to bend the pins into message holders (A), file markers (B), giant hooks and eyes (C), and much more.

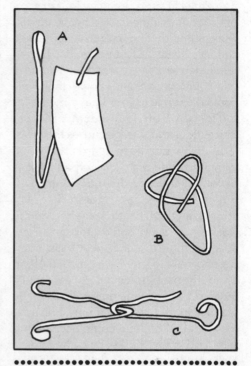

BODY WASTES

Most people don't feel any loss when they flush the toilet—but they should. With each flush we throw away pure organic matter, full of the nutrients and minerals that make plants grow. In an uninterrupted natural cycle, the waste would decompose into the soil, where it would nourish plants to be eaten by people, who would produce more waste.

The cycle that operates in most American cities goes more like this: Human waste is flushed away with water that carries it to a sewage plant, where it is separated from the water and becomes sludge. Nobody knows quite what to do with the 25 billion gallons of sludge produced each day in this country. Fifteen percent of it gets dumped in the ocean, 35 percent is burned, 25 percent is buried, and 25 percent is used as soil conditioner (landspread).

Every disposal method has its problems. Dumping pollutes the ocean, burning pollutes the air, and most communities are running out of landfill sites. Landspread, which seems appealing at first glance, can be lethal, because industries contribute 40 percent of the sewage. Though residential wastes may be relatively pure, industrial wastes are often contaminated with heavy metals like cadmium and mercury and toxic chemicals like DDT and PCBs. If contaminated sludge is spread on fields, the grain and vegetables grown there will contain chemicals and heavy metals.

The solution may seem obvious. Since industrial sewage causes the problems, why not keep it from mingling with its residential counterpart? Cities haven't figured out how to do that yet, but individuals can. How? By using composting toilets to transform body wastes into clean, safe humus.

An outhouse is the most basic composting toilet. The bacterial process in an outhouse, however, is essentially oxygen-free, and the anaerobic bacteria that live in such environments emit noxious odors. Modern composters eliminate bad odors by keeping the system well ventilated, so the decomposition is done by odorless aerobic bacteria rather than their smelly cousins. The most famous of the composing toilets, the Clivus Multrum, is a self-contained waste system as convenient and clean as any conventional toilet. Human wastes and kitchen garbage are deposited in a fiberglass container. As they move, "glacier-like," down the sloping bottom, they are worked over by bacteria. It takes a year or two for the bacteria to reduce the volume of the waste by 90 percent, but when they are finished, all that remains is a fine-grained, soil-like material, free of pathogens, artificial chemicals, and odors.

The Clivus was the first waterless toilet, but it now has several competitors. As with any new product, consumers must be critical before they buy. Ask the company for names of previous customers so you can find out how they like the system, and perhaps see it in operation. As an alternative, consider building your own system. Several organizations that specialize in appropriate technology now publish plans for composting toilets

★ BATHROOM READING ★

Several excellent publications provide additional information to homeowners who are thinking about buying or building a composting toilet. They include:

GENERAL INFORMATION:

Goodbye to the Flush Toilet, Carol Stoner, ed. (Rodale Press, 33 Minor Street, Emmaus, PA 18049), 1977, $6.95.

The Toilet Papers, Sim Van der Ryne (Capra Press, 631 State Street, Santa Barbara, CA 93101), 1978, $3.95.

Composting Toilets, Lane County (Office of Appropriate Technology, Lane County Public Service Building, 125 East 8th Avenue, Eugene, OR 97401), 1978, free.

Stop the Five-Gallon Flush: A Survey of Alternative Waste Disposal Systems (School of Architecture, McGill University, P.O. Box 6070, Montreal 101, Quebec, Canada), 1976, $2.00.

BUILDING PLANS:

Composting Privy, Technical Bulletin No. 1 (Farallones Institute, 15290 Coleman Valley Road, Occidental, CA 95465), 1975, $2.00.

Composting Toilets and Greywater Disposal—Building Your Own, Zandy Clark and Steve Tibbets (Alternative Waste Treatment Association, Star Route 3, Bath, ME 04530), 1977, $3.00.

Compost Toilets: A Guide for Owner Builders (National Center for Appropriate Technology, Box 3838, Butte, MT 59701), 1978, $2.00.

(see box). Of course, learning to live with a composting toilet requires some personal adjustment from those who have grown up in a "flush and forget it" culture. Nevertheless, in an era in which water is becoming scarce in many communities and fertilizer, a petroleum byproduct, is growing ever more expensive, flushing seems more and more like the shortsighted self-indulgence it is.

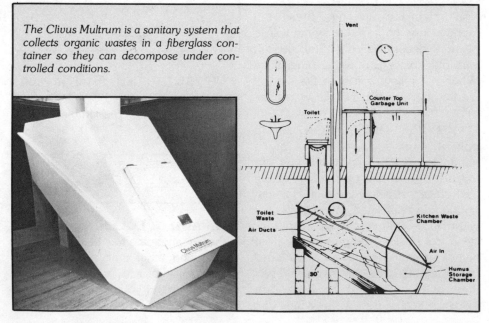

The Clivus Multrum is a sanitary system that collects organic wastes in a fiberglass container so they can decompose under controlled conditions.

★ SELLING SLUDGE ★

Many cities are starting to look at sewage sludge as a product instead of a problem. These clever people sterilize or compost the stuff, pack it in plastic bags, and market it as organic fertilizer. Nu-Earth comes from the good citizens of Chicago, Milorganite from Milwaukee, Grow-Rich from Vancouver, ORGRO from Schenectady, and Metroloam from Boston. Since sewage sludge can contain dangerous heavy metals, it should be used only on lawns and ornamental plantings unless the package states that it has been tested and found free of cadmium and other heavy metals.

★ WHERE TO GET ★ A COMPOSTING TOILET

Enviroscope, Inc.
711 West 17th Street, #F8
Costa Mesa, CA 92627

Clivus Multrum USA
14A Eliot Street
Cambridge, MA 02138

BONES

What can you do with fish, pork, poultry, and beef bones? Our Stone Age ancestors would have been shocked by the question. For centuries people have crushed bones for fertilizer and carved them into ornaments and implements. Modern meat eaters can revive those uses or invent some of their own. Here are a few suggestions:

STOCKPOT. To extract the last bits of flavor and nourishment from leftover bones, pop them in a pot, cover with water, and simmer. Fish bones (including the heads) should cook for no more than twenty minutes, but poultry and meat bones can cook up to three hours. When the cooking is finished, strain the stock and preserve it by freezing in ice cube trays (for sauces) or empty milk cartons (for soup).

WHEN YOU WISH UPON A BONE. Save the wishbones from your chicken dinners. Let them dry, then cover with glitter or paint. Fasten the wishbones on packages for good luck or hang them on the Christmas tree.

BONE MEAL. Bone meal, a common fertilizer, is made from crushed bones that contain 2–4 percent nitrogen and 20–25 percent phosphorous, two elements that are vital to plant growth. Most households aren't equipped to crush steak bones, but you can break up poultry bones by putting them in a burlap sack and smashing them with a hammer. Put the crushed bones in the garden or around your houseplants.

BUTTONS AND BEADS. Large bones can be sliced and drilled with power tools. Depending upon how thick you slice the pieces and where you drill them, the bits of bone can be buttons or beads. Smooth the edges of finished pieces with a file, sand with fine paper, and polish with jeweler's rouge.

★ BONES AND FOLK ART ★

Bone has always been used in folk art because it's easy to get and easy to work with. Anglo-Saxon artists turned bone into chessmen, Renaissance artists carved fanciful scenes on bone boxes, and American whalers traced intricate designs in their scrimshaw.

Today, bone is neglected by craftspeople, who seem to have forgotten that a carefully polished piece of bone can be as beautiful as ivory. Bone is a relatively soft material, so if you'd like to try your hand at carving, you need nothing more elaborate than a pocketknife and a pointed instrument for etching. Smooth rough spots with files, sandpaper, or jeweler's rouge. Try making tool handles, cuff links, needles, earrings, and inlays for boxes and game boards. For inspiration, consult *Bone and Horn Carving, A Pictorial History* by Carson I. A. Ritchie (A. S. Barnes, 1975) or *Scrimshaw* by Leslie Linsley (Hawthorn, 1976).

This unusual necklace is made from turkey and chicken bones painted with black satin acrylic paint.

BOOKS

Most people feel anxious about throwing out books, so don't. Books that bore you often have value to other people. And even if no one wants your old books, you may be able to think of new uses for them if you treat them as what they actually are—blocks of paper.

SECONDHAND PROSE. In large cities, some booksellers purchase secondhand books. They pay a fraction of what the books seem to be worth, but it is a way to turn reading matter into ready cash. Look in the Yellow Pages under "Book Dealers."

SSSSSSH. Schools, libraries, hospitals, and other institutions are often eager to receive old books as donations.

Even if they can't use the books in their collections, they may be able to sell them in fund-raising sales. Talk to the librarian and ask her to estimate the value of your gift so you can claim it as a tax deduction.

ANTIQUITIES. Some books, such as first editions, have unexpected value as antiques and collectibles. To find out whether your old tomes fall into that category, consult *Bookman's Price Index* (Gale Publishing) or *American Book Prices* (Bancroft-Parkman).

BOOKSHELF. If you have old hardcover books that have no value to you or anyone else, make yourself a bookshelf by stacking the books in neat piles about 12 inches high. Lay shelving across the stacks and arrange other books and knickknacks on the shelves. If the bookshelves seem unstable, drill ½-inch holes right through the books and shelves and pound in ½-inch dowels to steady them.

SECRETS. The hollow book is a classic hiding place and you can make one from a worthless old book that is at least 1 inch thick. Open the front cover and use a utility knife and straight edge to cut a rectangle out of the book's pages. Keep cutting until you've gone through all the pages. Paint thin wallpaper paste around the edges of the book so it soaks through and seals the pages together. When the paste dries, stash your secret treasures in the cavity, close the book, and set it inconspicuously on a bookshelf.

PAPERED. Some old books have no antique value but are printed in quaint typefaces with remarkable illustrations.

If you have such books, consider cutting out the plates and framing them. Or paper one wall of a study or office with the pages. Cut the pages apart evenly and glue them to the wall with wallpaper paste. Smooth the edges with a roller and seal the finished wall with clear acrylic. Just make sure—dead sure—that the book you're cutting up is worthless, or you'll never forgive yourself.

See also PAPER.

★ VOLUNTEER ★ BOOKS

People in third world countries are often hungry for books and have no money to buy them. An organization called the International Book Project matches the books you want to get rid of with individuals or institutions that need them. You pay the cost of shipping the books to the recipient. The Project needs technical books of all kinds, textbooks, children's books, fiction, and encyclopedias no more than twenty years old. For more information, write International Book Project, 17 Mentelle Park, Lexington, KY 40502.

BOOTS

Most people can't bear to throw away an old pair of boots. This leads to outrageous reincarnations—boots as planters (insert a tall narrow bottle and fill it with flowers) or pedestals (fill the boot with plaster and glue a wooden disc to the top). After a while, of course, this sort of thing can get tiresome, and if you don't want your house to look like a bootique, you might try taking your old boots apart and salvaging their components as useful raw materials. Here's what you can do with the parts you salvage:

LEATHER. Most boots wear out at the base, leaving a tube of relatively undamaged leather. To salvage the leather,

★ REREAD RIGHTS ★

If you find yourself throwing out favorite paperbacks because their pages are falling out, try this trick for holding them together. Line up all the pages and hold them in place with wood clamps. Use a coping saw to cut ¼-inch slits about 1½ inches apart in the spine of the book. Cut short lengths of string, press them into the slits, and dribble white glue in after them. Allow the glue to dry before covering the spine with a strip of cardboard.

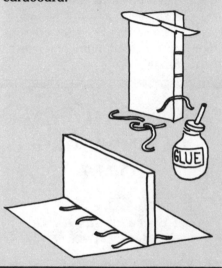

simply cut it away from the shoe of the boot with a utility knife. You may want to use the tubes as wrist protectors when you work with glass or metal or pick berries in the brambles. With zippered boots, try sewing up both ends of the tube and using the zippered pouch as a heavy carrying case for tools or hunting knives. If you can't think of a use for the leather in its tubular form, cut the side seam, flatten it out, and use it for any of the projects described under LEATHER.

ZIPPERS. Boot zippers tend to be long and tough, so it's worthwhile to cut away the stitching around them and save them for duffle bags (*see* BLUE JEANS) and other rugged items.

HEELS AND SOLES. Worn heels and soles are usually the reason you're getting rid of the boots in the first place.

You can, of course, ask your local cobbler to replace these parts if the rest of the boot is okay. You can also rescue a good pair of soles and/or heels from one old pair of boots and use them to repair another. To remove soles, cut the stitches that hold them to the shoe of the boot and peel them off the bottom. Pry heels off by pounding a wedge between the heel and the shoe. Attach heels and soles to the second pair of boots with a latex-based adhesive, perhaps an indoor/outdoor-carpet glue.

RUBBER. Now that inner tubes are scarce, the rubber in rain boots is a valuable household resource. Use it for any of the purposes listed under INNER TUBES.

GRIPPERS. The grippers on rubber boots can be detached by cutting through the little rubber tab that holds them in place. Reuse the grippers by sewing them onto backpacks, tents, duffle bags, and other gear.

See also LEATHER; SHOES.

BOTTLE CAPS

Screw-on bottle caps often find their highest usefulness when they maintain a relationship with their original bottles. A cap protects the contents of its bottle, allows you to turn a full bottle upside down, and turns an empty bottle into a float. Screw-on bottle caps that are unaccountably separated from their bottles can be used as little disposable dishes for mixing small quantities of glue or paint. Because many bottle caps are the same size as the ends of tall dinner candles, almost anything can be converted into a candleholder by glueing on a bottle cap and screwing in a taper.

Pry-off caps are more difficult to reuse because they are damaged during removal. However, if you buy your beer and soda in returnable bottles, they are plentiful and you'll want to reuse them by taking advantage of their roundness, their rough edges, or their colorful tops. Here are a few ideas:

SHOE SCRAPER. A bottle cap shoe scraper will come in handy on muddy days. Start with a piece of scrap wood at least 12 × 6 inches and tack bottle caps to it, fluted side up. Before people come indoors, they can rub the bottom of their shoes against the scraper.

GAME TIME. Use bottle caps as markers in homemade games or to replace lost markers from purchased games.

TAMBOURINE MAN. If you need a noisemaker for New Year's Eve, or a sporting event or a homemade band, make a jangly tambourine from bottle caps. Punch holes through the centers of a dozen caps, using a hammer and nail. Now remove both ends from a soup can and punch holes around each rim. Wire the caps loosely to the holes and shake, shake, shake.

BOTTLE CAP WASHER. Pry-off bottle caps can be used as emergency washers. Simply drill a hole of the proper size through the bottle cap and let the fluting face the bolt.

BUTTON BASE. Make campy, colorful buttons for outdoor clothing and equipment by punching two small holes through the cap with a hammer and a finishing nail.

HOT CAPS. Bottle caps make sensible trivets, because there's a little cushion of air under the surface of each cap. Glue caps to a hexagonal piece of wood, arranging the colors to make an interesting geometric pattern. Or cover individual caps with stretch fabric by cutting circles of material twice the diameter of the cap. Take little running stitches around the edge of the fabric, put the cap top down in the center of the circle, and pull the stitches so the fabric gathers around the cap. Then stitch the covered caps together.

FISH STORY. Make a scale scraper out of bottle caps and a 2 × 4-inch block of wood. Fasten the bottle caps, fluted side up, to one side of the block by nailing through their centers. Grasp the block and run the bottle caps lightly up and down the fish to get rid of scales.

See also JAR LIDS.

BOTTLES

See JARS AND BOTTLES

BOXES, CARDBOARD

If you look in the wastebasket of the average American household, most of what you'll see is packaging. Half of the packaging is paper, and two thirds of the paper is cardboard boxes. That's a lot of boxes—30 million tons of them per year—yet almost all could be reused or recycled.

In most households, cardboard boxes have two functions. First, they are classic containers used for storing everything from heirlooms in the attic to hardware in the cellar. Second, they are a source of cardboard that can be used for models, puzzles, backing, and many other things (*see* CARDBOARD). Good as these uses are, they do not exploit the full potential of the cardboard box.

To get more out of the boxes, you need to know about the cardboard that goes into them. Cardboard boxes come in two varieties—corrugated and paperboard. Paperboard boxes are made from a single layer of cardboard that can be creased easily by hand. The cardboard may be thick or thin, coated with wax or plastic, and printed with pictures or advertising messages. Paperboard boxes come in hundreds of shapes and sizes, and it's impossible to specify a use for each. The goal, though, is to match the new function with the form of the empty box (Function follows form!). For ideas, see box on page 20.

Corrugated boxes are tough packing containers with a little wave of paper sandwiched between two slices of cardboard. This cardboard does not fold readily, so it can be used in furniture, toys, and even small buildings (*see* CARDBOARD). Corrugated boxes are less common than paperboard in most households, so many people routinely save them for storage and moving. To minimize the space they take up, pack small boxes in larger boxes before sticking them in the closet or attic. Then you'll always have the right size available for projects like these:

BED BOX. To make a temporary bed tray for a sick person or a friend who likes breakfast in bed, start with a box as long as your lap is wide. Remove the top flaps from the box. Cut arches as wide as the patient's lap from the two long sides. When the legs are positioned on either side of the patient, the top of the box provides a flat surface for writing, eating, or craft work. Cover the top with cheery adhesive-backed paper.

★ TEN WAYS TO ★ CAMOUFLAGE A BOX

- Paint it
- Glue fabric to it
- Cover it with papier-mâché
- Wrap it in yarn or twine
- Tack carpet scraps to it
- Glue on a collage made of pictures cut from magazines
- Press adhesive-backed paper on it
- Cover it with leftover aluminum foil
- Glue gift wrap to it
- Leave it as is to make a Pop Art statement

PAPER CHESTS. Many of the storage chests in stores today are nothing more than corrugated boxes with tops. If you've already got a box, why buy? Just remove the top flaps and make a new top. Find a piece of cardboard 6 inches longer and wider than the top of your box, perhaps the side panel of

Never in Your Wildest Dreams

One empty corrugated box may not be worth much, but if you get enough of them together, they can be worth a fortune. That's the experience of Jesse Sims, a former produce manager in a Los Angeles supermarket. Sims started collecting and selling the supermarket's leftover boxes in 1975. Before long, he was collecting boxes from other businesses in his spare time. Finally, he resigned from his supermarket position altogether so he could devote himself full-time to cardboard recycling. It was a good decision. His gross annual income from recycling alone is around $80,000.

another box. Put the first box precisely in the center of the cardboard panel and draw around it. Use a ruler to extend the lines to the edge of the panel. Using a straight edge, score all the lines you've drawn by pulling a table knife along them firmly enough to dent but not cut the cardboard.

On each corner cut a 3-inch tab. Fold the panel along the score marks, tuck the tabs inside the cover, and glue with a latex-based adhesive. Fit the top over the box and tie with string until the glue sets. Finish all edges with tape and decorate the chest if you wish. This chest is fine for storing out-of-season clothes, tax records, wedding dresses, kid's toys, and lots of other things.

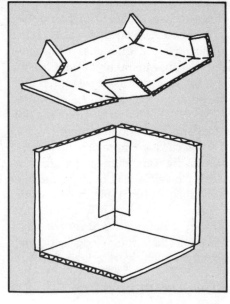

CORRUGATED FURNITURE.

Many people have tinkered with the idea of making simple furniture out of cardboard, but some of the most functional designs come from James Hennessey and Victor Pananek, authors of two volumes of *Nomadic Furniture* (Pantheon, 1974 and 1978). Their plans for a chair and a table base are reproduced here. If those plans seem complicated, camouflage a basic box as an end table, plant pedestal, or nightstand. Besides being very inexpensive, these accent pieces have an added advantage—when you want to redecorate, just recycle your furniture in the fireplace and make some more! To make a simple table, select a heavy box whose dimensions fit the area you want occupied. Put a weight in the box—a brick, or a plastic bag full of sand—and tape the top shut. Find something to cover the box—leftover wallpaper, the good part of a worn sheet, your favorite Sunday funnies—and glue it smoothly to the box using wallpaper paste. Conceal rough edges with a swatch of trim—macramé, lace, or bias tape, depending on the look of the room. Coat the table with several layers of acrylic to make it more durable.

This simple support for beds, tables, desks, and chairs can be built entirely from cardboard without fasteners or tape. It can support 400 pounds, according to the authors of Nomadic Furniture.

This chair, designed by Victor Papanek, can be constructed entirely from cardboard without fasteners or glue. In the pattern, x'ed lines should be scored, not cut, so the cardboard can be folded more precisely.

BOX BAGGAGE.

If you find yourself temporarily in need of an extra piece of luggage, make a sturdy suitcase out of a corrugated box. Select a box whose length and width approximate a suitcase and cut it down so the sides are 8 inches tall. Follow the steps under Paper Chests to make a top for the box, but make the flaps on the sides 8 inches wide. When you have assembled the top, run a piece of tape around the top, over the clamp string, to provide extra strength.

Now draw a light line around the suitcase as shown and punch three pairs of holes, on each side of the box. Thread a piece of heavy elastic through the holes and tie a square knot on the inside of the suitcase, leaving a little slack. Pack the bottom of the suitcase and slip the top over it. Pull an old belt through the loops and buckle it on one side, leaving a little slack at the top to use as a handle. If the suitcase is too large to be encircled by one belt, buckle two together.

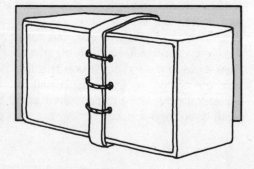

SOLAR DRYER. Drying is perhaps the most energy-efficient way to preserve food, especially if you use a solar dryer to dehydrate fruits and vegetables. To make a simple dryer, find two cardboard boxes of the same width. One should be long and shallow, the other square and about twice as deep. Cut 2-inch holes in both ends of the shallow box and one end of the deep box. Paint the inside of the shallow box with flat black paint and tape clear plastic over the top. When the paint dries, use tape and cardboard to connect the narrow end of the "collector" with the end of the other box that has the holes in it. Prop the shallow black box at an angle facing the sun and arrange the produce to be dried on a piece of screen that can sit on top of the larger box. The air that's warmed in the black box will rise into the second box and dry the food.

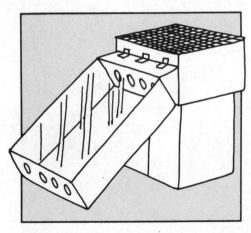

MAILER. Most corrugated boxes are sturdy enough to mail almost anything from Christmas presents to the appliance that has to go back to the factory. Cushion whatever you're sending with wadded newspaper or shredded Styrofoam from cups, egg cartons, and meat trays.

DUSTCOVERS. Corrugated boxes can be used to keep dust off appliances, power tools, sewing machines, typewriters, power mowers in the winter, and more. Cut off the flaps, decorate the sides, and slip the box over the appliance. Not only will it look neater than a plastic cover, but if you use the box the appliance came in, it will fit quite precisely. The top can serve as a work or storage surface.

★ BOXING MATCHES ★

Paperboard boxes come in an overwhelming number of shapes and sizes. What's more, the boxes that show up regularly in my trash are probably not the ones that show up in yours. But as a sampler, here are suggestions for things to do with fifteen common boxes.

Margarine Box. The flat box that holds four sticks of margarine side by side makes a crushproof sandwich box.

Cereal Box. Cereal boxes are just the right size for homemade in/out boxes. Cut off the top flaps and one large panel. Cut the short sides at an angle so it's easier to grab the papers in the box.

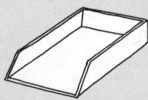

Tissue Box. Keep an empty tissue box on your kitchen counter to collect odd things like rubber bands, tacks, bottle caps, and other small items that you don't want to put away at the moment. (If you have a lot of tissue boxes, write for a free copy of "Arts and Crafts from Scotties," Scott Paper Company, P.O. Box 4255, Chester, PA 19016.)

Detergent Boxes. Detergent boxes are strong enough to hold back issues of your favorite

SOAP FLAKES

magazines. Cut the top off the box and cut a wedge out of the spine so you can see the titles.

Pasta Boxes. A camera bug once pointed out that a 1-pound spaghetti box holds exactly 400 color slides. Other pasta boxes can be cut down to hold lenses in a camera bag.

Aluminum Foil Box. When you make long rolls of dough for refrigerator cookies, freeze them in aluminum foil boxes.

Cake Mix Box. Cut one panel and the top off a cake-mix box to make a quick dustpan.

Cracker Box. Square saltine cracker boxes fit right around a loaf of bread. Stash the bread in the box and it won't get squashed when you freeze it.

Toothpaste Box. The average toothbrush fits right into the average toothpaste box, so use it as a traveling holder.

Envelope Box. If the envelope came out of it, it can go back in. Use this box as a file for letters.

Tea Bag Box. These boxes open with a flap on top, so they make nice organizers for gloves and scarves.

Aspirin Box. The small boxes that bottles of pills come in make fine stamp dispensers. Cut a slit in the top of the box with a razor blade, put a roll of stamps inside, and draw them out through the slit.

Powdered Milk Box. These boxes are large, heavy, and seamless. Cut off one panel, line the box with a sheet of plastic, and use as a roller tray on your next paint job.

Dried Soup Box. One dried soup comes in a low box just the size of recipe cards. With its flip lid, the box makes a handy recipe file.

Pizza Box. Next time you get a clean pizza box, keep it for storing tablecloths and other linens you don't use very often.

RECYCLE→RECYCLE→RECYCLE

Many community-run recycling centers accept corrugated cardboard, and some take paperboard, too. In addition, a few businesses are recognizing the wisdom of making money by recycling boxes rather than paying money to have them hauled away. A&P, Food Fair, and Shop Rite are among the supermarket chains that have experimented with recycling and might have a local collection center. Wherever you take your boxes, they must be free of food residues, tape, wax, plastic coatings, and other contaminants. Dismantle the boxes or open both ends and fold flat.

The recycling center won't make much on your contribution. The going rate for corrugated cardboard is about a penny a pound. To locate a market for scrap cardboard, look in the Yellow Pages under "Waste Paper."

The low price is misleading, because there are plenty of uses for recycled cardboard. One of the biggest is making new cardboard. Almost all cardboard packaging could be made from recycled boxes and paper, but only 20 percent is, largely because supply *and* demand are erratic, making it simpler for manufacturers to depend on virgin fibers.

Individuals can increase the supply of recyclable cardboard by separating boxes out of the household trash and toting them to the recycling center. And you can increase the demand for recycled cardboard by purchasing things packaged in it whenever possible. To identify products packaged in recycled cardboard, look for the symbol printed below. The symbol, developed by the American Paper Institute, indicates that the product is made with "a significant amount of recycled fibers." Another telltale sign is the color inside the box. White means virgin fibers were used; grey usually means the paperboard is made from recycled fibers.

To tell whether packages are made from recycled materials, look for this symbol, created by the American Paper Institute.

CARDBOARD CREEPER. If you happen to have an enormous appliance box, save at least one panel and use it as a creeper when you have to go under the car to change the oil or check out the tail pipe.

INSTANT EASEL. Any corrugated box can be turned into an easel to support art projects in progress. Draw a diagonal from corner to corner on both ends of the box. Cut along the diagonals with a kitchen knife and cut apart the edges that hold the two triangular sections together. Use the section without the open flaps as the easel by setting it on a table so its ridge end is in the air. Add a paper support by glueing a long, narrow strip of cardboard to the front edge of the easel.

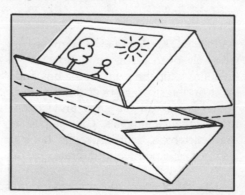

GREEN BOX. To make a greenhouse for starting seedlings in the spring, select a middle-size corrugated box with the flaps on the long side. Remove the flaps and cut out the center of each panel, leaving a skeleton like the one shown. Cover the sides with plastic—perhaps used plastic wrap or plastic bags that have been cut open. Fasten the plastic down with tape to make the greenhouse moisture-tight. Set the box over your seedlings and leave them in the sunshine. If you do a careful job of taping, this greenhouse will survive several spring showers before it turns mushy. In the fall you can use a similar contraption to extend the growing season of cool-weather crops such as lettuce.

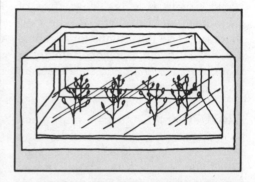

★ THE WELL- ★ ORGANIZED BOX

Here's a case where the whole is greater than its parts. To make an organizer from miscellaneous boxes, find boxes the size of the things you want to organize and cut them off so that they are the same height. Arrange and rearrange them to fit in the available space—perhaps a desk drawer, or a larger box with handles cut into the sides so you can carry it around. Glue the sides of the boxes together and cover the outside of your assemblage with acrylic to protect it. Use the organizer for storing all the odd items in the household catch-all drawer or for keeping tools or cleaning supplies at your fingertips. Or, turn the entire construction on its side to make a pigeonhole organizer.

BREAD AND OTHER BAKED GOODS

Even in the thriftiest homes, bread goes stale. To soften hard rolls and bread, sprinkle them with water, put them in a brown paper bag, and stick the bag in a warm oven for five minutes. When the bread is too far gone to respond to that treatment, it still has plenty of uses. Here are a few of them:

CRUMBS. The quickest way to make bread crumbs is to break up slices of stale bread and toss them into the food processor. Use the crumbs for breading meat or au gratin toppings. Remember that old potato chips and stale crackers also make tasty crumbs.

CROUTONS. Croutons are a French idea for recycling old bread and adding texture to soups and salads. Cut stale bread into ½-inch cubes. Sauté, if you like, in melted butter and season with onion, garlic, or other herbs. Toast the croutons in the oven until they are thoroughly dry.

STUFFING. Instead of buying fancy stuffing mixes in the store, make your own from stale bread. Keep slices of dried bread refrigerated in a plastic bag until you need stuffing for poultry or pork chops. Then break the bread into small bits, moisten with butter or milk, and add celery, onions, herbs, nuts, sausage meat, or mushrooms for extra flavor.

★ LET THEM ★ EAT CAKE

In most households, sweets don't stay around long enough to get stale. If, however, you do find yourself with a stale cake or a few rock-hard cookies, crush them into crumbs in the food processor and use them in crumb crusts or toppings.

FRENCH TOAST. For some reason, French toast is better than usual when made with stale bread. Soak the bread in a saucer of milk until it is soft but not spongy. Dip each piece of bread into beaten egg and fry in butter. Sprinkle with cinnamon before serving.

BREAD STICKS. Why pay premium prices for bread sticks when you can make your own from leftover bread? Trim the crusts from the bread and cut each slice into four sticks. Brush the sticks with melted butter and sprinkle with grated cheese, sesame seeds, or garlic salt. Bake in a 350-degree oven until the sticks are crunchy.

CROUSTADES. Croustades are cups made of stale bread, though it's easiest to make them when the bread is still semisoft. Cut an unsliced loaf of bread into 4-inch chunks. Scoop out the center of each chunk, leaving a ½-inch wall. Brush the cup with melted butter and bake for ten minutes in a 350 degree oven. Fill the croustades as if they were pastry shells.

••••••••••••••••••••••••••••••••

BREAD BOXES

In the days before preservatives, everyone had a bread box to keep baked goods fresh. I think it's still a fine idea. If you have an old bread box sitting in the cellar, scour off the rust, renovate it with a coat of paint, and stash your bread and cookies in it, or store homemade cheese, fruitcake, and other foods that need to age undisturbed. If that doesn't appeal, think about the box as a metal storage unit with convenient shelves. Then try reincarnations like the ones that follow:

OVEN BOX. A bread box makes a workable oven for a wood stove or a campfire. Strip the paint off the box and set it on the stove or over the fire. Put your goodies on the shelf and check them at regular intervals. This setup isn't as predictable as a kitchen range, but it's also not as expensive to operate.

SEED BOX. Most bread boxes are

---

metal, which makes them rodent- and insect-proof and a good place to store things like bird seed. Turn the box on its backside, fill it with seeds, and set it near the feeder.

SHELVE IT. If you remove the door from a bread box, you'll notice two shelves that can probably be put to good use in the bathroom. Drill two sets of holes in the back of the box. To keep the box from slipping off the nail, make the bottom hole a little larger and the top hole a little smaller than the head of the nail you intend to use. If you can, pound nails into studs to hang your shelf. Otherwise, use toggle bolts.

BREAD BOX BULLETINS. If you do remove the door of your bread box, don't get rid of it. Hang it on the wall and use it as a magnetic bulletin board.

READ BOX. Most bread boxes are wide enough to hold your average magazine. What's more, they have two handy compartments. Take advantage of this characteristic by removing the door, setting the box on its backside, and using it as a magazine rack.

See also METAL SCRAP.
•••••••••••••••••••••••••••••••

BROOMS

It takes a while to wear out a broom, but when you do, don't pitch it. With a little trimming, an old floor broom can be converted into a specialized cleaning implement. Even up the bristles with scissors and saw off the handle to make a whisk broom. Or cut off the bristles at a diagonal and use the new broom to get dirt out of corners. If the broom is too far gone for such alterations, cut off the handle and save it for the projects described under BROOMSTICKS AND OTHER TOOL HANDLES. Then use the bristles for projects like these:

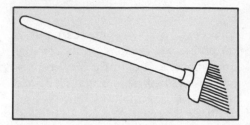

BRISTLING WITH IDEAS. The bristles of a broom can be cleaned by swishing them in warm soapy water and spreading them in the sun to dry. Then gather a handful and wrap a piece of wire around it one third of the way from one end. Twist the wire tightly and use the new brush for cleaning away crumbs in the toaster and other small jobs. Clean bristles can also be used for testing cakes, spreading glue, and other toothpick tasks.

STRAW DESIGNS. The straws in a broom are a fine craft material if you soften them in water and press them flat with a hot iron. Use the flattened straws to decorate small objects. Spread glue over a thin piece of paper and arrange the straws in geometric patterns. Dye some straws if you wish to add more interest to the design. When the glue has dried, cut out the design and glue it to a flat surface on the object. This technique is traditional in Mexico, where craftspeople often use it to make vivid patterns on the tops and sides of trinket boxes.

★ HELLO DOLLY ★

If you need to move something heavy, an old broom can be a big help. Tip the heavy object so one edge rests on the broom bristles. Have someone else push the object while you pull the broom. The object will move across the floor without leaving scuffs and scratches.

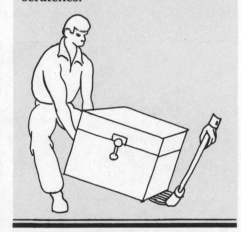

READY RACK. To turn a broomstick into a rack for towels, clothes, or tools, buy two brackets at the hardware store and install them under a cabinet, on the wall, or in the closet. Cut the broomstick to the proper length and slip it into the brackets. Use S-hooks to hang utensils from the rack.

FIREWOOD FRIEND. Broomsticks are the basis of a simple caddy that makes carrying firewood much easier. Cut two pieces of broomstick, 13 and 20 inches long. Salvage two 40-inch strips of webbing from an old lawn chair. Screw the webbing to the dowels as shown, with washers in between so the screws won't pull through the webbing. Pack firewood into the caddy and carry by the shorter stick.

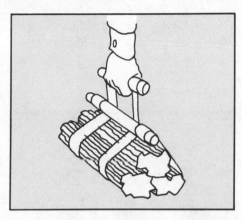

BROOMSTICK STOOL. To make a simple campstool, cut four pieces of broomstick 18 inches long and two pieces 1 foot long. Cut a 13 × 18-inch piece of heavy fabric (perhaps denim from an old pair of jeans). Make a ½-inch hem along the long sides and a 3-inch casing on the two short ends. Insert the foot-long pieces of broomstick into the casings. Drill each of the remaining pieces of broomstick—make one hole at the center and one hole 1 inch from the end. Bolt the two set of legs together at the center, leaving them loose enough to fold. Using 2½-inch screws, fasten the ends of the legs to the ends of the sticks inserted through the fabric.

BROOMSTICKS AND OTHER TOOL HANDLES

Broomsticks are almost legendary for the number of jobs they can do around the house. Here are a few examples:

TOOL SAVER. Use a broomstick to rescue a rake or hoe with a broken handle. Remove the old handle from the tool socket. If the old handle is narrower at the end, use a plane and a file to taper the broomstick to match. Drive the broomstick into the tool socket and secure it by inserting a wood screw through the pilot hole.

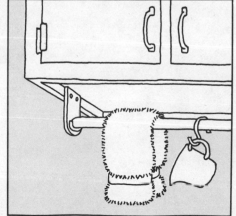

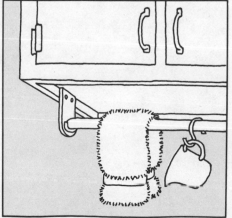

CURTAIN STICK. To make a simple curtain rod, cut a broomstick as long as the window is wide. Drill holes through the broomstick at either end and hang from finishing nails driven into the window molding. Use pliers to bend up the ends of the nails so the rod won't fall off. This simple broomstick rod can also be used to hang curtains in front of open closets or pantry shelves.

See also WOOD SCRAPS.

★ SIX QUICK ★ THINGS TO DO WITH AN OLD BROOMSTICK

- Stake plants
- Support a bird feeder
- Prop up a tent
- Roll up a map or chart
- Wave a flag
- Play stickball

BRUSHES

See PAINTBRUSHES; TOOTHBRUSHES

BUILDINGS

Ever since the price of new construction went sky high, Americans have been making better use of the buildings they have. In the process were rediscovered the charm of older buildings, many constructed with sturdy materials, and elaborate details which can't be matched today.

The simplest way to recycle an old building is to purchase an older home and renovate it. The days of bargain-basement prices are over—even in city slums the competition for sound housing stock has pushed prices up. Still, if you can do at least some of the renovation yourself, a rehabilitated older home will cost less than a comparable new one. The trick in such purchases is to be certain that the house is structurally sound before you buy. There's no point sinking money into windows and wallpaper if the foundation is shaky. One helpful publication is *Renovating an Old House*, published by the U.S. Department of Agriculture and available through your Congressperson. Other valuable guides include *How to Select and Renovate an Older Home* by Gerald Sherwood (Dover, 1976) and *How to Inspect a House* by George Hoffman (Delacorte, 1979). Once you've bought the house, one of the best sources of information about renovation is *Old House Journal*, 69A Seventh Avenue, Brooklyn, NY 11217.

Those with a flair for design can often convert an older building into a purpose for which it was never intended. By now, turning a train station into a restaurant, a church into an antique shop, or a barn into a home doesn't seem particularly imaginative. There's still room, however, for those who can metamorphose gas stations, laundromats, fire stations, and old mills. For inspiration, take a look at *Rescued Buildings* by Roland Jacopetti (Capra Press, 1977) or *Recycling Buildings* by Elisabeth Kendall Thompson (McGraw-Hill, 1977).

Sometimes an old building is too derelict or too clearly in the way to be sal-

This gas station on a back road in northern California was once called the White Palace. Now it's home for Larry Grasso, who recycled it.

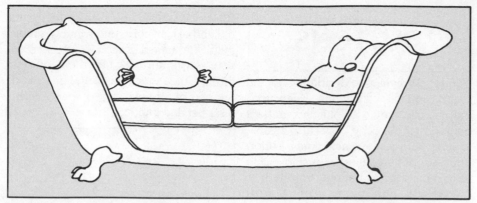

vaged. Even then, all is not lost. All around the country, smart designers, architects, and homeowners have noticed that the fixtures and details in older buildings simply can't be duplicated today. So they are rescuing stained glass panels, beveled glass doors, sweeping staircases, Victorian fretwork, claw-foot bathtubs, stone gargoyles, cast-iron register covers, cherry wainscoting, wide pine floorboards, brass doorknobs. What happens to all this material? Some is reused for its original purpose in period homes. Some extraordinary pieces like carved mantelpieces and Federal entrance ways are installed in new homes to provide individuality and distinction.

Still other materials are reincarnated with entirely new functions. Corbels, the L-shaped brackets under the eaves of flat-top houses, become shelf brackets. Fretwork is used to divide rooms. Fireplace mantels become headboards. A claw-foot tub with one side cut out and a cushion added is transformed into a loveseat. A newel post becomes a plant stand. Instead of treating these "architectural antiques" as permanent fixtures in their original buildings, think of them as independent objects whose new use is determined by their size, shape, and design.

★ WHERE TO SELL ★ ARCHITECTURALS

There's a brisk interest in odd bits from old buildings. So if you're renovating and have no use for an old staircase, cupboard, window, or fireplace mantel, an architectural dealer will probably be willing to buy it. Such dealers are a cross between antique dealers and demolition experts. There are over a hundred across the country, most located in major cities where materials are plentiful. To find out whether such a dealer exists in your community, look in the Yellow Pages under "Building Materials, Used." Or consult *Old House Journal*, published annually by *Old House Journal*, 69A Seventh Avenue, Brooklyn, NY 11217. Remember that many dealers prefer to dismantle interiors themselves, so ask around before you get going with the crowbar.

Never in Your Wildest Dreams

Don Carpentier collects buildings. Most are nineteenth-century structures that were in danger of being razed for new construction. He takes the buildings apart, stone by stone, clapboard by clapboard, carefully numbering everything so it can be reassembled. Then he carts the pieces home to a private village called Eastfield. When Carpentier started ten years ago, he was considered an eccentric, but now his village, which includes a working tin shop, a tavern, and a church, is a mecca for preservationists. Each summer Carpentier holds workshops on nineteenth-century crafts like housewrighting and fireplace construction. For a schedule, write Eastfield Village, Box 145 RD, East Nassau, NY 12062.

BUTTONS

Before consigning old clothing to the ragbag, rip off its buttons. Keep your button collection in an old glass jar. Not only will it look pretty, you'll also be able to see what you have next time a button pops off your favorite skirt or shirt. Aside from replacing lost buttons, your button collection can be useful to you whenever you want to join two pieces of fabric or related pieces of clothing. For example, sew buttons on the cuffs of your gloves so you can button them onto your coat for safekeeping. Or make buttonholes in your dish towels and sew buttons to your aprons so you'll always have a towel at your fingertips. You can unfasten it for washing.

If you don't use your buttons because you can't make buttonholes, try this trick. Cut two patches of iron-on mending tape a little wider than the button and 1 inch long. Put the patches directly over and under the spot where the button should be and press with a hot iron. When the patches are cool, use a sharp razor blade or utility knife to make a slit the size of the button right through the center of the patches. This technique may not look finished enough for tailored clothes, but it will allow you to make a button-down pocket for your knapsack or a button-on bandanna for your workshirt.

In some households buttons accumulate faster than the sewing projects on which they can be used. In that case, think of the buttons as attractive plastic discs with predrilled holes. Then try using them for projects like this:

CUTE AS A PICTURE. Little girls once learned to sew by making button samplers. Buttons can still be used to make homey-looking pictures, but you'll find that the project goes faster if you glue the buttons to a piece of fabric backed with cardboard.

BUTTON GAMES. Substitute buttons for lost counters in games ranging from backgammon to Parcheesi. Use large flat buttons to revive the game of tiddlywinks.

PERFECT ENDING. Tie buttons on the end of light cords and window-shade pulls. Tie a small button on the end of your sewing thread when the knot slips through the fabric. Tie a large button on the end of a drawstring to keep it from disappearing into its track.

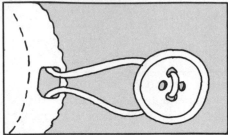

COSTUME BUTTONS. Button jewelry may seem like kid stuff, but some designs are attractive enough to warrant adult attention. Shirt buttons, for example, accumulate rapidly in most households. Strung side by side on two strands of heavy-duty thread, they make a pearly necklace. Add a bead or a larger button now and then for interest, and tie the thread ends with a square knot when the necklace is long enough to slip over your head. Fancy buttons also make attractive earrings (glue them to an old set of clips) and cuff links (attach two buttons with a short piece of fine chain).

HUMMER BUTTON. This old-fashioned toy amuses modern kids, too. Select a large button, about 2 inches in diameter. Find two thin dowels and drill holes through them at either end. Thread a piece of string through the dowels and the button, and position the button midway between the dowels.

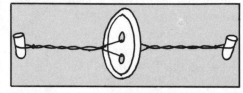

Twist the string and pull gently on both dowels to make the button hum.

CALENDAR, LAST YEAR'S

If you use your calendar as a diary, keep it. Make extra notes on it about the weather, places you go, people you meet, even tax-deductible expenses. Then save the calendar as a record of your year.

If you don't mark on your calendar, collect a complete set of seven. The difference between one year and another is, after all, the day of the week January 1 falls on. So if you collect all the possibilities, you'll never have to buy or throw away another calendar except in leap years.

If neither of those ideas works for you, think of the calendar as a collection of printed numbers and pretty pictures.

NUMBER GAME. Cut your old calendar into little numbered squares and use them to label things. Number the window screens when you take them down in the fall or the parts of an appliance when you disassemble it. Use the numbers to post important phone numbers or to make flash cards.

THE YEAR IN PICTURES. If your calendar is beautifully illustrated, use the pictures for decoupage projects (*see* GREETING CARDS).

See also PAPER.

CANDLE STUBS

If you are fond of candlelight, you probably have a drawerful of candle stubs, too short to be aesthetic, too long to throw away. The stubs are made of wax, a complex combination of hydrocarbons, alcohols, and fatty acids, which has a range of important properties. Wax melts into a liquid at low temperatures and burns at high temperatures. When wax cools and hardens, it forms a moistureproof barrier. Finally, wax is an excellent lubricant. All of these characteristics make wax a valuable household resource, so save those stubs and use them for jobs like these:

SLIP, SLIDING. To use candle wax as a lubricant, try running a candle stub along a stubborn saw or the bottom of a sticky iron. Make drills, needles, and nails work easier by sticking them through a candle before using them. Rub candle wax on the bottom of dresser drawers to make them slide smoother and on snow shovels to keep snow from sticking to them.

QUICK STICK. If you need a fast, temporary adhesive, use a blob of melted wax from an old candle. The wax will seal envelopes, stick candles to their holders, and do other odd jobs.

FIRE STARTER. One of the simplest ways to start a fire is to toss a couple of candle stubs into the kindling and light it. By the time the stubs are consumed, the fire will be blazing.

CHEAP BATIK. Candle wax can readily be used in batik, the art of painting wax on fabric before dyeing it. Melt candle stubs in a double boiler. Fish out wicks and skim debris off the surface of the wax. Tack a piece of fabric—perhaps a remnant from an old sheet—to a board and draw a design faintly in pencil. Apply hot wax to the design with a paintbrush and let it harden. Dye the fabric in cold-water dye and hang it up to dry. When the material is almost dry, lay it on a pile of newspaper and iron it until the wax melts and is absorbed by the paper. To make a more complicated design, apply more candle wax and repeat the dyeing process.

NEW CANDLES FROM OLD. True candle lovers will want to melt down their stubs to make new candles. Put candles of the same color in a coffee can and set it in a pan of hot water. Heat the pan until the wax melts, and scoop any debris off the surface of the wax. Find a mold for the candle—Styrofoam cups are good—and make a wick out of a

piece of string dipped into the hot wax. Tie the wick to a pencil and lay the pencil over the cup so the wick hangs straight to the bottom. Now pour the wax carefully into the cup and let it harden. Peel off the Styrofoam when the candle is thoroughly cool. These may not be boutique candles, but you can

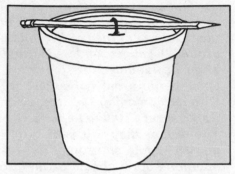

disguise them in pretty containers, stick them in jack-o'-lanterns, or save them for the next blackout. For more information, consult *The Complete Candlemaker* by Ann Hirst Smith (Van Nostrand Reinhold, 1974) or *Tie Dye, Batik and Candle-making—A Step by Step Guide* by the editors of Macmillan (Macmillan, 1976).

SEALER. Use wax to seal leftover paint or putty so it won't dry out. Simply melt the wax, pour it over the exposed surface, and allow it to cool into a protective skin. Caution: Do not use candle wax to seal jelly or other foods, since the wax may contain dyes or additives which could be harmful. Melted wax can also be used to close cracks in vases and other ceramic containers. Just pour the melted wax into the cracked crock and slosh it around so it coats the sides.

RUSTPROOFER. If you want to protect tools that you won't be using for a while, melt several candle stubs in a coffee can and dip the metal parts into the liquid so they are coated with waterproof wax.

CANS

The can was invented in 1810 by an Englishman named Peter Durand. Since then it has become one of the most prevalent forms of packaging, containing everything from soup to hair spray, car wax to fruit juice.

The possibilities for reusing cans are just as numerous. Cans can be cut, curled, punched, pounded, painted, or used as is. They can also be collected and recycled into new cans. An exhaustive list of all the ways to reuse cans would be a book in itself, so this brief section can only suggest some of the most promising ways to reuse the cans you might otherwise discard.

CANNED LIGHT. Cans have shiny reflective surfaces that make them naturals for lamps, lanterns, and candleholders. To make a simple but striking camp light from a one-ended can, fill the can with water and freeze. Use a small hammer and nail to punch holes through the metal in an arabesque pattern. Thaw the ice, turn the punched can upside down over a candle, and let the light flicker through the holes.

For a portable lantern, try making a "bug" from a lidless can with a 5-inch diameter. Punch three holes—one through the can near the rim and a pair of holes 5 inches away from it. Make a handle from an old coat hanger and loop it through the holes. Use a sharp

knife to make an X cut opposite the handle in the center of the can. The X should consist of two straight slices about 2 inches long. Force a 1-inch candle through the center of the X so it points to the inside of the can and is about 3 inches from the top. Light the candle and carry the lantern into

Never in Your Wildest Dreams

People who tinker with trash usually do it for their own satisfaction, but sometimes it turns into something bigger than that, something like a multi-million-dollar business. Take the case of George Ballas, a Houston homeowner, who hated trimming the grass around two big oak trees in his yard. Ballas had noticed that the local car wash used brushes with long nylon filaments to whip the dirt out of crevices on the cars, and suddenly he had an inspiration. He rummaged through the trash, found an old popcorn can, punched holes around the edges, and tied strands of fishing line through the holes. Then he mounted his invention on a motor and let it rip. Sure enough, the strands of nylon cut right through the grass and weeds without damaging the trees. Ballas called his contraption a Weed Eater, spent $10,000 to perfect it, and started distributing it himself. The rest, as they say, is history. The Weed Eater you'll find in your garden supply store may not resemble its popcorn can prototype anymore, but it should be an inspiration to all those tinkerers who turn to trash to solve everyday problems.

the night—you'll be surprised at its brightness.

In the age of electricity, cans can also be used to make track lights and bed lamps.

CLEANING CAN. To make the grimy job of cleaning stovepipe easier, find an old can slightly smaller than the dimension of your pipe. Use tin snips to cut around the open end to make a sharp cutting edge. At the other end of the can, use a can opener to make half-moon cuts on either side of the can, leaving a strip of uncut metal through the center. Fold down the two moons and wrap tape around the resulting handle so you won't get cut from the edges. Grasp the handle and push the scraper into the dirty pipe, turning it to scrape away the accumulated creosote.

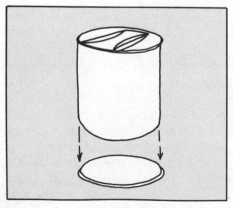

ORGANIZATION CAN

Cans make excellent storage containers because they don't crack, tear, or break. To reuse a can for storage, remove the lid entirely, file down any sharp edges, and wash the inside thoroughly.

CANISTERS. Cans, particularly those with plastic lids, make fine canisters for tea, coffee, sugar, flour, rice, and other staples. Make lids from pieces of scrap wood for cans that don't have them. Trace the top of a can onto the wood and cut out the circle slightly inside the line. Draw a second circle on the wood 1 inch wider than the first. Cut it out and glue the first circle to the center of the second. Finish the wood. Set the top on the canister so the first piece of wood slips into the can, forming a seal. If that seems too complicated, make gathered tops by cutting a circular piece of cloth or plastic 4 inches wider than the can and hemming it with elastic thread. Pull the elastic until the fabric hugs the can and tie off the ends.

THE FAMILY OF CAN. Grouping cans is an appealing way to make organizers for silverware, papers, office supplies, nails, and other small items. To make a handy pigeonhole organizer for lightweight objects, arrange half a dozen cans attractively and glue them at their

intersections with superglue. Paint the entire arrangement with bright enamel paint. Then hang the cans on the wall by pounding in a long nail and slipping it into one of the gaps at the back of the organizer.

For a portable organizer, select six cans of the same size. Drill holes through the sides of the cans 1 inch from the upper rim. Line the cans up in

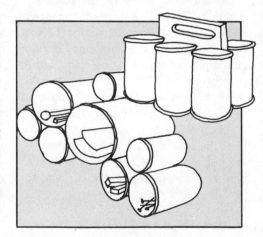

two rows and cut out a piece of scrap wood as long as the rows and 8 inches wide. Make a 1½-inch slot in the top of the wood to use as a handle. Thread three long bolts through the cans in one row and mark where the bolt hits the wooden handle when it is positioned as illustrated. Drill three holes through the handle and thread each bolt through a can, the handle, and then through a second can.

CANTAINERS. Open cans are also good for storing things, especially if they are fastened to the spot where they will do the most good. The easiest way to hold a can in place is to drill a hole through its bottom and a corresponding hole in the place you want to mount it. Put a lock washer over the hole in the can and use a long screwdriver, preferably one with a magnetic shaft, to screw the can in place. Attach a can to the top of your stepladder to hold hardware while you work, or bolt a can to your desk for paper clips, the kitchen counter for spoons, the telephone desk for pencils, and so on. It's also worth noting that if you bolt a horizontal can to the wall, it can serve both as a holder and as a peg for hanging things, like rope, wire, belts, and garden hose.

ADACAN. If you don't want to devise your own system for storing things in cans, you can turn to a prefab system called Adacan. The system consists of wire holders that support soup or soda cans at a slant and can be installed on regular pegboard. A set of twenty holders costs $5.95 from Pierce Products, Box 805, Marathon, FL 33050.

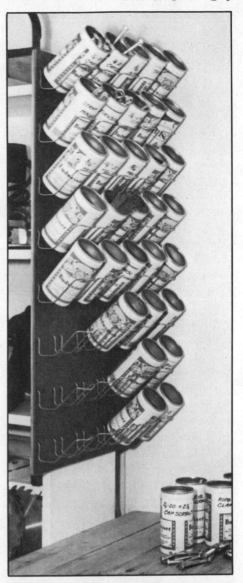

The Adacan system creates modular storage for a workshop using topless aluminum cans, pegboards, and specially designed brackets.

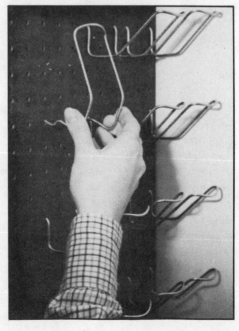

★ THE CRAFTY CAN ★

The possibilities for reusing empty cans increase dramatically if you invest in a few tools for shaping the metal. With a little practice and patience, these tools will help you turn your cans into anything from dollhouse chairs to a candelabrum. The following items belong in every can crafter's tool kit:

Tin Snips. A good pair of snips can be the difference between a hack job and a work of art. Buy middle-size snips with powerful jaws and comfortable grips. Practice until you can make a smooth, continuous cut.

Awls or Sharp Nails. An awl allows you to punch a clean hole in a piece of metal. Back the metal to be punched with a piece of wood—any scrap will do for a flat piece of metal. For a can, use a dowel (perhaps a broomstick) and brace it against the place to be punched with a second piece of square scrap. Then place the awl over the hole-to-be and strike it sharply.

Needle-nose Pliers. The long, narrow jaws on these pliers allow you to bend and curl strips of metal.

Ball Peen Hammer. A round-headed hammer is best for flatten-ing dents in the metal and for creating special textural effects.

Gloves. Cut metal edges can be sharp, and the beginner should wear gloves to prevent unpleasant cuts.

File. Use it to smooth off sharp edges.

Clear Acrylic. "Tin" cans are really made of steel coated with tin, so when you cut one open, the steel is exposed to moisture. To prevent rust, coat your work with clear acrylic. You can also paint cans with oil-based paints, cover them with fabric, and decorate them with decoupage.

You might also want to include a book on "canning" in your kit. Two of the best are *Tin Craft* by Lucy Sargent (Simon & Schuster, 1972) and *Can Crafts* by Earl Fowler (Chilton, 1977). Mr. Fowler creates his projects by cutting the sides of cans into thin strips and curling or twining them together. Ms. Sargent pays special attention to the enameled finishes of different cans and the decorative effects that can be created with a ball peen hammer. Both books are full of project ideas—if you tried them all, you'd use up a year's supply of cans in no time.

A CAN FOR ALL REASONS

★ LABELED ★

Even if you throw out the can, you may be able to reuse the label. Most labels are designed to please the eye and they can do that even after you've consumed the product. Glue a collage of colorful labels to the door of an old refrigerator, the sides of a wastebasket, the valence above the cabinet or any other surface in need of color. Protect your work with a coat of clear acrylic.

If you don't chose to decorate with labels, save them for more utilitarian reasons. Labels with valuable information about how to use a product—recipes, for instance—can be clipped and filed. Or start a label file in anticipation of those manufacturer's refund offers that require so many proofs of purchase. At the very least, tear the labels off the cans you empty, stuff them in an envelope, and use them as an instant shopping list.

One type of label deserves special attention. Many schools collect labels from Campbell's and Franco American products because the parent company will redeem them for equipment ranging from overhead projectors to plaground balls. To register for the program, schools should write to Campbell's Labels for Education, PO Box 1608, Maple Plain, MN 55348.

All cans are useful but some cans are more useful than others. Because of their special shapes and/or sizes, the following cans should be salvaged whenever possible:

PAINT CANS. Don't let the last half inch of paint cake in the bottom of a paint bucket. Instead, empty it into a glass jar (so you can see quantity and color), wipe out the paint can with newspaper, and clean out the last traces of paint with an appropriate solvent. Now you have a clean bucket with a sturdy handle. Fill it with roofing nails when you have to replace shingles. Let your kids use it as a sand pail on the beach. Strap it on your belt so you can use both hands when you go berry picking.

Or, turn a large paint can into a simple stove for burning sawdust by cutting a two-inch hole in the bottom. Stick a length of broomstick through the hole and hold it upright while you pour dry sawdust around it, packing the sawdust as tightly as possible. Pull out the broomstick by twisting it gently. Twist several pieces of newspaper and stuff them into the hole at the center of the sawdust until a ''tail'' sticks out the bottom. Cut off the paper at the top and set the can on three bricks arranged so air can reach the paper on bottom. Then light the paper wick from underneath. This simple stove will give off heat for several hours—enough to heat the garage or workshop on chilly days.

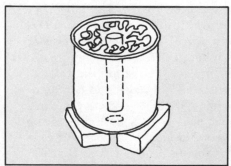

JUICE CANS. Cooks can use the large cans from tomato and pineapple juice for baking specialty items like Stovepipe Bread (see RECIPE IN BOX). Gardeners can use them to ripen melons in cool climates by opening each can as little as possible to remove the contents and then refilling it with water. When melons develop on your vines, set each one on a water-filled juice can. The cans collect solar heat during the day and release it at night when melons do their best ripening.

Actually, juice cans are so sturdy that you can also build simple furniture from them. For starters, try a simple hassock made of seven large cans and a length of fabric. Cut a piece of fabric as long as the circumference of a can and several inches wider than the can is tall. Wrap the fabric tightly around the can and whipstitch a seam in the side. Take running stitches around the edge of the fabric at the top and bottom of the tube and pull the fabric shut. Cover all seven cans

the same way. Then arrange them in a petal pattern so the seams don't show. Take several stitches with sturdy thread to attach the cans to each other. Trace the top of the footstool on a piece of foam and cut it out. Trace the same pattern on a piece of fabric adding two inches in all directions. Position the foam on top of the cans and the fabric on top of the foam. Whipstitch the fabric to the cans and conceal the stitching with trim.

SQUARE CANS. What you use a square can for will depend upon whether its contents were edible—like olive oil—or inedible—like turpentine. A can with edible contents can be turned into a popcorn popper if you cut off the

★ CAN IT ★

The pencil can is a classic, but empty cans are ideal for storing many other things, particularly if you match the size of the can to the things that need to be contained. For instance:

Large can (from juice or shortening) screwdrivers, kitchen utensils, marbles,

Medium can (from soup or vegetables) nails, matches, crayons, clothespins

Shallow cans (from tuna or cat food) rubber bands, snaps, bobby pins, springs

front panel with a metal snipper. Smooth any rough edges with a file and clean the can thoroughly. Punch four holes in a square pattern in the end of the can opposite the spout. Bend a straightened coat hanger in half, stick one end of wire in one hole and out the one above it. Repeat for the other end and wrap the metal handle with tape. To use the popper, cover the bottom with oil, add popcorn, and cover the pan with aluminum foil. Jiggle the pan over an open fire until the corn is popped. To turn a square can with a handle into a lunch pail, use a saber saw with a metal-cutting blade to cut a 5 × 5-inch square from one side of the can near the top. Hinge the panel to the can at the top and attach a butterfly fastener at the bottom.

Square cans with inedible contents make fine window boxes. Cut off the front panel and file down any rough edges. Paint the can inside and out with rustproof paint, punch drainage holes in the bottom, fill with soil, and plant your favorite flowers. If you are a boating enthusiast instead of a gardener, make your rowboat more buoyant with empty square cans. Cement the caps on the cans and hold them underwater to be sure they don't leak. Then lash several cans under each seat in the boat. If the

boat overturns, the air-filled cans will keep it from sinking.

SARDINE CANS. You can always use an empty sardine tin as a kitchen soap dish (coat with clear acrylic first to prevent rust), but the real find here is the key. Uncoil the metal from it, wearing gloves to prevent cuts. Next time you open a tube of toothpaste start squeezing from the bottom until you have about half an inch of flat tube. Smooth the tube further by rubbing it with the key. Cut two quarter-inch slits in the end of the tube and slip the tab you've made into the slit in the key. Now turn the key so the tube rolls up around it. As you use the toothpaste, keep turning the key—the pressure will squeeze out more toothpaste and you'll get an extra week of brushing. Sardine can keys with flat ends can also be used as screwdrivers for tiny screws, and those with round ends can be used as needles for poking laces through holes in leatherwork.

★ WHAT TO DO ★ WITH AEROSOL CANS

Much as I wanted to find a sensible secondary use for empty aerosol cans, I couldn't. These cans have to be very strong to withstand the pressure inside—sometimes up to 100 pounds per square inch—so it's tough to get into them. What's more, they are dangerous because you can never tell whether a can is still under pressure. You can't even send empty aerosols to a recycling center because they are likely to blow up in the crusher. When a package is so utterly beyond redemption, the inevitable conclusion is that it makes sense to buy an alternative whenever possible—hair spray in pump bottles, paint in buckets and so on.

★ STOVEPIPE ★ BREAD

Nut and fruit breads baked in coffee or fruit juice cans come out with a pleasant, plump shape. Make up a recipe like the one that follows. Grease the can, drop in the dough, let it rise until it peeks over the rim of a No. 2 can. Then bake at 325 degrees for 45 minutes.

⅓ cup milk
1 package yeast
1 teaspoon honey
3 tablespoons raisins
2 tablespoons water
2 cups flour
⅓ cup honey
½ teaspoon vanilla
3 egg yolks
¼ cup butter
3 tablespoons nuts
3 tablespoons dates

Warm the milk to 80 degrees and dissolve the yeast and honey in it. Set it aside for fifteen minutes. Soak the raisins in the water during the same period. Mix together the yeast, egg yolks, vanilla, and flour. Knead until smooth. Add the raisin water to the dough and knead in the butter. Let rise once. Add the raisins, nuts, and dates before putting the dough into the can.

HAM CANS. The top from a large ham can is just the size of the bottom of a household iron, so you can use one as an iron rest. If you prefer, leave the lid on the can and use it to store cookies, crackers, and other baked goods. In both cases, tape the sharp edge so no one gets cut. Small ham cans with both lids removed make festive candle holders. Glue a small can to the flat inner edge of the can and poke two small holes through the can at the opposite edge. Insert a metal ring through the holes and clamp it together so you can suspend the can, perhaps in a window. Paint the assemblage, put a votive candle in the small can, and light it.

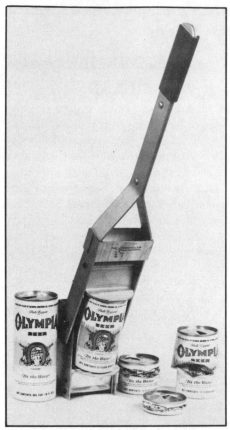

The Recycler® can crusher is a convenience for people who recycle a lot of cans.

RECYCLE→RECYCLE→RECYCLE

Someone once estimated that the average American uses 389 cans per year. All 389 could be recycled.

A goodly percentage of those cans are made of steel with some sort of coating, usually tin. Though tin is a very small part of the can, most of the momentum for recycling comes from detinners. The United States has no natural source of tin, so the more we reclaim from cans, the less we have to import. Each year about 3,000 tons of tin are reclaimed through recycling. Old cans are also used by copper mines in refining. And the detinned steel can be reused in reinforcing steel.

In a few communities giant magnets are used to separate cans from the rest of the garbage, but in most places individuals must take responsibility for collecting the cans and hauling them to a recycling center. The center, in turn, sells the cans to a scrap dealer. To find a market for cans, look in the Yellow Pages under "Scrap Metal."

If you plan to recycle your cans—and you should—rinse them, strip them of their labels, and crush them. The simplest way to crush a can is to remove both ends, put it on the floor, and stamp on it (don't wear tennis shoes!). If that seems too physical, you can buy a can crusher called The Recycler, a wall-mounted unit that reduces cans to one fifth their original size and costs $19.95. It's available from The Recycler, P.O. Box 8437, Spokane, WA 99203.

CAN STAND

Cans fastened end to end have even more reuse possibilities. The only question is how to make them stay together. There are three possibilities, and the one you choose will depend upon the strength of the bond you need and the exterior appearance you want. The simplest method is to wrap wide plastic tape around the intersection. For better appearance and a little more strength, spread one of the superglue compounds on the rim of a can and press the second rim into it. Secure the joint with tape until it sets. To make a really strong connection, mix up a batch of epoxy putty and spread it thickly over the top of a can (leave the lid in place to strengthen the bond). Press a second can with lid into the putty and let it set overnight. Now what do you do with your connected cans? Some ideas:

PEDESTALS. To make a pedestal for plants, a lamp, or a statue, glue together a stack of wide cans. Screw a piece of

wood into the bottom of the top can before attaching it to the others. Weight the bottom can with rocks or sand so the pedestal won't tip over.

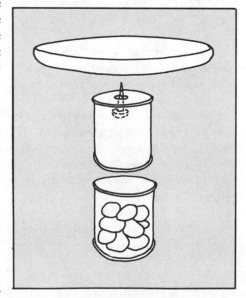

LIGHT UP. A stack of cans without ends makes a convenient lamp base be-

cause you can run the wiring right through the center. Just be sure to weight the bottom can so the lamp won't tip over.

BOOT STAND. To help tall leather boots hold their shape, make two supports using three soup cans for each. Fasten the cans together and stick them in the boots to hold them upright.

UMBRELLA CAN. To make a container for drippy umbrellas, save four 3-pound cans from coffee or shortening. Cut top and bottom out of three cans and only the top out of the fourth before cementing them together.

TABLED. To make larger tables and pedestals, glue cans into stacks of the same height. Then use superglue to attach the cans side by side in a rectangle. These can bases are surprisingly strong and look very contemporary if you use cans with striking labels.

KITCHEN CANS

Most discarded cans originate in the kitchen, and many can be reused there. Before cooking with any can, remove the paper label and scrub away the glue.

POTS AND CANS. Convert cans into simple pots by punching a hole just under the rim on both sides. Cut a straight piece of wire from a coat hanger and loop one end through each hole. Use small can pans for melting butter and larger ones for warm-up jobs. These free pans are ideal for camping, and they make good backup pans when all your regular cookware is in use.

BAKE CANS. Some round breads and cakes are supposed to be baked in cans. Muffins, pot pies, and fruit tarts fit nicely into tuna and sardine cans. Grease the sides of all cans thoroughly before adding the food.

MEASURING CAN. Cylindrical cans are standardized to hold a premeasured volume. If you know the volume (see chart), you can use the can as a measuring cup.

MEAT CANS. Bake individual meat loaves in small soup cans. When you're ready to serve, open the other end of the can and shove the meat loaf out. To make perfect burgers, pat a wad of meat flat and trim off the edges with an empty tuna can. Or pack and freeze individual burgers in tuna cans.

COOKIE CANS. To make distinctive cookies, start with custom-made cookie cutters. After removing both lids, use tin snips to cut a can down, starting at the top and cutting an arc toward the bottom. When you are 1 inch from the rim, level off and cut around the can with a continuous motion. If there are jagged bits of metal on the edge of the cut, smooth them down with a file. Then bend the circle into cookie cutter shape with needle-nose pliers.

KIDDY CANS. Make sure the kids get their share of cans for toys and games. Bury a couple of small soup cans in the backyard so just the open top shows and let the kids use them as golf holes. Be sure to punch holes in the bottom of the cans so rainwater can drain out. Bolt six larger cans to a piece of wood, prop it at a slant, and let kids throw beanbags into the cans. Or set up ten tall potato chip containers in a bowling triangle and have the kids bowl them over with a rubber ball. Cans can even be used as blocks if you're careful to file off all sharp edges. Or punch two holes at opposite sides of the rim of a can and tie a long string through each hole. Do it with a second can and you'll have kid-size "stilts"—just stand on the cans and hold them under your feet when you walk by pulling on the strings. Or try the old walkie-talkie trick by punching holes in the bottom of two cans and tying them together with string. Hold the strings taut while one person talks into a can and another person listens on the other end.

See also COFFEE CANS; SODA AND BEER CANS; SPICE CONTAINERS; TUNA CANS.

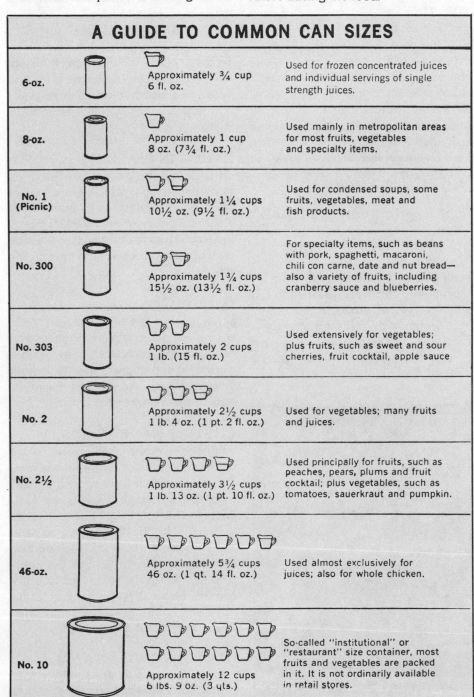

A GUIDE TO COMMON CAN SIZES

6-oz.		Approximately ¾ cup 6 fl. oz.	Used for frozen concentrated juices and individual servings of single strength juices.
8-oz.		Approximately 1 cup 8 oz. (7¾ fl. oz.)	Used mainly in metropolitan areas for most fruits, vegetables and specialty items.
No. 1 (Picnic)		Approximately 1¼ cups 10½ oz. (9½ fl. oz.)	Used for condensed soups, some fruits, vegetables, meat and fish products.
No. 300		Approximately 1¾ cups 15½ oz. (13½ fl. oz.)	For specialty items, such as beans with pork, spaghetti, macaroni, chili con carne, date and nut bread—also a variety of fruits, including cranberry sauce and blueberries.
No. 303		Approximately 2 cups 1 lb. (15 fl. oz.)	Used extensively for vegetables; plus fruits, such as sweet and sour cherries, fruit cocktail, apple sauce
No. 2		Approximately 2½ cups 1 lb. 4 oz. (1 pt. 2 fl. oz.)	Used for vegetables; many fruits and juices.
No. 2½		Approximately 3½ cups 1 lb. 13 oz. (1 pt. 10 fl. oz.)	Used principally for fruits, such as peaches, pears, plums and fruit cocktail; plus vegetables, such as tomatoes, sauerkraut and pumpkin.
46-oz.		Approximately 5¾ cups 46 oz. (1 qt. 14 fl. oz.)	Used almost exclusively for juices; also for whole chicken.
No. 10		Approximately 12 cups 6 lbs. 9 oz. (3 qts.)	So-called "institutional" or "restaurant" size container, most fruits and vegetables are packed in it. It is not ordinarily available in retail stores.

No need to buy measuring cups when you have a set of empty cans.

CARDBOARD

Cardboard is the most common form of packaging because it's tough, cheap, and easy to work with. These same properties make it valuable to the household recycler. Cardboard is tough enough for constructing casual furniture and even small buildings. Working with cardboard requires no special tools, so it is an ideal material for models, odd-size boxes, and other made-to-order objects. Finally, it is so readily available that you can afford to experiment. If a project fails, you can toss it out and start again.

Cardboard is such a versatile material that we can mention only its most general uses. Think of cardboard whenever you have a problem that could be solved by something flat, thin, and semiflexible.

PAINTER'S PAL. Use cardboard strips to mask moldings and other surfaces when you paint. Hold the cardboard flat against the surface to be protected and paint right up to it. When the strip of cardboard gets too messy, replace it with another. Even if you use up a year's supply of cereal boxes, this method is cheaper than masking tape.

TOY TIME. If you have nothing but cardboard in the house, the kids can still have fun on a rainy day. Start by making sewing cards. Draw or paste a picture on a piece of cardboard and use a nail to poke holes at ½-inch intervals all around the picture. Use scrap yarn or string with its end dipped in nail polish to "stitch" through the holes. Next, make game boards. Use a piece of cardboard as the base and draw or paint a checkerboard on its surface. Better yet, give the kids some bottle caps, a set of dice, and a blank board and let them invent their own game.

Older children can make everything from dump trucks to dollhouses out of cardboard. For detailed instructions, check out *Building Cardboard Toys* and *Building Cardboard Dollhouses*, both by Jeff Milstein (Harper & Row, 1979), a craftsman who has figured out how to make cardboard toys that are colorful, fun, and surprisingly durable.

STIFFEN UP. When making tote bags and other carriers, stiffen the sides and bottom by inserting two or three layers of cardboard between the bag and its lining.

EATING IN PLACE. Pieces of 12 × 18-inch cardboard can be used as placemats if you paint them or cover them with decoupage. To make more elaborate placemats, cut parallel slits all the way across the placemat and weave yarn or raffia back and forth through the slits.

PUZZLED. Want a clever way to send a birthday or get-well message? Print your message on a piece of paper and back it with cardboard. Then cut the cardboard into puzzle pieces, stick them in an envelope, and let the recipient assemble them to get your greeting.

CUSTOM-MADE BOXES. When you have an odd-shaped object to wrap or store, pack it in a custom-made box. Put the object on a piece of cardboard and draw a rectangle that encloses it entirely. Measure its height and draw sides to match. Use the illustration (see page 18) to indicate where you should score and where you should cut the cardboard. Fold up the sides and glue the corners. Make a top for the box in the same way, with the sides 1 or 2 inches deep. Trim all cut edges with tape.

DIVIDED WE STAND. Use cardboard panels as dividers in recipe, check, and correspondence files. Cut a piece of light cardboard as wide as the paper to be filed and ½ inch taller.

Never in Your Wildest Dreams

Because corrugated cardboard is lightweight, strong, and readily available, it's an ideal building material, according to Roger Sheppard, author of Paper Houses *(Schocken, 1974). His book explains how to make domes and other structures out of cardboard panels, using the principles of geodesics developed by Buckminster Fuller. The panels are cut in the shapes of precisely measured templates, assembled into small buildings, and covered with protective plastic coatings. Durable cardboard houses have been built on college campuses in Canada, park sites in England, and vacant lots in New York City. If you'd like to attempt one in your backyard—they make dandy toolsheds or summer guest houses—start collecting cardboard and check out this book!*

Cardboard structures like this 42-foot geodesic dome built in Milan are surprisingly durable.

★ TECHNIQUES FOR WORKING ★ WITH CARDBOARD

Working with cardboard is easier if you master a few simple processes:

Folding. To make a sharp crease in a piece of cardboard, put it on a flat surface and set a straight edge on the fold line. Score the cardboard by running a knife or the point of scissors along the line so it is dented but not torn. Fold along the score mark.

Cutting. Don't cut cardboard with scissors—it's hard on your hand and leaves a damaged edge on the cardboard. Instead, use a metal ruler and a razor blade or mat knife. Go over the cutting line lightly several times until the two parts of the cardboard separate.

Pasting. Although cardboard can be glued with ordinary white glue, your work will be more durable if you use bookbinder's glue or wallpaper paste. Apply the adhesive with a brush so it spreads evenly. To strengthen joints, especially corners, glue a strip of brown paper over the intersection on the wrong side of the project.

Decorating. Cardboard projects can be decorated with almost anything: paint, feathers, crushed eggshells, fabric, bits of leather, wrapping paper, yarn, ribbon, strips of colored tape, wallpaper, glitter, buttons, and anything else that strikes your fancy.

Create a tab in the ½-inch margin and label it.

NEAT WORK. Use cardboard instead of newspaper to cover the work surface when you are painting, refinishing, glueing, or doing other messy jobs. You can cut on it without going through to the table, and it's less likely to leave telltale smudges than newspaper.

BACK IT UP. Cardboard has obvious value as a backing, especially for its flimsier cousin, paper. Use cardboard to support notepads made of scratch paper, to reinforce covers on paperback books, to mat pictures and photographs for framing, and for other backup jobs.

LITTLE LOOMS. Many people dismiss weaving as an at-home craft because they think they would need lots of space and money for a loom. Not so. With a piece of cardboard, you can make a perfectly adequate loom for weaving napkins, small bags, headbands, and other little things. Start with a piece of cardboard the size and shape of what you want to weave. Cut an odd number of ½-inch notches in opposite sides of the cardboard. The distance between the notches should be determined by the thickness of the fiber you

plan to use. Tie your thread to the first notch and run it across the front of the cardboard to the first notch on the opposite side. Pull the thread around the notch and run it back across the front of the board to the second notch on that edge. Continue until the entire board is covered with parallel threads. Now tie a new thread to the first row and weave it over and under the parallel threads, then turn around and weave back in the other direction, going *over* the threads you went *under* on the first row and vice versa. Continue weaving until the entire board is covered and then tie off the thread. Cut away the cardboard to liberate your creation. For more information consult *Weaving on Cardboard: Simple Looms to Make and Use* by Marthann Alexander (Taplinger, 1971).

CARDBOARD TUBES

You probably throw away a cardboard tube every week, if not from paper towels then from toilet paper or plastic wrap. Instead of treating the tubes as leftovers, think of them as rings, protective sheaths, and containers without

ends. Suddenly, you'll see new uses for them. For example . . .

MAILING TUBES. To send something that can't be folded, roll it up and insert it into a cardboard tube. At the ends of the tube, pinch one side in and press the other side on top of it. Secure with wide tape. If you like sending personalized greetings, make up fancy scrolls for birthdays or anniversaries and ship them off in cardboard tubes.

CARDBOARD CURLERS. Cardboard tubes are acceptable hair rollers for large, soft curls. Cut the tubes into convenient lengths, roll up hair when it is almost dry, and fasten with long bobby pins.

JIFFY POTS. Rather than spending several cents apiece on starter pots for seeds, make them from cardboard rolls. Use a serrated knife to slice the rolls into 4-inch sections. Don't worry if they squash a little. At one end of each section, make four 1-inch-long cuts at equal intervals. Fold over the flaps you've created and secure them with waterproof tape. Fill the little pots with dirt and plant your seeds. The cardboard deteriorates after a month or two of watering, so when transplant time comes you can set the pots right into the garden.

NEAT NAPKINS. If you've switched from paper to cloth napkins, keep them neat between meals with homemade napkin rings. Slice a cardboard tube into 1-inch sections with a serrated knife. Cover the outside of the tube with white glue and wrap it with scraps of yarn or string, pressing the strands close together until the tube is entirely covered.

LINT PICKER. Wrap two-sided tape around a tube. Insert two fingers into the end of the tube and run it over clothing to remove lint and dust.

HANDY HANDLE. If you have to carry a parcel that's tied with string, run the last loop across the top through a cardboard tube. Carry the package by the tube so the string won't bite into your hand. When you get to your destination, simply tear off the handle.

STRING THING. Cardboard tubes are ideal storage reels for bits of string, ribbon, and yarn. Wind up each piece on the tube and cut a slit in the tube to secure it.

RUFFLES. Turn a cardboard tube into a quick decoration by putting it on a cutting board and slicing almost but not quite through at ½-inch intervals. Bend the connections between the slices and form the tube into a circle. Paint and use the ruff around candles or as a Christmas tree ornament.

COLLAR IT! Most kitchens and workshops are full of extension cords, skeins of yarn, hanks of clothesline, etc. To prevent unnecessary entanglements, fold each flexible thing into even sections and then slip a cardboard tube around it.

WRINKLE PREVENTION. Slit a long cardboard tube lengthwise and slip it onto the bottom of a hanger to keep pants from creasing when you lay them over the bar.

EXTEND YOURSELF. Here's a neat trick: If you need to remove a burned-out light bulb from a fixture that's too high to reach, just locate a long cardboard tube, slip the end over the bulb, and turn. To install the new bulb, press it gently into the open end of the tube, raise it to the socket, and twist it into place.

••••••••••••••••••••••••••••••••••••

CARDS

See GREETING CARDS

CARPET SCRAPS AND WORN-OUT RUGS

A carpet worn in high traffic paths shouldn't be thrown away when it's replaced. Turn it over and use a linoleum knife to cut out good sections that were hidden under furniture. To prevent raveling, buy heavy plastic tape in a matching color and fold it lengthwise over the edges, or ask the local carpet store to bind the edges. Carpet can be sewn by hand with a curved upholsterer's needle and a thimble. Or stitch up seams on your sewing machine using a heavy needle and your longest stitch. For detailed instructions about using carpet remnants, consult *Creating Rug Art with Remnants* by Betty Rayside (Crown Publishers, 1975).

THROWAWAY RUGS. Cut old carpets into smaller rugs to be used in hallways, bedrooms, bathrooms, or entrance ways. If the rugs slip, secure them with double-sided tape. Long sections, cut from the edge of an old rug, can be used as runners over a new carpet.

PET CARPET. Cut a section of carpet to fit into a pet's bed. Staple other pieces to a scratching post for the cat.

NOISE CONTROL. Muffle the noise of typewriters, sewing machines, and other appliances by cutting pieces of carpet to fit under them.

CAR CARPET. Carry two 2 × 4-foot pieces of carpet in the trunk of your car. Kneel on one piece next time you change a tire. If you own a station wagon, line the back with scrap carpet; it's more comfortable for passengers, especially kids.

SLIM MAT. Cut a piece of old carpet as long as you are tall and 3 feet wide. Use it as an exercise mat and roll it up for storage.

CARPETBAGS. Carpetbags are an American tradition, perhaps because they can be made so easily from rug remnants. The simplest version is made from a large rectangle of carpet folded in half, right side out. Get a piece of 2-inch canvas webbing twice as tall as the bag plus about 3 feet. Fold the webbing over the open sides, pin in place, and stitch, leaving the slack as a shoulder strap. For a roomier bag, try adding pleats at the base of the bag, or perhaps side panels of carpet.

BUFFERS AND ERASERS. Find a piece of scrap wood 3 inches wide and 6 inches long and a piece of carpet 7

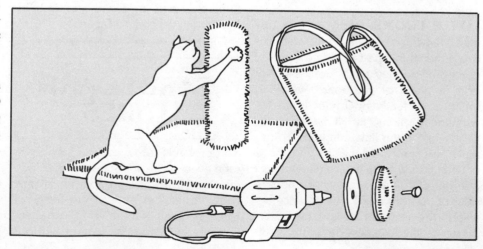

inches long. Staple the ends of the carpet to the ends of the wood and use it for buffing shoes or erasing blackboards. If you have an electric drill, make a quick polishing attachment by cutting a circular piece of carpet and backing it with a disc of heavy cardboard. Punch a hole precisely in the center of the circle so you can screw it to your drill disc.

RUGGED CLOTHES. Large scraps of shaggy carpet can be fashioned into vests and jackets that resemble sheepskin. Follow a purchased pattern and use scraps with flexible backing.

This vest may look like sheepskin but it's really made of carpet remnants.

WONDERFUL WALLS. If you have a large amount of leftover carpet, accent a wall with it. Cut the carpet into strips and hang it as you would wallpaper. When the adhesive dries, brush the seams so they don't show. Glue smaller pieces of carpet to window seats or platforms on the floor.

SOFT SHOE. Trace your feet on the back of a carpet scrap and cut the soles out. Insert the carpet sole into boots for warmth. Slip another pair into your work shoes to cushion your feet. Or put a set in a pair of slippers that has a hole in the sole.

●●●●●●●●●●●●●●●●●●●●●●●●●●●●●●

CARS

People usually trade their old cars in for new ones. Before you do that, consider that most cars can be totally reconditioned for less than $2,000. For that money, according to Scott Sklar of the National Center for Appropriate Technology, "engine and transmission can be rebuilt, new peripheral engine parts, brakes, tires and exhaust system can be installed, body damage can be repaired and the car can be painted, rust-proofed and reupholstered." After getting the works, your new old car should get another 50,000 miles.

Of course, if your old car is disabled from accident or extreme old age, you won't be able to recondition it and a dealer may be less than eager to accept it. In that case, call a salvage company, usually listed in the Yellow Pages under "Auto Parts, Used." These companies stockpile old cars so they can sell the used parts, and the price you'll get depends upon the condition of your car and the demand for parts from that model and year.

If the price seems pathetically low, you may want to do your own salvage job before consigning your heap to the junkyard. An old car is like a candy store for mechanical types—all those motors, pumps, and fans waiting to be reused. Even if you don't know a carburetor from a spark plug, you can still salvage plenty of useful material from an old automobile. Don't be intimidated by the complexity of the engine. Once the car has stopped running, it's not a well-tuned whole but an assemblage of reusable parts and pieces. Take out anything that looks promising. The items that follow should get you started, but don't confine yourself to them.

TIRES. Do any of the tires, including the spare, have life left in them? Will they fit your next car or that of someone you know? If so, take them off and save them (otherwise, *see* TIRES).

★ ADVANCED CAR ★ COURSES

People who build their own shop equipment and backyard machinery often turn to an old automobile as a source of parts. The price is right, and individual components may be less worn than the vehicle as a whole. The procedures for adapting car parts to large projects are too detailed for this book, but here are a few suggestions:

• The body of the car can be converted into a "pickup truck." For instructions, send $3 to Ralph C. Bowden, 240 East Scott Avenue, Knoxville, TN 37917.

• The gasoline engine in the car can be hooked up to run a power saw, lathe, or generator.

• Exhaust pipe that's in good condition can be bent into a long U and used as a heat exchanger in the fireplace. (You may also want to install a small fan to keep air circulating through the pipe.)

• The car's horn can be hooked up to a homemade alarm system.

• The drive shaft and alternator can be used in a windmill. For more information on alternator reuse, get a copy of *The Auto Alternator Technology Handbook,* available for $5 from ESSCOA, Box 318C, NFLD, NJ 07435.

• The starter can be converted into a small motor for running homemade machines, such as the heat exchanger made from exhaust pipe.

• The front wheel assembly can be used as the base of a trailer for a boat or a snowmobile.

• Radiators can be incorporated into solar stills.

• The water pump can be used in a homemade wood splitter (directions available in issue number 60 of *Mother Earth News,* available for $3 from *Mother Earth News,* P.O. Box 70, Hendersonville, NC 28739).

★ BUMPER CAR ★

Jason Seley, a sculptor, has been using nothing but car bumpers in his work since 1958. At Cornell University, where he teaches art and architecture, he is best known for his bumper car. Fashioned entirely from bumpers, the car runs nicely, thank you, and holds five passengers.

BATTERY. If the battery is still good, remove it by loosening the bolts that clamp the cables to the terminals. If the bolts won't budge, use a terminal puller to remove the cables from the battery. Lift the battery out of the car and store it until you need it in another car. Check the water level now and then, and store it with its terminals up so it doesn't leak. (*See also* BATTERIES.)

SEATS. Car seats can be reused as furniture in camps, clubhouses, and basements. A good tug should free most backseats. For the front seats, locate and loosen the bolts that hold them to the floor.

KNOBS AND HANDLES. Remove window cranks, knobs on the front panel, door handles, and other fixtures. You never know when you'll need a handle for a screen door or a knob for a pot lid that's lost its original.

BRAKE SHOES. Brake shoes have a very rough, abrasive surface, so if you can get them off the car, you can grab them by the spine and use them to grind oil stains off concrete floors.

HOOD. Some people remove a car's hood by loosening the nuts near the hinge. These same people then turn the hood upside down and use it behind a snowmobile as a sled for hauling firewood.

WINDSHIELD WIPER. Make a squeegee to clean moisture off the inside or outside of your car window by clamping a short section of windshield wiper in a large paper clamp.

WHEELS. A heavy wheel is just the thing for anchoring the pole at the end of your badminton or volleyball net. Use a thick pole that fits tightly into the center hole and fasten the net to it. Then just wheel your net to the court and wheel it away when the game is done. Or mount a movable wheel on the garage wall and use it for rolling up the garden hose. Or bury it in the ground under a downspout and fill the center with gravel so rainwater will run into the ground without eroding the lawn.

★ HOMES FOR UNWANTED AUTOS ★

No matter how tempting it may be, don't walk away from an unwanted car. Every year 170,000 cars are abandoned, congesting city streets and blighting the countryside. This is littering with a vengeance, and it costs local governments—and taxpayers—plenty to clean it up.

If your community is plagued by derelict vehicles and the local government can't afford a cleanup operation, you can recruit volunteers to seek out the cars and tow them to a central location. Then rent a portable flattener that will crush the cars so they can be shipped to the nearest scrap processor. For more detailed information about how to organize such a campaign, write for this booklet: "The Junk Car, From Field to Foundry," available from Ashley Mack, TVA, 274 Summer Place Building, Knoxville, TN 37902.

When a car is abandoned, thieves may "recycle" the parts that are the easiest to sell, but the stripped down shell will continue to scar the landscape.

Never in Your Wildest Dreams

Bomb shelters fell out of favor in the fifties, but there are some people who never stopped worrying about what would happen if nuclear war were declared tomorrow. A few years ago, researchers at the Oak Ridge National Laboratory in Tennessee developed plans for "expedient shelters" that could be built by ordinary people in case of nuclear attack. To construct one of the shelters, appropriately called "Car Over Trench," you dig a trench 40 inches deep and 30 inches wide. Then you drive your car over the trench and fill the car with 2 tons of dirt. In case of attack, you get into the trench. The researchers called this shelter a "last resort," but claim that it provides better protection than the average basement. It took this couple fourteen hours and twenty-seven minutes to build their shelter.

This couple created an emergency bomb shelter by digging a trench, driving an old car over it, and filling the car with two tons of dirt.

WINDOWS. The glass in car windows can be reused in cold frames, light tables, even picture frames. To remove the glass from a door, unscrew the door panel. Inside you'll find lots of nuts and screws. Remove them until you can work the glass out of its track. To take out a windshield, get two friends to stand on either side of the car while you climb up on the hood and loosen the chrome with a screwdriver and a mallet. Under the chrome you'll find a strip of weatherproof rubber. Pry it up all the way around the window and have your friends lift out the glass.

HINGES. The hinges from a car's doors, trunk, and hood can often be reused on gates, lids for bins, shed doors, and other projects.

LIGHTS. The headlights, taillights, and dome light in a car can be removed by unscrewing them from the front or from behind the fender. Hook the lights to a 12-volt battery, and include an on-off switch in the wiring. Now you have an emergency light to use during power failures. The plastic reflectors on top of the lights are also useful. Nail one to a stick to mark the edge of the driveway. Or screw one to your mailbox to keep the snowplow from running it down in the winter.

CARPET. If you didn't use your backseat much or if you kept rubber mats on the floor, the carpet may be worth salvaging. Use a utility knife to cut the carpet free around the edges and pull up gently. Clean with rug shampoo and trim the pieces into throw rugs for the front hall or silencers for the basement steps. (*See also* CARPET SCRAPS.)

The Ghost Parking Lot, a sculpture in a Hamden, Connecticut, shopping center, consists of twenty old cars that appear to be sinking in asphalt.

MIRRORS. Mount car mirrors as extras in the bathroom or bedroom. If you position them right, you'll get an automatic view of the back or side of your head. Parents of small children might want to mount a mirror in a strategic corner so they can, for example, see the playroom from the kitchen.

RADIO. The radio in a car can often be detached—just follow the wires under the dashboard—and installed in a new car.

HUBCAPS. Mounted on short legs and covered with a grill, a hub cap makes a fine little outdoor stove. Drill 1-inch holes through the bottom for ventilation.

BRAKE DRUM. A brake drum makes a fine mushroom anchor for a small boat. Bolt a socket for ¾-inch pipe to the center of the drum on its concave side. Drill a hole through one end of a foot-long piece of ¾-inch pipe and screw the other end into the socket. The anchor rope is passed through the hole at the end of the pipe.

★ ★ ★

If you have more advanced automotive skills, you can salvage engine parts from the car and sell them to a secondhand-parts store. The price you'll get for the parts separately is sure to be more than you'd get for the car as a whole. Generally, the most sellable parts are the fuel pump, starter, radiator, alternator, voltage regulator, core charger, carburetor, and transmission. If you have really advanced skills, you may want to save some of those parts for your own use. And while you're taking the car apart, don't forget to salvage all those hoses, belts, wires, screws, springs, and bolts.

Once your car has been stripped, it can still be used as a greenhouse for spring seedlings, a storage shed for tools, or a winter palace for your dog. More likely you'll want to sell it to a scrap processor, who will reprocess it into steel. If you can't locate a scrap processor who will haul away your car, your options are few and fanciful. Maybe you can find an architect who will want to use your car in a sculpture like the *Ghost Parking Lot* constructed by SITE in the Hamden Plaza Shopping Center in Connecticut. Other people donate useless cars to carnivals where people pay a quarter to bash them with sledgehammers. Apparently lots of people have pent-up hostility toward cars, because these events always attract participants. If all else fails, organize a community cleanup and ask that your old wreck be the first to go.

See also METAL SCRAP; TIRES.

CARTONS

See BOXES, CARDBOARD; EGG CARTONS; MILK CONTAINERS; PLASTIC CONTAINERS

CHAIRS

See FURNITURE

CHEWING GUM

Don't stick your used chewing gum on the underside of your chair! There are better uses for it. Gum is, after all, an adhesive that dries rock hard, so in an emergency it can be used for sealing punctures in hoses, holding a loose heel on a shoe until you can hobble to the cobbler, and other purposes. In fact, you may want to save (and sterilize) some prechewed gum by storing it in a small bottle of rubbing alcohol. Don't rechew stored gum! Instead, try one of these ideas:

LIKE ATTRACTS LIKE. The only way to remove chewing gum from hair or fabric is to use more chewing gum. Take a fresh wad and dab it over the gum spot. The old gum will adhere to the new.

CLEAN KEYS. To clean the keys of your typewriter, dab chewing gum on them. The gum will pick up the ink and gunk that accumulates around the type and makes for fuzzy impressions.

GUM TO THE RESCUE. You'll be very glad you've saved your chewing gum next time you're faced with a light bulb that broke in its socket. After breaking off the sharp edges of glass with pliers, jam a large wad of soft gum into the metal part of the bulb. Let the gum harden, then grab hold of the gum plug, twist, and remove the bulb.

CHRISTMAS TREES

Every Christmas millions of little evergreens are sacrificed for a few weeks of merriment. That sacrifice will seem less pathetic if you reuse your tree when the holiday is over.

BLAZING BRANCHES. Use the branches from your tree for kindling, but be careful, because the dry needles ignite quickly and burn intensely. Although you shouldn't make a habit of burning softwood, because it causes creosote buildup, you can saw the trunk of the tree into fireplace logs.

GARDENER'S CHOICE. Trim the branches off the trunk of your Christmas tree and use them to mulch around bushes.

SWEET DREAMS. Make little pillows out of sheer scraps of fabric and fill them with needles from your Christmas tree. Use the pillows to freshen drawers and closets. Pillows filled with balsam are especially fragrant.

CHRISTMAS QUERL. A querl is a traditional German cooking whisk, used for beating eggs, stirring gravy, and other kitchen operations. To make a querl from a Christmas tree, look for a spot near the top of the trunk where several branches grow opposite each other. Saw through the trunk just below the branches. Cut the handle of the querl to be about 12 inches long and the beaters to be 2 inches. Peel off the bark and smooth down the wood. To use the querl, put the branched end in the pot and twirl it by rubbing the handle back and forth between your hands.

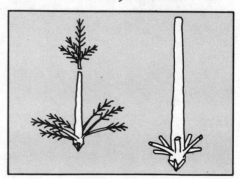

★ A TREE FOR ★ ALL HOLIDAYS

Next year, instead of buying—and discarding—a cut evergreen, consider purchasing a potted tree. Decorate it for the holidays and plant it outdoors in the spring.

GOODWILL TOWARD BIRDS. Put a Christmas tree on its side in a protected spot where the birds can use it as a winter sanctuary. The birds will be especially grateful if you've trimmed your tree with popcorn and cranberries.

SNOW HEDGE. If the wind drives snow over your driveway or sidewalk, collect trees from several neighbors and line them up as a windbreak. Anchor the Christmas trees by tying them to cement blocks and burying the blocks in the snow.

See also WOOD SCRAPS.

CIGARETTE BUTTS

Yes, even a cigarette butt can be recycled—as a natural insecticide to kill mealybugs, the wispy white pests on your houseplants. Open up several cigarette butts and empty the tobacco into a small container. Soak the tobacco in water overnight. In the morning, strain the tobacco water, pour it into a pump container, and spray it on the plants. Good-bye mealybugs.

★ DON'T ASH ★

For some reason, cigarette ashes mixed with a little water turn into a paste that can be used to polish silver. Rub the silver vigorously with a soft cloth dipped in the paste. Rinse and dry.

CITRUS PEEL

Although citrus peelings can go into the compost heap (*see* GARBAGE), the rinds from lemons, tangerines, limes, oranges, and grapefruits are fragrant and tasty, so they can be used in many special ways. Here are a few:

SWEET AIR. Citrus peels are a natural air freshener. Put them in a warm oven or toss them onto a wood fire. The citrus oils, released by the heat, will permeate the house with their sweet scent.

ZEST. Seasonings made from citrus peelings are called zest because they add just that to food. Use the colored outer layer of the rind—the white part is bitter. Grate citrus rinds fresh for cookies, cakes, sauces, fruit salads, rice, and main dishes. To preserve zest spread it on a cookie sheet and leave it in a warm oven for an hour or so. Powder the dried rind and store in a tightly capped spice bottle.

CANDIED PEEL. This luscious-looking sweet is easy to make. Cut citrus peels into narrow strips until you have 2 cups. Put the peels in a pan with 2 cups water and simmer for ten minutes. Drain, add more water, and simmer again. Repeat the process two more times. Now make a thick syrup from ½ cup water and 1 cup sugar. Add the peel to the syrup and boil until the liquid has been absorbed. The peel turns transparent but retains its bright color. Spread it on a rack to dry. Later you can roll the candied peel in sugar, dip it in chocolate, or eat it plain. Store in an airtight tin.

CLEANSER CANS

Cleanser cans come in two varieties—cardboard cylinders with metal tops (*see also* CARDBOARD TUBES) and plastic containers with snap-off tops (*see also* PLASTIC CONTAINERS). The cardboard contain-

ers biodegrade more readily, but the plastic ones are easier to reuse. Snap off the top, wash with hot sudsy water, and refill with something that should be dispensed from a shaker, perhaps baking soda to smother grease fires or insecticide to sprinkle on garden plants. Be sure to cover the old label with brown paper and mark the new contents on it.

The holes in the top of cleanser cans lend themselves to other uses. Here are a few suggestions:

BUG TRAP. A cleanser can is a cheap alternative to the exterminator. Open the can and put bug bait and poison inside. Snap on the plastic top or tape on the metal top. Set the poison can in the path of the bugs so they'll crawl through the holes, eat the bait, and die inside. Instead of sweeping up tiny corpses, just throw away the can. This method has the added advantage of keeping the poison away from kids and pets.

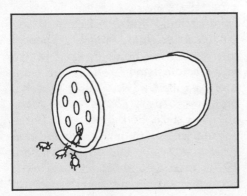

DISENTANGLED. If you want to keep a set of strings or other fibers from getting tangled, keep them separated by slipping each one through one of the holes in the cover of a cleanser can.

DRAIN SAVER. Remove the plastic top or cut the metal top out of a cardboard cleanser container with a pair of scissors. Put the disc over an open drain to keep hair and small objects from clogging it.

HEAVEN SCENT. The holes in the top of the cleanser can make it a natural container for odor killers, sachets, and other air fresheners. Fill the container with mothballs for the attic or potpourri for the linen closet.

CLOTHES

Fashion dictates that we throw out our clothes before they wear out. Good sense contradicts the notion but rarely wins the argument. Most of us exile perfectly good clothes to the back of the closet for simple crimes of cut and color.

There are alternatives. Damaged clothes can be repaired, clothes that bore you can be camouflaged, and outdated clothes can be reconstructed. Clothes that have been outgrown—physically or psychologically—can be given away, and hopeless cases can be dismantled for parts. Here's how:

REPAIR. For want of a button, the shirt was lost. If you've ever had to say that, you need a remedial course in mending. Most mending is a matter of common sense.

Replacing buttons is equally easy, especially if you've saved the extras from clothing you've discarded (*see* BUTTONS). Use sturdy thread and bring it through all the holes at least twelve times before tying it off. If you want more explicit advice about specific problems, consult *The Mender's Manual* by Estelle Foot (Harcourt Brace Jovanovich, 1976) or *A Guide to Basic Sewing*, edited by Ethne Rose (Nelson, 1979), two no-nonsense volumes full of contemporary tips and hints. Once you master the basics, think of mending as a creative as well as thrifty exercise. Use it to improve your clothes—cover small holes with appliqués, make patches of contrasting fabric, embroider over rips. Inventive mending can make a sad schmatte into a favorite ensemble.

★ SON OF AN ★ OLD FAVORITE

Some clothes fit so well we grieve when they wear out. If you find yourself faced by the demise of an old favorite, take it apart very carefully, making notes on its construction. Then use the pieces of fabric as the pattern for a new favorite.

★ SEVEN WAYS TO FOOL YOURSELF ★ INTO THINKING YOU'VE NEVER WORN THAT SHIRT BEFORE

<u>Appliqué.</u> Appliqué is a fancy name for a patch. Cut an interesting shape out of fabric, or cut out several pieces and arrange them in a patchwork pattern. Baste the appliqué in place and sew around all the edges with the zigzag attachment of your sewing machine. If you prefer, cut your patches from iron-on material and skip the sewing.

<u>Beads and Buttons.</u> Beads and buttons are another way of enlivening dull clothes. Use heavy thread to sew them on. Make designs with the buttons themselves or use them to accent embroidery and appliqué.

<u>Dye.</u> Dyeing is perhaps the most dramatic way to camouflage an old garment. Dyes are cheap, and you can do the job in the kitchen sink or a washing machine. Experiment with tie-dyeing and batik.

<u>Embroidery.</u> Embroidery adds a delicate touch to old clothes. Though you can get a pleasing effect with a simple cross stitch, you may want to consult a book like Anchor Embroidery's *100 Embroidery Stitches* (Scribner's, 1971) for fancier ideas.

<u>Paint.</u> Painting is one of the quickest ways to redecorate an old garment. Use textile paint or washable acrylics for large splashy patterns. For more delicate work, try embroidery paints, which come in little tubes with writing tips.

<u>Printing.</u> Hand printing is a real pick-me-up for old clothes. Make simple patterns with linoleum blocks and indelible ink. Or use stencils and acrylic paint.

<u>Ribbons, Lace, and Rickrack.</u> Sometimes all an old garment needs is a row of lace at the hem or a touch of rickrack on the collar. Topstitch along the edges of the trim.

CAMOUFLAGE. Camouflage is altering the look of clothes without altering the clothes themselves. It reached a high point in the sixties, when people were inspired to cover their old blue jeans with paint, mirrors, macramé, and various other materials. Less flamboyant forms of camouflage are still good techniques for extending the wearable life of your informal clothes.

RECONSTRUCTION. Reconstruction, the magical process of making new clothes from old, requires more sewing skill. Those who have it can convert dresses into smocks, dressing gowns into skirts, skirts into dresses, and almost anything into children's clothes. Boldness is the key to reconstruction. Take a hard look at the obsolete garment. Decide what you despise about it and figure out how to alter the despicable feature. Then rip into those seams. If the project is an abysmal failure, you haven't lost an outfit—you've gained hanger space (and, if you're lucky, a reusable zipper or a handful of buttons). For specific reconstruction ideas and instructions, check out one of these books:

How to Recycle Old Clothes into New Fashions by Fenya Crown (Prentice Hall, 1977);
New Clothes from Old by Gloria R. Mosesson (Bobbs-Merrill, 1977);
Oldies but Goodies by Donna Lawson (Butterick, 1977).

GIVEAWAYS. Hand-me-downs are a delicate matter, always tainted with condescension. Adults as well as children could wear the clothes their friends are finished with, but they don't. That reluctance probably explains why most people would rather give their clothes away to strangers.

Happily, there are plenty of strangers waiting to receive them, including the

★ FIVE THINGS ★ TO DO WITH A SOW'S EAR

Tastes differ, styles change, so there's no point in giving detailed instructions about what to do with a Nehru jacket or a cowl neck sweater. Suffice it to say that these five strategies have added years to the lives of millions of garments.

Shorten. Cut off long sleeves to make short sleeves, short sleeves to make vests. Shorten a dress into a tunic. Cut off pants to make shorts or bloomers.

Lengthen. Add cuffs to sleeves, ruffles to dresses, flared bottoms to pants. Use a contrasting fabric for fun.

Change the Neckline. Change a turtleneck to a scoop neck. Add a collar. Remove a collar. Try V-necks, round necks, keyhole necks.

Change the Sleeves. Gather the sleeves at the wrist. Make them puff at the elbow. Leave them long and loose. Cuff them.

Mix and Match. Graft the good parts from one garment onto the good parts of another. Take sleeves from one shirt and sew them to the body of a second shirt. Replace the top of a dress with a sweater.

★ NOTIONS ★ COUNTER

Before consigning old clothes to the rag bag, strip them of their valuables:

- Buttons
- Collars
- Elastic
- Hooks and eyes
- Sleeves
- Snaps
- Zippers

Salvation Army, Goodwill Industries, your local church, thrift shops, theater groups, and even nursery schools where the kids use them for dress-up. Be sure everything is clean and mended before you give it away. And ask for a receipt so you can claim the value of the clothing as a tax deduction.

DISMANTLING. After exhausting the first four possibilities, you're left with one drastic alternative—dismantle your clothes. Use a single-edge razor blade or a seam ripper to open the seams. Salvage the fabric (see FABRIC SCRAPS) and the notions.

See also BELTS; BLUE JEANS; COATS AND JACKETS; GLOVES; NECKTIES; PANTS; SHOES; SOCKS; SWEATERS.

★ KIDDIE ★ CLOTHES

If you are a parent, one of the best things to do with your old clothes is remake them into children's clothes. An adult coat usually has plenty of fabric for a toddler's snowsuit. Mommy's worn-out slip can be converted into a fancy nightgown for a little girl. And the sleeves from Daddy's workshirt can be converted into a pair of shorts for Junior. Although you can dismantle the adult clothes and recut the fabric following a child's pattern, there are easier ways of transforming adult duds into kiddie clothes. For advice, consult *Kid's Clothes for Under $5* by Donna Lawson (Music Sales, 1978).

CLOTHES HANGERS

See HANGERS

CLOTHESPINS

In many homes the tumble dryer has driven clothespins into retirement. Yet quite a few people still have a bag of them stashed at the back of a closet. Their reuses depend upon whether you are facing two-piece clothespins that are fastened with a wire spring or single-piece clothespins. The spring clothespins are handy for clamping jobs; the single-piece clothespins are actually wooden dowels split open on one end.

CLAMP DOWN. When glueing thin objects, use spring clothespins as clamps. Position them evenly around the glued area and leave in place until the glue sets.

ELECTRIFYING. With two spring clothespins, you can make a quick set of terminal clips to check electrical connections. Unfasten the two wooden sections. At the pinching point of one, screw in a small bolt and file the head flat. At the pinching point of the other, screw a bolt right through the wood. Put two washers and a nut on it. Reassemble the clothespin. The two bolts should make contact. Now simply loosen the nut, wrap electrical wire around the bolt between the washers, and screw down. For testing purposes, the other end of the wire can go to a simple light fixture.

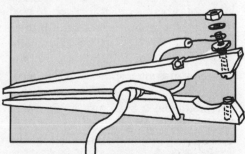

CLOTHESIPHON. When siphoning gas out of a tank, the hard part is getting the flow of gasoline started through the tube. A clothespin can help. Stick one end of a flexible plastic tube into the gas tank. Double over the end of the hose and clamp a clothespin over it. Wind up the hose on the clothespin, flattening the hose as you go. The flattening presses out the air, so when you unwind the resulting vacuum sucks the gas right into the hose.

SCREW ANCHOR. Use one-piece clothespins to anchor large screws in plaster. Cut off the head off a pin and measure the diameter of the stub. Drill a hole that size into the wall and drive the clothespin into the hole. Insert the screw into the clothespin and turn. The screw will bite more readily into the wood and the pressure will create a tight plug.

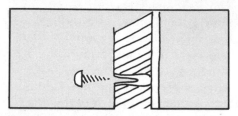

HANDY HANDLES. To make a simple knob for a screen door or a drawer, cut off a one-piece clothespin just below the cleft. To make or replace a handle on a small tool, insert the handle end of the tool between the legs of the clothespin. Drill a small hole through the

"sandwich" and insert a wire through the hole. Twist the wire to keep the handle from slipping and wrap it tightly around both legs of the clothespin.

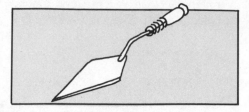

CLIPBOARDS. A set of clothespins screwed to a piece of wood makes a convenient rack for small objects that might otherwise go astray. Use spring clothespins to hold messages, dish towels, and other flimsy items. Use one-piece pins for small tools, toothbrushes, kitchen utensils, and even the tips of fishing poles.

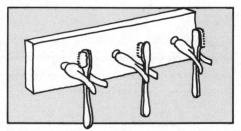

CANNED STORAGE. The number one use for coffee cans is undoubtedly storage, since the metal keeps out moisture and pests and the snap-on lid preserves freshness. In the kitchen, use the cans for pasta, lentils, popcorn, nuts, and other loose foods. When you go camping, use coffee cans for a small supply of cereal or flour. Or give gifts of homemade cookies and candies packed in decorated coffee cans.

In the workshop, coffee cans make ideal storage for the heavier nuts, bolts, and nails, as well as leftover bits of paint, turpentine, and other liquids. To use one as a paintbrush cleaner, cut a slit in the plastic lid and force the brush handle through it so the bristles are suspended in the liquid in the can.

This list could continue until it hit everyone's favorite thing to put in coffee cans, but it concludes with a classic—using coffee cans to hold bait for fishing. To improve on this idea, cut both ends out of the coffee can and cap them with plastic lids. Then when the worms crawl to the bottom of the can—as they always do—you can turn the can upside down and dig into the new bottom.

COATS AND JACKETS

The warming capability of a coat usually outlives its appearance. That's why coats in most households go through an informal progression from "good" coat to everyday coat to weekend-in-the-woods coat. In fact, with a little alteration you can save yourself much of the expense of winter sportswear by recycling coats and jackets. Try cutting off a full-length city coat to turn it into a hip-length hiking jacket. Turn an old raincoat into a gardening or fishing jacket by cutting it off and using the extra fabric to make roomy pockets for your gear. If the sleeves and collar get tatty before the rest of the coat, make a heavy vest by removing them and facing the edges with the extra fabric. Other coats are roomy enough to be converted into capes.

The only rule is to look at the coat's

design and see how it can best be modified. Then rip into the job. Even if you ruin the coat as a whole, you can still use the parts. Down, for instance, can be salvaged for stuffing pillows, sleeping bags, or new clothing made from kits. Save fur for hats and muffs and leather for patches and bags. Coat cloth can be treated like any other salvaged fabric (*see* FABRIC SCRAPS).

COFFEE CANS

Coffee cans are a favored branch of the can family. Their size is handy, and the snap-on lids guarantee them a spot on the "save this" list in most households. In fact, coffee cans have so many uses that they may be hard to come by. If that's your problem, remember that 46-ounce juice cans and 3-pound shortening cans are good substitutes.

★ CAMPING CANS ★

The resourceful camper can make an entire cooking kit from empty coffee cans.

Fire Starter. To start a charcoal fire without lighter fluid, cut out both ends of a coffee can and punch holes in the sides for ventilation. Crumple a wad of newspaper in the bottom of the can, light it, and fill the can with charcoal. Once the coals are glowing, remove the chimney with tongs or cook right over it.

Vagabond Stoves. The Girl Scouts have always sworn by this simple tin can stove: Remove one end from a large-size coffee can. Cut a "door" 3 inches wide and 3 inches tall with a pair of tin snips. Punch holes in the top of the stove for ventilation. Now press the stove into the dirt so it makes a ring. Remove the can and build a twig fire inside the circle. Put the stove over the fire, feed it through the door, and fry your eggs on top.

A variation of this stove uses charcoal. Use a can opener to punch air holes around the top and bottom of a coffee can. Roll a narrow strip of wire mesh into a coil and place it at the bottom of the can. Cut a second piece of mesh the size of the can opening and lay it flat on top of the coil. Cut a third piece of mesh larger than the can opening and use it as a cooking surface. Put your charcoal on the inside mesh platform, light, and cook.

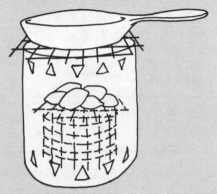

Camping Kettles. To make a kettle from a coffee can, punch holes just under the upper rim on opposite sides of the can. Loop an old hanger through the holes.

Toasty Idea. Making a toaster from a coffee can is equally easy. Punch eight evenly spaced holes around the can's rim. Straighten two coat hangers, cut them in half, and insert the pieces of wire through the holes to make a tic-tac-toe pattern. Set your toaster over a bed of hot coals and get out the jam.

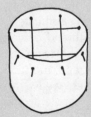

Cheap Light. Need an extra lantern on a camping trip? Fill an old coffee can with clay or heavy dirt, packed tight to within an inch of the rim. Wrap a thin rag around a stick and push it into the dirt. Then pour the fat from bacon or other meat into the can. Light the rag. You'll be surprised how long and bright this hobo lamp will burn.

Solar Can. On a bright summer day the sun can make your coffee with the help of a coffee can. Paint the can flat black on the outside. Fill with water and cover with a black lid. Set the can on a sheet of foil in the bright sun. Now go for a hike. When you come back, you'll have hot water for coffee.

Canned Potatoes. If you find that the potatoes you bake in the campfire always get a little scorched, try putting each spud in its own can before roasting. The can acts like a miniature oven, evening out the heat.

Can-Do Tripod. If you want to support a pot over the campfire, make a tripod from a coffee can with a hole near the rim and three green sticks about a yard in length.

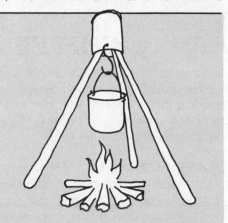

Wedge the ends of the sticks into the can so their free ends form a tripod. Bend a piece of coat hanger wire into an S-hook and slip one end of the hook through the hole in the coffee can and use the other end to hold the handle of your pot.

Camper's Potty. Last, but not least, don't forget that a large coffee can with a lid makes a convenient, in-tent toilet for the middle of the night.

COFFEE CUPS, STYROFOAM

All over America, coffee shops are sending out millions of Styrofoam coffee cups with little plastic lids. It's not easy to reuse 250 of them every year, but here are a few ideas:

LUNCH CUP. Rinse out the coffee cup you got in the morning and make instant soup in it for lunch. Then take it home and store the leftovers from your supper in it. If they are the kind of leftovers that can be eaten cold, pop the cup into a bag the next morning and take it to work for lunch.

COMMUTER CUP. If you drink coffee while driving, cut a triangular wedge in the lid, fasten it on the cup, and drink through the notch. No more sloshed coffee!

COFFEE MATE. A Styrofoam cup can substitute as a coffee maker when you want a single cup of java. Cut four small holes in the bottom of the cup, line the inside with a paper towel, and add a tablespoonful of ground coffee. Hold the cup over another cup and fill it with hot water. The water will drip through, making exactly one cup of coffee.

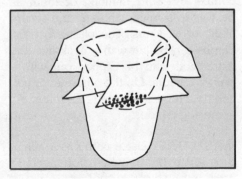

BAIT CUPS. When you go fishing, store your live bait in Styrofoam cups so they'll stay cool and lively.

See also STYROFOAM.

COFFEE GROUNDS

Coffee grounds are organic matter, so they can be composted with the apple peels and eggshells (*see* GARBAGE). They can also be used in other ways.

PLANT PICK-ME-UP. Most houseplants respond well to a light sprinkling of coffee grounds on top of the soil. Don't overdo this treatment, because the acid from the grounds can harm the plants.

ODOR EATER. For some reason, coffee grounds absorb odors, so they can be used to freshen smelly places. Dry the grounds by spreading them out on a cookie sheet and leaving it in a warm oven. Then set a can of grounds in the refrigerator or sprinkle some in the cat box.

DYEING FOR COFFEE. Even when they're too weak to make a cup of coffee, used grounds will produce a warm brown dye for fabric or paper. Soak the

★ THE THREE- ★ YEAR FILTER

Coffee filters can also go into the compost heap. On the other hand, if it irritates you to spend a cent or two on each throwaway filter, switch to a reusable variety. Sold under the names Filtertek and Perma-Brew, this filter fits all coffee makers, can be cleaned in the dishwasher, and is guaranteed for three years. It's available in many supermarkets for about $3. If you can't find one, write to the manufacturer: Tops Manufacturing Company, 83 Salisbury Road, Darien, CT 06820.

This reusable coffee filter can be washed in the dishwasher between uses.

grounds in water for an hour to get the best color, then filter carefully through a strainer lined with cloth. Try using a coffee tint on homemade stationery (*see* PAPER). Or use it to dye dingy lingerie a sexy shade of beige.

COMBS, TOOTHED AND TOOTHLESS

Old-fashioned combs used to make a delightful ping when their teeth broke off. Newer combs are made of sterner stuff. They don't wear out as easily, but they do accumulate at the bottom of dresser drawers. Bring out those old combs and start thinking of them as devices to scratch, smooth, and secure fibers of all kinds. The plastic in most combs can be cut with a hacksaw, and extra teeth can be clipped out with a pair of scissors. On the other hand, you can do a lot with a comb as is. Here are some suggestions:

WASH DAY. Use a comb as a miniature scrub board when you need to wash out a stubborn spot.

BACK SCRATCHER. Anyone who's had an itch in the center of his or her back knows that back scratchers are no joke. To make one from old combs, find

a stick of wood at least 18 inches long and 1 inch in diameter, perhaps a section from a broomstick. Drill two holes in the backs of the combs and screw them to either side of the broomstick. Then scratch away.

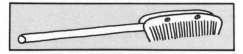

THUMB PROTECTOR. Next time you have to pound a small nail, hold it in place by supporting it between two teeth in an old comb. If you miss the nail, you'll pulverize the comb and not your fingers.

SINGING COMB. A comb with or without its teeth makes a good kazoo. Fold a piece of waxed paper over the teeth. Hold the comb teeth up between your lips and hum to make the paper buzz. Play "She'll Be Combing Round

the Mountain," "There's No Place Like Comb," and other down-comb favorites.

COMB LOOM. Find two combs whose teeth are the same size. Drill three holes through the backbone of each comb. Screw the two combs to opposite ends of a piece of wood 1 inch thick and as long as the item you wish to weave. Wind thread or yarn back and forth between the teeth of the combs, starting at one end and working toward the other. Then weave an over-and-under pattern parallel to the combs.

NO-SLIP SLICER. A comb that has been cleaned and sterilized in boiling water can be used to hold slippery objects in place when you slice them. Insert the teeth into the item to be sliced—perhaps a slippery onion—and hold the spine while wielding the knife.

CORD

See STRING

CORKS

Real corks are becoming scarce, so those you pop out of your wine bottles should be treated like the household resource that they are. You can, of course, use your corks to stopper new bottles. Or you can devise other uses which take advantage of the fact that corks are soft enough to carve and light enough to float. Here are a few possibilities:

SHARPIE. Run the edge of an almost dull razor blade through an old cork and you'll be able to use it for a few more shaves.

FLOATER. Boat freaks and fishers should drill holes in corks and string them on their key chains so the keys will float if they go overboard.

STAMP OF APPROVAL. Like to leave your imprint on things? All it takes is an old cork with one smooth end. Draw a simple design—perhaps your initials—on the end of the cork and cut away the material outside the line with the tip of a sharp knife. Press the cork on an ink pad and leave your mark on notepads, fabric, clothing labels, and other personal possessions.

UNDER CORKS. Make handsome coasters and trivets out of whole corks turned on their sides or corks sliced into ½-inch rounds with a sharp thin knife. Drill holes in the corks and assemble them Tinker Toy fashion with toothpicks or bamboo sticks.

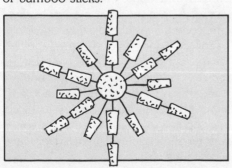

CORK CUSHION. A cork is an obvious place to stick pins, tacks, and little nails. Or glue a cork to the top of your workbench or recipe file. Slit the top with a razor blade and insert the directions you're following at the moment.

SHINE ON. For some reason, dull metal objects begin to gleam when you rub them with a cork. This trick works wonders on brass lamps, old knife blades, and kitchen cutlery, among other things.

CORNCOBS

Most people know that corn is best fresh picked and eaten right off the cob. Everybody knows what to do with the corn, but what about the cobs? First, spread them in the sun and let them dry. Then make use of their rough texture and absorbency. Here are three suggestions:

GROUND COB. If you have a grinder, chop the corncobs into coarse chunks. Use the chunks as a soil conditioner, in the compost heap, or as kitty litter.

CORNCOB TORCH. To make a bright torch for summer evenings, soak a dry corncob in kerosene or used motor oil for about six hours. Drill a hole in the bottom of a small tomato paste can and screw the can to the end of a broomstick. Ram the soaked corncob into the can and light it. It will burn for a surprisingly long time.

SCRUB COB. Dried corncobs are rough enough to make short work of dirty cleanup jobs. Next time you have a grimy task—cleaning the barbecue grill or scrubbing the mud off a bicycle fender—grab a corncob, dip it in water, and use it to scrub away the dirt.

CRAYON STUBS

Anyone who spends much time around children knows that crayons that start out as straight, bright, pointed sticks of color end up as dirty little nubs. Prolong the life of short crayons by wedging them into the tubes left over from empty felt-tip pens. Even when they are too short to hold, crayon stubs have uses if you think of them as short sticks of colored wax. Scrape off the dirty flecks and use them for . . .

TRANSFERS. To transfer a pattern to wood or fabric, use a crayon stub to trace it onto tracing paper. Turn the crayoned side of the paper toward the material and press with a warm iron. The wax will melt, leaving a mirror image of the pattern.

CANDLE COLOR. Add color to homemade candles by shaving off a bit of old crayon and adding the flakes to the melted wax. This is a good way to camouflage the fact that you are making new candles out of stubs (*see* CANDLE STUBS). Don't try making candles exclusively from crayon wax, because they'll sputter and smell.

CRAYON CREATIONS. One way to decorate recycled cans, bottles, boxes, and fabric is to cover them with brilliant blotches of crayon wax. Clean the surface to be decorated and remove the paper from the crayons. Melt the crayon wax by putting several crayons of the same color in a frozen food tin—the partitioned ones are perfect—and putting it in a 100-degree oven. Or hold the candle stubs with tweezers and pass them through the flame of a candle. Drip the melted wax onto the object or spread it with a stiff brush. Vary the colors and overlap layers of wax. The final result will be a colorful, textured surface that's durable as long as it doesn't get hot.

DANDELIONS

America's most ubiquitous weed, the dandelion, is much maligned by gardeners and lawn growers. If you've always imagined that there's more to do with dandelions than swear at them, you're right. In fact, there's so much more that you may want to turn the entire front yard over to their cultivation.

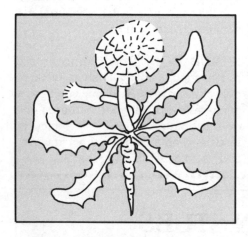

WEED WINE. The most famous dandelion byproduct is wine, made from the golden blossoms before they turn fuzzy. For detailed recipes consult:

   Super Easy, Step-by-Step Winemaking by Yvonne Tarr (Random House, 1977).
   Wild Plants for Wine-Making by Edwin Belt (British Book Center, 1974).
   Wine-making at Home by Bruce Palmer (Workman, 1975).

GREAT GREENS. Dandelion leaves are a desirable green in the spring when other salad makings are in short supply. They contain plenty of Vitamins A and C, iron, calcium, and even protein. Gather the greens before the plant blossoms, when they are most tender. Toss them with other greens in salads or cook them like spinach.

ROOT BREW. Dandelion roots make a coffee substitute much like chicory.

Dig the roots, scrub carefully, and roast in a low oven until they are dark brown. Grind in a blender or a coffee grinder. Mix a little dandelion powder into your regular coffee before brewing, or boil a teaspoon of powder with a cup of water for about two minutes to make a stimulating coffee alternative.

FRIED FLOWERS. For a distinctive springtime dish, try fried dandelion flowers. Pick fresh new blossoms, rinse, and drain. Cut off all the greenery and dip each blossom into tempura batter. Deep-fry until golden. Then salt and serve. Who knew weeds could be so tasty?

★ POISONED ★ POSIES

Since dandelions are considered a weed, some people use herbicides to get rid of them. Dandelions may also be contaminated by sprays used on other plants. For both these reasons, pick dandelions and their leaves only in places where you can be sure they are free of poisons, preferably in your own yard.

DEODORANT BOTTLES

If you buy your deodorant in pump bottles, turn to PUMP CONTAINERS. If you buy your deodorant in aerosol cans, shame on you—there's no way to reuse them. If you buy your deodorant in little bottles with big round balls, be sure you make use of those remarkable containers. To separate the plastic top that holds the roll-on ball from the container itself, find the line of separation and pry

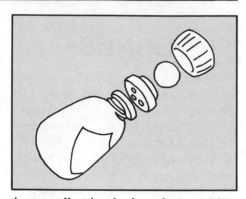

the top off with a knife or fingernail file. Once the top has been removed, the bottle can be refilled with all kinds of liquids and the top snapped back in place. Try filling empty deodorant bottles with:

- Bath oil: spreads more easily
- Liquid starch: roll on collars and cuffs before ironing
- Paint: kids can paint all afternoon without making a mess; use poster paints and thin if necessary
- Suntan lotion: roll it onto your body so your hands don't get sticky
- Water: for moistening tape and postage stamps.

See also JARS AND BOTTLES.

DETERGENT SQUEEZE BOTTLES

Dishwashing detergent always comes in tall plastic containers. Some have snip-off lids and some have clever lift-up valves. All are made of pure polyethylene, so in a sensible society they would be collected and recycled into new bottles for more dishwashing detergent. In our society, you'll have to rinse the bottles, soak off the labels, and reuse them, either whole as squirt bottles or sliced into open-mouthed receptacles for a variety of household items. Here are suggestions:

SQUEEZE FOR SUDS. Even after the detergent is gone, the squeeze bottle can be used for soap. Break up the remnants of old bars into pieces small enough to fit through the neck of the bottle. Cover the soap bits with water and let them sit for a day or so. Then shake the bottle and squeeze out suds to wash hands, dishes, and lots of other things.

TWO FOR ONE. Cut a plastic squeeze bottle in half with a sharp knife. Use the bottom as a starter pot for plants and the top as a funnel.

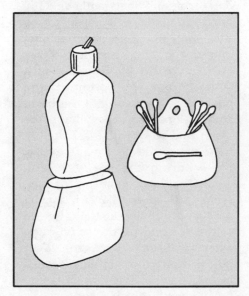

SECRET FORMULAS. Many people save money by making their own cleaning products. Store those homemade solutions in plastic squeeze bottles—just be sure to label each bottle. For recipes, consult *The Formula Book* by Norman Stark (Sheed, Andrews, McNeel, 1975).

WATER, WATER. Keep an extra squeeze bottle full of water all the time. It's handy for watering plants, filling the steam iron, spot-cleaning the floor, and other chores. Keep another water bottle in the car for cleaning the windshield when you run out of wiper fluid and rinsing your hands after you change a flat.

SQUIRT FUN. In the summer, give the kids squeeze bottles full of water and let them have an old-fashioned water fight. In the winter, add a few drops of food coloring to each bottle and let them paint the snow.

SQUEEZE BREEZE. An empty detergent bottle isn't really empty—it's full of air. You can put that fact to good use by squeezing a puff of air over figurines, gears, and other delicate parts that need to be dusted.

See also PLASTIC CONTAINERS.

DISHES AND COOKWARE

Somehow well-equipped kitchens have a way of becoming overequipped. Sets of dishes break one by one until only a few orphans sit forlornly on the shelf. Faithful old pots and pans, retired in favor of newer, more specialized utensils, sulk in the dark corners of the cupboard. Instead of letting these extra items occupy needed space, reassign them. Here are a few suggestions:

CUPS

If you find your cupboard cluttered by extra coffee cups and mugs, exploit their dipper shapes and handy handles.

GETTING A HANDLE ON IT. If you have more cups than bowls, serve soup and even cereal in coffee cups and mugs. Make individual servings of Jello gelatin and pudding in them, too. Kids, especially, find it easier to eat when they can grab hold of the bowl.

FINGER CUPS. China cups without handles can be rechristened as finger bowls. Set one beside each person's plate when you serve fried chicken or spareribs.

GET THE SCOOP. Use extra cups or mugs as scoops for flour, sugar, cat food, and other dry staples. Keep one mug in each container or bag.

GLASSES

Drinking glasses accumulate in most houses, perhaps because we can't resist saving the ones that come with jelly and cheese. There is, however, no law that says these glasses must be used for beverages.

SHELVE IT. Glass shelves show off knickknacks to advantage, and you can make a set with four matching glasses and three pieces of 12 × 5 window glass. Turn two glasses upside down, spread "superglue" on their rims, and set them on a sheet of glass. Now spread glue on their bases and place another sheet of glass on top of them. Glue two more glasses directly over the first set and add another shelf. Let the glue dry thoroughly before using the shelves.

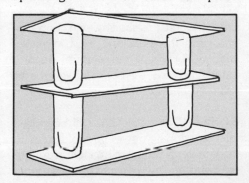

JELLY GLASS. Fill your extra glasses with homemade jelly for gifts or for yourself. Pick the fruit at U-Pick farms (call the county extension agent for farms in your area), and cook according to the recipes in any cookbook. Wash the glasses in hot water and sterilize them with boiling water before they cool. Fill with hot jelly and seal with melted paraffin.

CHIPPED LIPS. A glass with a chipped lip is dangerous for drinking, but it's fine for container jobs like holding toothbrushes or combs in the bathroom.

Just wrap a piece of plastic tape around the rim and no one will be the wiser.

VICTORIANA. Turn extra glasses with interesting shapes into miniature bell jars by inverting them over tiny arrangements of dried flowers.

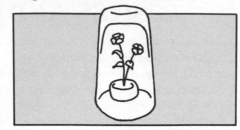

POTS

If you can afford it, buy good pots. The extra expense is justified by the pleasure of cooking in responsive containers. Eventually, of course, even good pots must be demoted. When that day comes, think of them as durable containers, with or without lids and handles, to be used for jobs like these:

PANISTER. An old pan with a tight lid makes an extra canister for flour, tea, pasta, and other staples. Don't need a container in the kitchen? Send the pot to the garage to hold pet food, bird seed or potting soil. Don't hesitate to paint the pot a bright color and add a decal or two.

DOUBLE TROUBLE. Use a disreputable pot to hold the water in an improvised double boiler. Put two inches in the old pot and add several marbles. Set the second pot into the first and turn on the fire. Why the marbles? If the first pot is boiling dry, the marbles will alert you with their noise.

BAKE-OFF. An old pot that's lost its handle can be used as a baking dish in the oven. Make round breads, casseroles, and puddings.

MIX UP. Or use that old pan as a mixing bowl. If it has a handle, grab it with one hand while you stir with the other.

BIG SCOOP. An old pot with a handle is a scoop for bailing water out of anything from a boat to a stopped sink, dipping animal food out of a sack, or scooping up just enough compost to go into a hill of squash.

ODD JOBS. Keep an old pot around for inedible cooking jobs like making soap and candles.

GARBAGE POT. An old pot makes a perfect on-counter receptacle for gloppy garbage that should go to the compost heap. For that matter, convert an old pot into a kitchen composter.

PANS

Shallow pie and cake pans that have left their baking days behind them can be used for anything from feeding dishes for your pets to drip catches for your paint can. Or try ideas like these:

SQUIRREL DEFLECTOR. If the neighborhood squirrel insists on raiding your bird feeder by climbing up the support pole, drill a hole the size of the

pole through the shallow pan. Slip the pan onto the pole and hold in place with nails or wire. Then remount the bird feeder on top of the pole and your birds will feed undisturbed.

BIRD BATH. The birds will be grateful if you donate one of your old pans to their athletic club. Drill a hole through the bottom of the pan and screw it to the

★ AMERICANA IN YOUR CUPBOARDS ★

Lots of people decorate their kitchens by hanging up utensils and cookware that they buy at auctions or flea markets. Why not use your own worn or obsolete kitchen equipment to get the same effect? Pull out the potato ricer you never use, the wooden spoon that got singed, the egg beater that hasn't been touched since you got the food processor. Hang objects like these on a blank wall to create a three-dimensional collage.

Disreputable pots and single dishes can also be decorative. Paint problem pots or pans bright colors. Then decorate with tole painting, stencils or decals. Turn a pie plate or skillet into a "sampler" by painting your favorite quotation in the center. Similarly, individual plates can be displayed with plate racks. If you have several plates with different but appealing patterns, group them together. If the plates are dull, paint fanciful designs on them.

top of a post, using a thick rubber washer to prevent leaks. Paint the pan with rustproof paint before filling it with water.

DUSTPAN. Turn an old square or rectangular cake pan into a dustpan for the shop by cutting out one side with a coping saw. To make a handle, drill two holes through the opposite side and bolt onto an old broomstick.

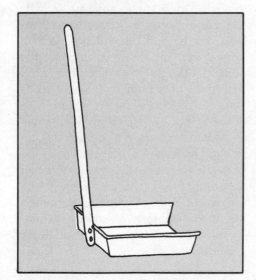

BROKEN DISHES

Naturally, if you've simply decided to replace a set of perfectly good dishes, you should give the old set to Goodwill so someone else can get some use from them. But if the dishes are broken, your options are limited to projects that require bits and pieces. Here are suggestions:

THERAPY. Many people find that

WEE GARDEN. Use old cake pans for seedlings in the spring. In the winter, try planting a miniature formal garden in a pan, complete with gravel paths, tiny statues, and Lilliputian plants.

HARDWARE HELPER. Keep a retired cake or pie pan in your workshop. When you need to sort through that can of miscellaneous nuts and bolts, dump its contents into the pan. The pan will make it easier to hunt for the piece you want and easier to pour everything back in the can when you're through.

PAINT PAN. Although you can use any old pot as an extra container for paint, a 13 × 9 cake pan will accommodate a wall roller.

WATER! If your house becomes unbearably dry in the winter, you can use your extra pans to add humidity to the air. Set pans of water on radiators, woodstoves, even the vents from central heaters. Water in shallow pans actually evaporates faster because more surface area is exposed to the air.

smashing dishes is a good release when they are frustrated or angry. Keep a supply of broken dishes on hand so you can hurl a couple at the basement wall.

THE WHOLE IS GREATER THAN THE PIECES. Fragments from old dishes can be assembled into mosaics to be used as wall plaques, or trivets, or patio tiles. Save your broken dishes until

you have a nice selection of colors and textures. Break the dishes into penny-size pieces by putting them in a bag and hitting it with a hammer. You can use the jagged pieces, or you can smooth their edges by tumbling them in a rock polisher. Either way, arrange the fragments on a piece of scrap wood the size and shape of your finished project. When the arrangement pleases you, glue it down with white glue. Wait for the glue to dry; then fill the cracks with grout. For more information about mosaic work, consult *Mosaic Making Techniques* by Helen Hutton (Scribner's, 1977).

POT ROCKS. Use broken dishes to provide drainage at the bottom of flowerpots. Break up the dishes so the pieces fit inside the pot and cover the drainage holes.

★ DON'T CRY ★ OVER BROKEN DISHES

When a favorite dish breaks, sweep up all the pieces and put them in a paper bag. Later, when you're calm, reassemble the pieces. When you understand how they fit together, coat the edge of the break with epoxy and add one piece, allowing it to dry thoroughly before you add the next. Be sure to wipe excess glue off the crack with nail-polish remover and support the two pieces with Plasticine or masking tape.

Minor chips can be removed from dishes by sanding with a fine abrasive paper. Keep using finer and finer grades of paper and finish by polishing the area with jeweler's rouge. If you have more serious chips or missing pieces, you'll have to purchase a Master Mending Kit from the Atlas Minerals and Chemicals Division, Farmington Road, Mertztown, PA 19539. The kit costs $21.95 but it has supplies for mending porcelain, china, glass, and pottery.

Never in Your Wildest Dreams

Broken dishes, bottle bottoms, pebbles, shells, and junk tiles are embedded in the glittering masterpiece of Simon Rodia known simply as the Watts Towers. It took Rodia thirty-three years to build the towers in his Los Angeles neighborhood. He started with a structure of bed frames and pipes, salvaged bits of concrete and steel. Year after year he added to it, until one of the towers stood over sixty feet high, constructed entirely from cast-off materials. Although Rodia's towers are a powerful statement about waste and the possibilities of reuse, he never intended them as that. "I had in mind to do something big," he said, "and I did it."

DISPOSABLE ANYTHING

A product whose chief virtue is that it's easy to throw away should make you pause. Think about whether the labor you're saving is worth the waste of resources. Perhaps it is for disposable diapers, but the small inconvenience of replacing blades in a razor or refilling a lighter doesn't really warrant disposable products.

DOORKNOBS

You may not replace your doorknobs every day, but when you do, you certainly won't want to throw the old ones out. Think of them as hooks and handles and you'll suddenly see plenty of uses besides the ones mentioned here.

HEFTY HOOK. Everybody hangs things on doorknobs anyway, so why not use old ones as hooks for jackets, belts, cords, and other things. With a screwdriver, remove the setscrew that holds the doorknob to its shaft. File off the edges of a number 8 screw so its head fits precisely into the square hole at the end of the doorknob. Wedge the screw into the hole and pour epoxy glue through the setscrew hole until it fills the cavity inside. Allow the doorknob to set for twenty-four hours, then screw it into the wall or a rack. If your old doorknob was made of brass, ceramic, or wood, these hooks will look good enough for the front hall.

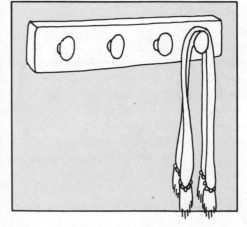

TOOL KNOB. A doorknob can often make a comfortable, high-leverage handle on a file, screwdriver, or brace bit. Loosen the setscrew, insert the shaft of the tool, and tighten the screw back down.

SANDER HANDLER. To make a sander that makes short work of long flat sanding jobs, follow the instructions above for fixing a screw in a doorknob.

Screw knobs on either side of a 2 × 4-inch block of wood, wrap sandpaper around the block, and staple it to the ends.

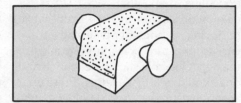

★ DON'T THROW OUT THE DOOR ★ WITH THE DOORKNOB

True, old doors can always be used as scrap wood (*see* WOOD SCRAPS), but some are sturdy enough and others beautiful enough to command other uses. Here's a sampling of possibilities:

- Room divider
- Workbench or desk top
- Picnic table top
- End of a cabinet
- Surface for a single bed
- Closet door

cartons, you can tack them up on the walls of the garage, chicken coop, doghouse, or basement as a cheap form of insulation. For best results, overlap the cartons so the top of one goes over the cups of the next.

BUMPER WALL. Even if you don't need their insulating value, egg cartons make a striking wall covering. Create a molded plastic look in an entrance or hallway, on the kitchen valance or the bedroom ceiling by trimming away the lip and top of each carton. Then glue or tack the cartons to the wall, side by side, bumpy side out. Paint for an ultra-modern textured look.

HOLD IT. Egg cartons make fine temporary holders for pins, thumbtacks, nails, scissors, and small tools. Trim the cup side of the carton, turn it upside down, and poke things into the cups.

EGG CARTONS

Egg cartons have an eccentric shape that has inspired an entire school of crafts. As a result, schools, scout troops, senior citizen centers, and other craft-oriented places will always be glad to take your extras.

Before giving away your cartons, consider the many uses they might have around your own house. The most obvious is organizational. Egg cartons make super containers for all kinds of small objects that need to be sorted. If an entire carton seems too large for what you want to store, use a kitchen knife to slice off the number of cups you need.

Though organization is their number one talent, egg cartons have many other uses. Here are a few examples:

STARTER CARTON. Egg cartons are

ideal starter trays for seedlings in the spring. Punch a small hole in the bottom of each cup for drainage. Then fill the cups with potting soil, set on a water-proof tray, and plant one or two seeds in each compartment.

SNUG AS AN EGG IN ITS CARTON. Styrofoam has some value as an insulator, so if you have a lot of

BRIGHT AND CLEAN. When making homemade candles (*see* CANDLE STUBS) or soap (*see* FATS AND GREASE), use egg carton molds for votive candles and guest soaps.

ICE COLD CARTONS. Styrofoam egg cartons can double as ice cube trays when you need extra ice for parties or picnics.

★ THINGS (OTHER THAN EGGS) ★ TO KEEP IN YOUR EGG CARTONS

- Cuff links, fine chains, and other jewelry
- Paper clips, pushpins, rubber bands, and other office supplies
- Small Christmas ornaments
- Small screws, nails, bolts, and other hardware

- Buttons of different colors
- Loose change
- Seeds and bulbs
- Beads and baubles
- Apricots, plums, and cherry tomatoes that are going to a picnic
- Collections of rocks or shells

PACK IT. Sending breakables? Styrofoam egg cartons provide cheap, lightweight, and crush-resistant packaging. Cut the cartons into bits, or use the cups themselves to cushion the contents of the package.

See also STYROFOAM.

••••••••••••••••••••••••••

EGGSHELLS

For sheer genius in packaging, you can't beat eggshells. The delicate inner membrane preserves freshness, and the tough outer container provides protection. Even when its egg-keeping function is finished, an eggshell has secondary uses. Some depend on its shape and some on its chemical composition. Here are a few examples:

INSTANT FUNNEL. To make a quick, disposable funnel, grab half an eggshell and poke a small hole in the center of the bowl with a nutpick. Center the hole over your container and pour the liquid through the eggshell.

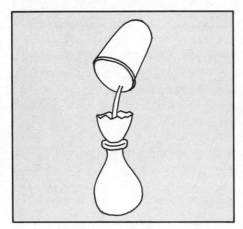

STAIN REMOVER. When you have china or glassware that's stained from coffee or other foods, clean it by soaking in a vinegar and eggshell bath.

PLANT BREAKFAST. Eggshells are an organic material, rich in the same minerals that make bone meal so valuable in the garden. Add eggshells to the compost heap. Or dry them in the oven, crush them with a rolling pin, and sprinkle the powder around your houseplants. No plants? Add powdered eggshells to dog or cat food as a calcium supplement.

EMPTY EGGS. Eggshells have an appealing shape that is a natural for decorations. Keep the egg intact while removing its contents by using an ice pick to puncture holes in both ends of the egg. One hole should be ¼ inch and one should be slightly larger. Press your lips to the smaller hole and blow gently. A somewhat scrambled egg will emerge through the hole at the other end. Let the shell dry for several days. Then decorate with paint, dye, or felt-tip markers. Hang the eggs by tying a matchstick to a thread and inserting it in the egg, or string them together like giant pearls.

EGGS OF FORTUNE. To make memorable gifts or favors with eggshells, blow out the insides as described above. On occasions when you want to give money as a gift, fold the bill in half lengthwise, roll it up, and insert it into an eggshell decorated for the event. Or write fortunes on small pieces of paper, roll them up, and slip them into eggshells. Keep a basket of "fortune eggs" beside the front door and offer them to guests.

EGG PLANTER. Eggshells can be biodegradable pots for seedlings. Break the shells so one end is larger than the other and use the large section as a pot. Punch a tiny drainage hole, fill each pot with soil, and plant your seeds. Support the eggshell pots in egg cartons. When the plants are ready for transplanting, crack the shell a little, then set plant and shell into the garden.

EGG GLUE. To make a general-purpose glue, throw a bunch of eggshells into the blender with an egg white and blend into a smooth paste. Use the gritty egg glue for paper and for simple household repairs. This glue will keep for a few days in a covered container.

EGGSHELL MOSAIC. Eggshell mosaics give a delicate texture to reclaimed boxes and bottles. Clean and dry several dozen eggshells. Crush them in a paper bag. Spread white glue all over the object to be decorated and sprinkle the eggshells over the glue until the entire surface is covered. Paint the shells (a pearl color is especially nice) and protect them with several coats of acrylic.

THE EGG AS ART OBJECT. The shape and delicacy of eggshells has appealed to craftspeople ever since Fabergé. Those with steady hands and a fascination for miniatures may want to create their own tiny scenes inside empty eggshells. A helpful book on the subject is *The Splendid Art of Decorating Eggs* by Rosemary Disney (Hearthside Press, 1972).

HANGING EGGS. Eggshells can also be eye-catching rooters for plant clippings. Use a nail scissors to cut a large hole at one end, remove the egg, and seal the interior with melted paraffin. Make a macramé holder for the egg (*see* STRING) and put a plant clipping in the shell. Fill the egg with water and add a little plant food.

••••••••••••••••••••••••••

ELECTRICAL APPLIANCES

No matter how inventive you are in recycling their broken parts, appliances are worth more when they are working. Most are designed for such specific tasks that even if you do turn your vacuum cleaner casing into a planter, there will be telltale signs of its origins. Given all this, extend the lives of your appliances as long as possible by cleaning them regularly and keeping them away from corrosive conditions like moisture and heat. When an appliance quits, you may be able to resuscitate it if you understand how it works. Basically, all appliances depend upon electrical connections. When an appliance doesn't work, it's probably because the flow of electricity through it has been interrupted. People with a little electrical knowledge can trace the path of electricity through an appliance, but anyone can check for external problems with this three-point plan.

Check the Obvious. Repairpeople could entertain you for hours telling stories about people who didn't notice the oven was turned to Timed Bake or the television wasn't plugged in. Before doing anything else, run through the "How Could I Be So Stupid" checklist in the box.

Check the Owner's Manual. Never throw out a manual for an appliance. Most manuals include a troubleshooting chart explaining the most probable causes for various malfunctions. Check your warranty, too. Appliances often seem programmed to break within thirty days after the warranty expires, but it's worth looking to see if the company will take care of your problem.

Check the Cord and Plug. The most common cause of trouble in appliances is a damaged cord. Sometimes the problem will be obvious at a glance—the cord will be frayed or the plug will be cracked. Other times the appliance may work if you jiggle the cord. In either case, go to your hardware store and buy a plug and/or wire like those on the appliance. Snip off the damaged plug or cord. In the case of the cord, leave a 3-inch tail on the appliance.

Now you are ready to attach the good plug to the good cord. Pry out the plastic disc inside the plug, exposing two screws underneath. Separate the two strands in the wire for about 2 inches and tie an underwriter's knot (see illustration). Leave about 1½ inches of wire above the knot. With a kitchen knife, trim away the insulation from the wires, being careful not to clip off the tiny strands of copper. Wrap each wire clockwise around one of the terminal screws and tighten the screws. Be sure there are no stray wires sticking out from under the screws. If you're dealing with a three-prong plug, attach the ground

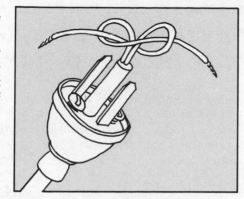

wire to the third screw, which will usually be green. Replace the plastic cap inside the plug.

If you are replacing the entire cord, turn your attention to the appliance end. Sometimes the cord unplugs from the appliance and you can remove the screws that hold the plastic end together. Inside you'll find more terminal screws. Unscrew them, remove the old wire, trim the new wire, and wrap it around the screws. Tighten the screws and close up the plastic housing. If the wire leads directly to the appliance, you'll have to go inside, a task that may prove impossible if the appliance has been sealed shut. Look carefully around the housing for the telltale screws that will admit you to the interior. If you don't find any, you'll have to splice the new wire onto the tail that you left hanging from the appliance just in case this happened. Strip the insulation from both wires for about an inch. Now twist one set of wires from each cord together. Twist the second set together, being absolutely certain that no wires from one set touch wires from the other. Cover the splices with wire nuts and electrical tape.

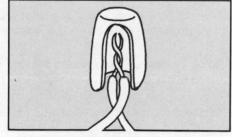

If you can get inside the appliance, trace the old cord to its terminal screws. Unscrew them, remove the old wire, and replace with new.

Check the Innards. If you replace the plug and cord and the appliance still doesn't work, the problem is internal. At

★ HOW COULD I ★ BE SO STUPID CHECKLIST

- Is the appliance plugged in?
- Is the outlet working? Find out by plugging in a lamp that works.
- Is the switch, button, or dial firmly in the "on" position?
- Is there some special function that could prevent the appliance from going on? For instance, is the stereo tuner set for phonograph? Is the dishwasher set for rinse and hold?

★ WHAT TO ★ SALVAGE FROM AN APPLIANCE

When an appliance breaks it usually means that one of many components has failed. Even though the motor is kaput, the pump and timer may be okay. If you know a little about electrical work, you can pull out these parts and reuse them in appliances that break in the future or in your own projects. Key parts to look for include:

- Cords and plugs
- Thermostats
- Motors
- Pumps
- Relay switches
- Timers
- Fans
- Heaters and burners

Even if you don't know a thing about electricity, you can still salvage parts that will be useful in other projects. Look for:

- Knobs
- Wires
- Gears
- Belts
- Hoses
- Screws
- Washers

★ COMMON APPLIANCES AND WHAT (IF ANYTHING) ★ TO DO WITH THEM WHEN THEY BREAK

APPLIANCE	PARTS TO SALVAGE	SECONDARY USES
Blender	Pitcher, motor, fan, contact switch, cord	If the blender still turns, use it for mixing paint, plant fertilizer, wallpaper paste, household cleaning formulas, etc.
Broiler oven	Door hinges, heating element, motor, thermostat, contact switch, sheet metal	Remove all electrical components from unit housing and use it as a bread box.
Can opener	Grindstone, gears, cutter, motor, contact switch, cord	No apparent reuse. Consider using a hand-powered model.
Clock	Motor, gears, hands, face, case, cord	Remove hands and face and use them to help preschooler learn to tell time. Replace face of clock with a favorite photograph cut to size.
Coffee maker	Heating element, contact switch, filter cup, pot	No apparent reuse. Consider using a pour-through coffee system such as Melitta.
Dishwasher	Pump, heating element, sprayers, strainers, motor, pipes, spring, latch, timer, switch	Remove metal door panel and use as a magnetic bulletin board.
Dryer	Drum, motor, heater, gasket, thermostat timer, centrifugal switch	Dryer drum is a giant strainer. Use it for making lye (see ASHES), rinsing fruits and vegetables, etc.
Fan	Basket, blades, switch, motor, washers	If the fan still turns, convert it into a strobe by removing the frame and blades. Cut out a heavy cardboard circle with the circumference of the blades and cut a second circle in it, 3 inches across and 2 inches from the rim of the cardboard. Attach the cardboard circle to the fan base with the original hardware. Put a bright light bulb 6 inches behind fan and turn both on.
Frying pan	Pan, cord, thermostat, contact switch, heating element, ceramic insulators	Pry or cut plastic legs off bottom of pan and use it as an extra stovetop pan.
Hair dryer	Bonnet, air hose, fan, motor, thermostat, contact switch	If dryer blows warm air, use it to thaw pipes, defrost refrigerator, dry out shoes, etc.
Microwave oven	To avoid accidental exposure to microwave radiation, do not disassemble your unit or use it for any other purpose. Repairs should be done only by an authorized service representative.	
Percolator	Thermostat, basket, cord, heating element, pot	Use covered basket as a self-draining sprouter (see MARGARINE TUBS).
Record player	Jacks, wires, needle, motor, housing, cover, rubber from turntable	If the turntable turns, remove all other mechanical parts from the top of the set and use the turntable as a revolving base for birthday cakes, centerpieces, small Christmas trees, etc.
Stove	Heating elements, sheet metal, knobs, timers, burner bibs, thermostat, switches	Remove top from stove and use oven and bottom drawer for insect-, rodent-, and water-proof storage.
Toaster	Spring, thermostat, heating element, wire bread guides, contact switch, crumb tray	Cut cord off toaster, paint it, and use it as a sorter for bills and mail.
Vacuum cleaner	Hose, brushes, motor, fan, switch, housing	Remove motor and other hardware from housing. Use wheeled canister as a caddy for tools, cleaning supplies.
Waffle iron	Grill, heating element, thermostat, hinges, ceramic insulators, contact switch	Most grills are reversible. Turn two flat sides out and use griddle to press things that have been glued.
Washing machine	Timer, hoses, motor, agitator, gaskets, belts, baskets, tub, sheet metal, solenoid, pump	Remove all hardware except for basket. Plug tub and use it for dyeing clothes, soaking old tools, making compost tea (see GARBAGE), etc.

★ MAKING THE ★ MOST OF MOTORS

The two types of motors found in appliances are universal and induction. Universal motors are compact, low-power motors, often found in vacuum cleaners, sewing machines, mixers, electric drills, and other small appliances. Induction motors, on the other hand, are usually found in refrigerators, washing machines, and other large appliances.

A motor can usually be removed from a dead appliance by detaching the two wires that lead in and the two wires that lead out. Once the motor is free, it can be reused in another appliance that requires the same horsepower. Or it can be used in homemade projects such as fans, grinders, sanders, rock tumblers, compressors, and pumps.

For more information about motors, consult "Selecting and Using Electric Motors," U.S. Department of Agriculture Bulletin No. 2257, available for 85 cents from the U.S. Government Printing Office, Washington, DC 20402.

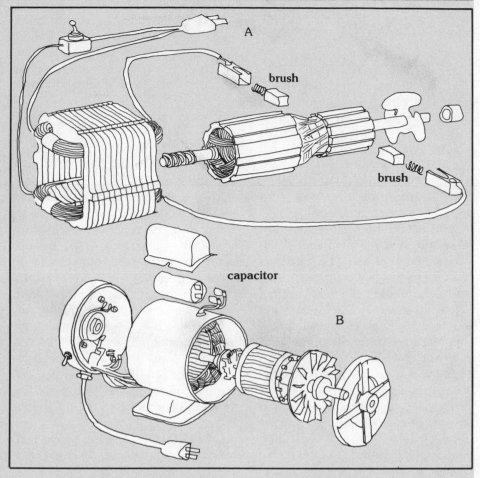

The universal motor (A) is often found in electric drills, vacuum cleaners, and blenders. It can be recognized by the carbon brushes on either side of the commutator. The split phase motor (B) is usually found in heavier equipment such as dishwashers and air conditioners and can be recognized by the capacitor that usually sits on top of the motor housing.

this stage, you'll have to come to terms with the nature of your appliance. Essentially, all appliances fall into two categories: those which heat up (toasters, irons, frying pans) and those in which something turns (fans, record players, vacuum cleaners). Heating appliances convert electrical energy into heat by passing it through a series of resistors. Turning appliances contain motors, devices that convert electrical energy into mechanical energy. Both can often be repaired with a little internal cleaning.

In a heating appliance, follow the path of the electricity through the appliance. Usually, the current will make a beeline for the switch that turns the appliance on and off. If the switch is dusty or rusty, the current may not be able to cross it, so clean it by blowing off the dust or filing off the rust with an emery board. The second stop for the current may be a thermostat, a bimetallic strip that switches the appliance on or off according to temperature. Check that too for dust. Otherwise, look at all connections for tightness and be sure there are no loose or broken wires. Check too whether wires or terminal screws can touch the appliance housing. If they can, reposition them or have a qualified repairperson check the appliance.

Appliances with motors have different requirements. Since the average home has fifteen to twenty motors, it's useful to know their basic maintenance. For example, keep the motor clean by wiping away grease and oil on the outside. Inside, remove dust with a vacuum cleaner or a soft brush. Some motors also need to be oiled, though too much oil can be as damaging as too little.

Sometimes you'll find a plate on the motor explaining how much and how often the appliance needs oil; otherwise consult the owner's manual. In general, use a few drops of household oil once a year for lightly used appliances and four times a year for heavily used ones.

Beyond such basic care, most appliance owners will need technical advice about bringing dead appliances back to life. There are many fine fix-it-yourself manuals on the market, but the following three are up-to-date and understandable.

Fix-It-Yourself Book of Electrical Fixtures, Wiring and Appliances (Peterson Publications, 1977).

Fix-It-Yourself Manual (Reader's Digest Association, Inc., 1977).

Simple Appliance Repair by Ross Olney (Doubleday, 1976).

Of course, you can also take your

★ NEW LIFE FOR ★ OLD APPLIANCES

Few people have the skill and patience to repair an old appliance, much less strip it for parts. As a result, the dumps are full of appliances which are sound except for one broken part. In Herkimer County, New York, the Association for Retarded Children saw that problem as an opportunity.

The association advertised that it would pick up and recycle unwanted appliances. The response was staggering—dealers and individuals called to contribute washers, dryers, stoves, and other old appliances. The association collected the appliances and trained retarded members to analyze and repair their problems. The restored appliances are sold at low prices, and appliances which cannot be restored are stripped for working parts. The hulls are sold to scrap metal dealers.

The program has been a tremendous success, according to its director, because it solves two problems simultaneously: It provides useful, therapeutic work for retarded people in the community, and it makes good use of waste appliances that would otherwise clog the dumps and create a public eyesore.

problem appliance to a qualified service dealer. If your worst fears are confirmed, you can still cannibalize the thing and salvage its components. Or you can try converting the appliance into something completely different (see chart).

See also METAL SCRAP; REFRIGERATORS; WATER HEATERS.

ENVELOPES

You can, of course, use an old envelope as a simple scrap of paper for a message, a love letter, or a doodle, but there is more, much more. At its most basic, an envelope is a container for letters, but why stop there? Carefully opened, an envelope can become a container for anything that's compact and/or skinny.

What's more, envelopes can be opened into flat sheets of paper, joined to each other, and snipped into new shapes. Their versatility is limited only by the imagination of the addressee. Here are some ideas to get you started:

WHITE BUSINESS ENVELOPES

RETURN TO SENDER. The basic rule about recycling paper is "use both sides." Apply that rule to envelopes and you'll see that there's an entire inside, clean and waiting to be addressed. Open the envelope into a flat piece of paper by steaming the seams or slipping a nail file between the edges of the paper. Now fold the envelope backward so the clean side is out and the addressed side is in. Glue your seams, insert your letter, and seal with tape. You may not want to use secondhand envelopes for send out job résumés, but they're fine for paying bills or mailing letters to your mom.

ACCORDION FILE. Stationery stores sell accordion files for several dollars, but you can make your own out of old envelopes. Open the envelopes carefully to preserve the flaps. Fold the flaps back and place two envelopes side by side. Glue the flap of one envelope to the front of the other. Glue other envelopes to the first pair in the same way. Tie the file with a scrap of yarn.

EMERGENCY CUP. Open an envelope by slitting it across the short end. Squeeze it open and what do you have? A short-lived container for water and other liquids.

SHOPPING PAL. Write your shopping list on an envelope and tuck the relevant coupons and advertisements inside.

MANILA ENVELOPES

LITTER ENVELOPE. Open a manila envelope carefully, leaving the flap intact. Enlarge the hole at the top by making two crosswise slits. Hang the envelope on a knob in your car and use it for candy wrappers and other trash.

ON FILE. The standard manila envelope is slightly larger than the standard file folder. To convert the former to the latter, slit both sides and trim the top so it has a tab for labeling the contents. These folders may be flimsier than the real thing, but they're cheaper, too.

SEND AGAIN. Manila envelopes can also be remailed by covering the original

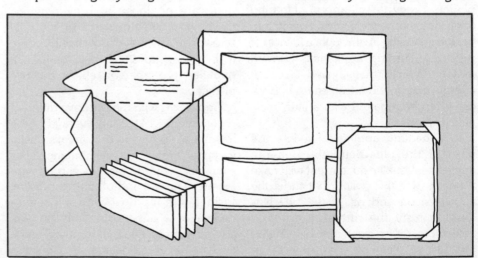

address label with your own. Or cut off the top third of the envelope, slit the sides about 3 inches, and cut away the flap on the addressed side of the envelope. Fold down the new flap, insert your letter, and seal with tape.

ANY KIND OF ENVELOPE

READER'S GUIDE. Clip the corner off any envelope and slip it over the page of your current book to mark your place.

CUTTING CORNERS. Snip off corners from old envelopes. Add a dab of glue and use them to mount photos and souvenirs in scrapbooks.

POCKETS ON MY WALL. Create an eye-level filing system by fastening old envelopes on the wall in your workroom or study by folding back the flap and taping or tacking to the wall. The addressed side of each envelope should lie flat against the wall and the clean side can be labeled to indicate the envelope's contents.

★ WHAT TO PUT ★ IN AN OLD ENVELOPE

- Stamps
- Coupons
- Photographs
- Negatives
- Bills
- Receipts
- Old letters
- Letters to be answered
- Tickets
- News clippings
- Warranties
- Souvenirs
- Meeting notes
- Recipes
- Road maps
- Tax records

★ SAVING STAMPS ★

If you can't think of any use for the envelope, be sure to cut off the stamp before you discard it. Stamp dealers are willing to pay for used stamps, particularly commemoratives, and many churches and charitable groups collect and sell stamps to raise a little money. This isn't a high-stakes proposition— dealers often buy by weight and pay only a few cents a pound. Still, if several hundred people save two or three stamps a day, it begins to add up. To locate dealers who buy stamps, look in the classified section of magazines for stamp collectors.

EYEGLASSES

Eyeglasses are so expensive that few people can throw them away without a twinge. Happily, the Lions International collects old eyeglasses and redistributes them to needy people in Asia and South America. Frames, loose lenses, and even sunglasses are acceptable. The recipients repolish the lenses, determine their prescription, and distribute them to patients who come to free clinics or eye camps in third-world countries. If your local Lions Club doesn't participate in this program, contact the national headquarters at 300 22nd Street, Oak Brook, IL 60570.

★ SPARE PAIR ★

In your passion for recycling old eyeglasses, don't forget to keep your most recent pair of specs as a temporary replacement in case you break your current pair. Or ask your optometrist to tint the lenses in an old pair of glasses to make prescription sunglasses.

★ FREEBIES ★

Sometimes people get self-addressed stamped envelopes or preaddressed business reply envelopes that, for one reason or another, they don't mail. Don't throw them away, either. Remove the uncanceled stamps from envelopes with a drop of lighter fluid and glue them onto another letter. Use the gummed sections of reply envelopes as lick-and-stick labels, notebook reinforcers, etc.

FABRIC SCRAPS

Fabric scraps can come from sewing projects, clothes that have been dismantled, worn linens, or deupholstered furniture. Whatever the source, they have dozens of uses. Launder all items that go into the scrap bag. Remove and save zippers, buttons, hooks and eyes and cut through most seams. Cut away areas with serious rips and snags so you'll have a selection of good, flat fabric. You needn't be a seamstress to reuse fabric scraps. Depending on the project, fabric can be tied, pinned, glued, or stapled to good effect.

PILLOW POWER. A pillow is nothing more than a pocket of fabric, stuffed and sewed shut. For a simple pillow, cut a piece of fabric twice as large as the pillow should be, fold it in half, right sides together, and stitch up two sides. Stuff the pillow with old stockings, more fabric scraps, or polyester fill. Whipstitch the open end closed. After mastering the basic pillow, experiment with size, shape, and decorative effects. Remember that a stuffed animal is just a pillow with a funny shape.

CAPE ROYAL. A large square of fabric can easily be converted into a cape. Cut a piece of string six inches longer than the length from your shoulder to your ankle. Tie one end of the string to a pencil and the other to a piece of chalk. Fold the fabric into four even quarters and make a quarter circle on it by placing the pencil at the center and drawing with the chalk while the string is taut. This step is easier if you get a friend to hold the pencil while you do the drawing. Make a second circle using the same center and a five-inch piece of string. Cut along both lines. Then cut a neck to hem opening in the cape. Trim all the edges with binding or ribbon and add a clasp at the neckline—perhaps a large antique button and a loop of elastic.

RAG ROLLERS. Long ago ladies curled their hair with cloth curlers, and you can try the same idea by tearing ½-inch strips of fabric twice as long as your hair. Moisten the hair and part off a section. Beginning at your scalp, wrap the hair around the strip of fabric in a sort of candy cane spiral. Tie the ends of the fabric strip together to secure the curl.

NO SEW CLOTHES. Large flat pieces of fabric lend themselves to no-sew clothing. Many of these styles were invented before zippers, buttons, and hooks, so they have a primitive appeal. Try making a halter top from a piece of fabric one foot wide and five feet long. Drape it around your neck, cross it over your bosom, and tie behind your back. Or make a turban from a band of material two feet wide and four feet long. Start with the fabric centered at the back of your head and pull the

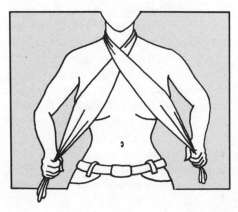

★ SCRAP BOOKS ★

A number of books have been written on using bits and pieces of fabrics. Here's a sampling:

Sewing with Scraps by Phyllis Guth (Tab Books, 1977) is directed at high school students but has ideas that would be useful for anyone.

Creating from Remnants by Ethel Beitler (Sterling, 1974) is specifically about using flawed fabric.

Rags by Linda and Stella Allison (Clarkson N. Potter, 1979) is about making things from every type of old fabric—T-shirts to doilies.

two ends toward your forehead. Wrap the fabric ends around to the back, twist them together, and tuck under the turban.

COVER UP. Use fabric to cover books, picture frames, filing cabinets, table tops, found containers, walls, lampshades, shelves, and much more.

When covering wood or other porous materials use a staple gun to attach the fabric, stretching it smooth as you go. Spray the finished job with water so the fabric will shrink slightly, eliminating any last wrinkles. If the staples are conspicuous, cover them with rickrack or molding.

Fabric covers can also be glued in place. Use Sobo fabric glue for small jobs. For large projects, mix up a batch of wallpaper paste. Spread a thin film of paste evenly on the object with a paintbrush. Then press the fabric firmly into the paste and rub over every part of it to be sure it adheres to the object underneath. To go around corners, cut out wedges of fabric (see illustration) so you won't have bulky double layers. Again, conceal seams under ribbon or rickrack. If the object will get much use, protect the fabric covering with several layers of clear acrylic.

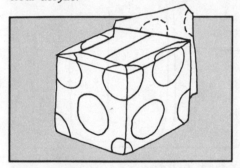

PATCHWORK PASSION. In Colonial America, where fabrics were scarce, patchwork was a decorative and utilitarian way of using bits and pieces left over from sewing and worn-out clothing. The early patchwork quilts with their thousands of tiny stitches are treasured today, but few twentieth-century people have patience for that kind of work. Happily there are other ways of doing patchwork. The simplest is perhaps the crazy-quilt approach. Lay out your most interesting scraps on an old sheet the size of the quilt you want to make. Try to select fabrics of comparable weight and don't use badly worn fabric. Cut and piece the scraps until you have a pleasing pattern. Then pin them in place. Using the zigzag stitch on your sewing machine, run around the edges of the pieces stitching them right to the sheet. Once the cover of the quilt is complete, you'll need to fill it.

★ 30 THINGS ★ TO MAKE FROM FABRIC SCRAPS

If you have sewing skills you can make almost anything from a bag of cloth scraps. Even if you don't have sewing skills, you can make most of the things on this list. Trim edges with pinking shears so they won't ravel, and use fabric glue to hold your seams together.

Aprons	Kerchiefs
Bandages	Napkins
Bean bags	Patches
Belts	Placemats
Bibs	Pockets
Bows	Potholders
Collars	Pouches
Cuffs	Rags
Facings	Ruffles
Handkerchiefs	Scarves
Hats	Shawls
Headbands	Ties
Hobo pouches	Tote bags
Hoods	Tourniquets
Hot pads	Wallets

Some quilters purchase batting made of polyester or cotton, but you can just as easily use a worn blanket, a flannel sheet, or a batch of baby blankets pieced together. Place a piece of solid fabric on the floor, lay the filling over it, and place the quilt on top. Stitch all around the edges to hold this sandwich together. To keep the filling from slipping around, you can either stitch along the outline of your patchwork or you can take occasional "ties" all over the quilt. To make a tie, thread a large needle with yarn and insert it through all three layers of the quilt, leaving a long tail on top. Bring the needle back through the quilt a quarter of an inch away from the first tail, cut off the yarn and tie a square knot. Although patchwork is usually associated with quilts, it can also be used to make beautiful clothing, placemats, bags, and other items. For more information, consult *The Contemporary Crazy Quilt Project Book* by Dixie Haywood (Crown, 1977) or *Patchwork Appliqué* by Pauline Chatterton (Dial, 1977).

RAG RUGS. Rag rugs are another American tradition that grew out of thrifty times when nothing went to waste. There's no reason why contemporary savers can't recycle their clothes in the same way. If a full-size rug seems too ambitious, make smaller items to be used as coasters, placemats, throw rugs, or wall hangings. Remember that collecting fabric for a large rug may take several years. Experts estimate that a 3 × 5 braided rug requires ten pounds of fabric and a 9 × 12 rug will consume seventy-five pounds. Traditional rugs were made from wool, but today's rug makers use anything from stockings to plastic dry-cleaner bags. The only rule is that the material should be consistent so the rug will wear evenly.

There are several techniques for mak-

RECYCLE→RECYCLE→RECYCLE

Fabric, like paper, can be broken down into fibers that can be reprocessed into new fabric. One hundred years ago, the rag man showed up regularly to collect scraps of wool and other fabric to be recycled into new cloth. As recently as World War II, householders saved their old clothes for the war effort.

Today, laws discriminate against reused fibers, making it cheaper and easier for manufacturers to use virgin wool and cotton and synthetics. As a result, the only way to recycle old clothes is to pass them on to other people who can use them. Hand clothes down to people in your own family, exchange them with friends, or donate them to charitable organizations.

Many fabrics can be woven into rugs, but old stockings are particularly durable.

ing rag rugs. The simplest is, perhaps, the tied rug that uses a piece of "monk's cloth" as a base. The monk's cloth is so coarsely woven that you can "stitch" strips of cloth into it. Begin by cutting or tearing your fabric into narrow strips, six to twelve inches long. The strips should all be the same length, determined by how shaggy you want your rug. Thread each strip through a large-eye tapestry needle and pull it through adjacent holes in the monk's cloth so the ends are both equal length on the front of the rug. Continue this process until the entire rug is full and fluffy.

Braiding is a more traditional method for rug-making. For this type of rug, tear or cut all fabric into three-inch strips and fold both edges of each strip into the middle. Now fold the entire strip in half so no rough edges can be seen from the outside. Press or stitch the strips so they will stay folded. When you have gathered plenty of strips, start braiding with three strips of different lengths. Tack two strips together with a diagonal stitch, and stitch on the third perpen-

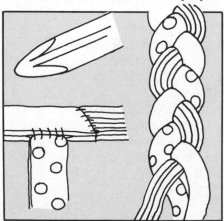

★ FINAL IRONY ★

The fabric from ironing-board covers deserves special attention. The covers, of course, always wear out in the center leaving perfectly good material at either end. Take advantage of the heat-resistant properties of this material to make yourself a free set of mitts for taking dishes out of the oven, using the fireplace poker, or cooking on the backyard barbecue. Trace around your hands allowing an extra two inches all around. Cut out the pattern, turn it over, trace again, and cut again. Back each piece of material with several layers of scrap fabric. Then place the two parts of each mitt right sides together and stitch around the outside. Turn inside out and finish the bottom edge with facing or trim.

dicular to the first two. Anchor the beginning of the braid to a chair with a piece of string and a safety pin and begin braiding, right over, left over, right over, and so on. Make the braid tight and even. When you get to the end of one strand, add the next one to it by stitching the pieces together on the diagonal. After you've completed several feet of braid, hold the loose end tight with a clothespin and coil the braid into a rug. Slipstitch the coils together. These instructions may get you started on a basic throw rug, but before tackling a larger project, consult *How to Make Braided Rugs* by Sally Clark Carty (McGraw Hill, 1977).

Those who know how to crochet can make still another type of rug. Tear strips of cloth about one and a half inches wide and crochet them together with a wooden needle that you buy or whittle from a ¾-inch dowel. Begin with three chain stitches and continue with a single crochet stitch in concentric circles. As you run out of fabric, simply tie on another strip. For more detailed instructions about making these and other inventive rugs, consult *Rag Rugs* by John Hinchcliffe (1977, Brook House, Chatsworth, CA 91311).

GARMENT BAGS. If you need a cover to protect out-of-season clothing, you can make one easily from a large piece of flat fabric, five feet square. Lay the fabric on the floor and fold two opposite edges into the center so they overlap by two inches. Center an old hanger over the top of the bag and trace its shape onto the fabric. Sew along the line you've drawn leaving a three-inch opening at the top. Stitch the bottom of the bag closed. Turn the bag inside out, insert clothing through the flap, and smooth it down. Add snaps or Velcro if necessary to keep the bag closed. If you simply want to keep dust off the shoulders of clothes you don't wear very often, cover them with old shirts or blouses.

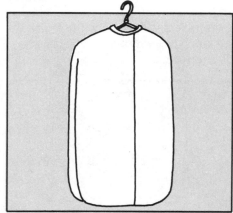

DUST PUPPY. One of the quickest ways to stop the drafts that sneak in under doors is to sew up a dust puppy. Cut a piece of scrap fabric 4 inches wide and 2 inches longer then the width of the door. With right sides together, stitch up the long side and one end. Turn the tube right side out and fill with sand so the puppy is floppy, not stiff. Sew up the open end and lay the puppy snugly against the bottom of the door. Make dust puppies for all doors between warm rooms and cold ones, and even for windowsills if they are drafty.

PLANT RAGS. Scraps of old fabric have a place in the garden, too. Use fabric to wrap the trunks of young saplings to protect them from rabbits during the winter. Tie up tomatoes with strips of fabric, and use old fabric to cover garden plants on chilly nights.

POCKETS FOR EVERYTHING. Banish clutter with a pocket wall hanging. Lay a piece of heavy material flat on the floor. Now cut smaller pieces of fabric to make pockets for all the things you want to organize. Fold under the top edge and stitch each pocket to the backing with a zigzag stitch. To make a pocket for a fat object, add little pleats on either side of the pocket before stitching. When all the pockets have been attached, back your creation with a piece of cardboard from a shipping carton, using Sobo glue and turning the edges under for a neat look. Hang one organizer on the wall beside the bed for glasses, magazines, tissues, and pencils. Put pockets in the bathroom for razor, hairbrush, Q-Tips, tissues, and make-up. And so on.

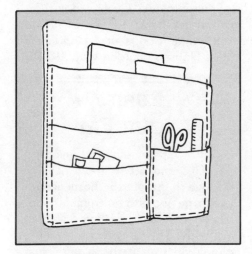

WINDOW WARMERS. One of the best things to do with extra fabric is turn it into thermal shades that will keep cold air from coming through your windows during the winter. One simple design is a Roman shade, made from quilted fabric so it can be pulled into loose folds above the window during the day. Plans for constructing a Window Warmer are available for $3 from the Center for Community Technology, 1121 University Avenue, Madison, WI 53703.

BAGS, BAGS, BAGS. A household with a good collection of scrap fabric need never buy another bag. In half an hour, you can make a bag to fit your running clothes, laundry, pajamas, tent stakes, silver dollars, boots, diapers, toys, tools—even your fabric scraps. To make a basic drawstring bag, start with a

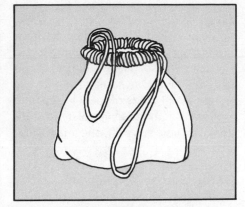

piece of fabric twice the size of the final bag and sturdy enough to hold its intended contents. Fold the fabric in half, wrong side out, and stitch up two sides. Make a 1-inch hem around the top. Make buttonholes in either end of the casing or press on two 1-inch iron-on patches and cut slits through them. Thread two pieces of cord through the casing and tie them so a large loop of one hangs outside one slit and a large loop of the other hangs out the other slit. Pull on both cords to close up the bag. To make more complicated bags, see *The Bag Book* by Lois Ericson (Van Nostrand Reinhold, 1977) for inspiration and instructions.

See also BLANKETS AND OLD QUILTS; BLUE JEANS; CLOTHES; COATS AND JACKETS; PANTS; SHEETS; SOCKS; SWEATERS; TOWELS; T-SHIRTS.

FAST FOOD CONTAINERS

Fast food companies are addicted to packaging. Most of the paper is covered with goop, so it can't be salvaged. The plastic burger containers, however, can be washed. Think of them as handy hinged boxes that can be used in projects like those described below.

NO-TIP SODA. If your children are always knocking over soda cans and glasses, help them out with tipproof bases made from burger boxes. Cut the top off the box, cut a hole the size of the soda can, and press in the can.

STYRO-FLYERS. Thin pieces of Styrofoam are the best material for model airplanes since balsa wood, and now someone has come up with an entire book about how to make aircraft from leftover fast food containers.

Styro-Flyers: How to Build Super Model Airplanes from Hamburger Boxes and Other Fast-Food Containers by Platt Montfort (Random House, 1981) is ostensibly for kids, but adults may also be intrigued by the aerodynamic possibilities of burger boxes.

Fast food cartons may replace balsa wood as the material of choice for model planes.

FATS AND GREASE

★ CORPORATE ★ ECOLOGY

Some fast food companies are at least trying to stem the flood of packaging. Burger King, for example, uses predominantly paper, which is the form of packaging that biodegrades most readily. In fact, the only plastic containers Burger King uses are plastic coffee cups. The company suggests that you turn them into flowerpots.

HEY, KIDS! LEARN HOW TO GROW YOUR OWN FLOWERS!

Those foam cups you were about to throw away are great for growing flowers and plants in. So you can start a garden right inside your house. Here's how to do it.

IF YOU WANT TO PLANT A BULB: Take the foam cup and use a pencil to punch a hole in the bottom. Then fill the cup with soil. Place the bulb in the soil, roots down and sprout up as shown in the picture. Next, put the cup in a saucer ashtray, or anything else that will hold water. Place the cup, saucer and bulb in a dark, cool place until you see shoots coming through the top of the soil. Water the bulb regularly, but try not to use too much water. As the plant begins to grow, you may need a small stick to keep it from drooping. An ice cream bar stick is perfect.

IF YOU WANT TO PLANT A SEED: Punch a hole in the bottom of the foam cup with a pencil, and fill the cup with soil. Then poke a hole in the soil with your finger—make the hole about an inch deep. Next, drop the seed in the hole and cover it up. And proceed as explained above. In just a short time, you can have a whole garden that will be the envy of all your friends. When they ask you how you did it, just say, "It's simple. All you need is some foam cups."

One fast food company with a conscience printed these fliers to encourage recycling.

SPARE BOWLS. Cut through the hinge on the burger box and what do you have? Two bowls perfect for soup, dip, nuts, and other edibles. Use them for parties, picnics, and other throwaway occasions.

CRUSHPROOF SANDWICH BOX. If you carry sandwiches for lunch, package them in used burger boxes. Not only will you save on sandwich wrap, but you'll never have to eat a squished sandwich.

POOPER SCOOPER. If you live in a city with a dog litter ordinance, use burger boxes to scoop up your pet's droppings and deposit them neatly in the nearest trash. (For that matter, conscientious pet owners can use this trick to clean up after their dogs no matter where they live.)

See also COFFEE CUPS, STYROFOAM.

Cooking fat is a resource most of us casually toss away. Better to keep all fats left over from chicken, bacon, burgers, and other meats. Pour liquid fat straight into a can with a snap-top lid; solid fat should be rendered into liquid by cooking over a slow fire. To keep fat from turning rancid, store it in the refrigerator, where it will resolidify. If you plan to use the leftover fat in cooking, keep fats from different kinds of meat in separate containers. Otherwise, it's okay to store whatever you have in one main dripping can.

GREASE. Use secondhand fats for small greasing jobs—muffin tins, cookie sheets, cake pans, and so on.

SHORT ORDERS. If you keep pork, beef, and chicken fats separate, they can be reused for odd cooking jobs like sautéing onions or mushrooms, frying potatoes and eggs, or for flavoring vegetables like spinach or baked beans.

TWEET TREAT. Birds get quick energy from eating animal fat, and they enjoy seed cakes all year round. To make a batch, fill an old coffee can with kitchen fat, melt it down, and mix in bread crumbs, sunflower seeds, and other bird tidbits. Pour the mixture into a used Styrofoam cup. When the fat hardens, peel away the cup and put the seed cake in a mesh bag like those onions come in. Hang the bag from the branch of a tree and wait for the birds to arrive.

SOAP. Colonial homemakers turned their cooking fats into soap and you can too. Making soap is no more difficult than baking bread, and the results are just as wholesome, since homemade soap is biodegradable and free of phosphates. Collect and purify 6 pounds of fat (see box). Now you'll need 6 cups of liquid lye. If you make your own lye (*see* ASHES), it should be strong enough to float an egg. You can also purchase lye crystals in most hardware stores and mix them with water according to the directions on the can. Either way, treat lye

with respect, because it is caustic and can cause severe burns. Have running water handy. Melt the fat and cool it to 85 degrees. Slowly, heat the lye to 85 degrees in an enamel pan. Remove both pans from the heat and gradually add the lye to the fat, stirring with a wooden spoon or stick. As the soap thickens, you can add food coloring or fragrant oils.

When the soap reaches the consistency of honey, pour it into wooden or cardboard boxes lined with fabric. For fancier shapes, use found containers like the plastic liners from cookie boxes. Rub the mold with oil so the soap will come out. Let the soap cool for about twenty-four hours. Fresh soap is caustic at first, so let it cure for about a month in a cupboard, stacked loosely so air can get to the cakes. More information about soap making is available in a 20-cent pamphlet entitled *Homemade Soap*, available from the Oregon Department of Environmental Quality, Box 1760, Portland, OR 97207, or in *Making Homemade Soaps and Candles* by Phyllis Hobson (Garden Way, 1974).

★ PURIFY ★ YOUR FAT

Leftover fat usually contains food particles and other impurities. To remove them, put the hardened fat in a large pot with an equal amount of water. Heat to boiling and then set aside. The fat will cool as a big chunk on top of the water. Next day, cut the fat into pieces and scrape the impurities off the bottom of each piece. If necessary, repeat the process. To make the fat smell good, add citrus peel during boiling.

FELT-TIP PENS

See PENS

FILM CANISTERS

Thirty-five-millimeter film comes in compact little containers with snap- or screw-on lids. When the film is gone, turn the containers into—what else?—containers for your pocket, purse, backpack, desk, or glove compartment. For example, you can make emergency kits of various sorts. Here are six suggestions:

- First-aid kit: two Band-aids, six aspirins, tiny tube of antiseptic cream
- Car kit: nickels, dimes, and pennies to use in parking meters
- Fix-it kit: assorted brads and screws, small hammer, and screwdriver with detachable handles
- Sewing kit: two needles, black, brown, and white thread wrapped around a toothpick, two shirt buttons, safety pin
- Survival kit: compass, matches, razor blade, bouillon cube, fish line and hook
- Key kit: duplicate keys to the house, car, strong box; (bury the canister in the flower bed in case of emergencies)

FLASH CUBES

Shutterbugs throw away thousands of spent flash cubes. The electrical part doesn't have much use after it's flashed, but the plastic shell is worth salvaging.

To remove the insides of the cube, turn it upside down and grasp the black knob on the bottom with a pliers. Twist it off. Now insert a nail file into the hole at the center of the cube and pry the innards out. It may take a couple of tries, but eventually the back panel will pop out bringing four little light bulbs with it. Use a pliers to loosen the wires that attach the bulbs to the panel.

Once the bulbs are removed, you have a clear plastic box with a black lid. What you do with it will depend upon the number you have and, probably, your hobbies. You could glue a hundred of them into a frame and use it as a shadow box for tiny collectibles or you could use one as a mixing bowl for small amounts of paint and glue. Aside

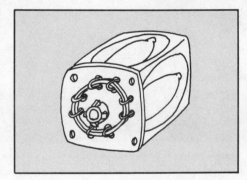

from their potential as Lilliputian containers, the flash cubes are transparent, which inspires uses like those that follow:

DUST COVER. If you build models, take apart appliances, or work on craft projects, cover small and delicate parts with empty flash cubes so they won't be lost or damaged.

PHOTO CUBE. To make a miniature photo cube, cut out photographs the size of the panels in an empty flash cube. In some cases, you may need to cut apart group photographs to get small enough faces. Press the pictures against the clear insides of the cube and stuff crumpled foil in the center to hold them in place. Glue the black platform to the bottom of the photo cube and keep it on your desk. Or give one to your grandma.

CHRISTMAS CUBES. For a holiday variation on the photo cube, cut out small details from Christmas cards and glue them inside the panels of an empty flash cube. Thread a piece of ribbon through the holes in the black panel before glueing it on and hang your Christmas cubes on the tree.

TINY TREASURES. If you collect miniatures, coins, mineral specimens, or other small objects, protect them by fastening them to the black base of a photo cube with two-sided tape. Then place the clear cover over the base and arrange your miniature display cases on a shelf.

FOIL, ALUMINUM

Aluminum foil is durable enough to be used several times. Clean it by rinsing under running water, wiping with a dishcloth, or sticking it in the dishwasher, dirty side down. Instead of stuffing crumpled wads of used foil in a kitchen drawer, roll the flattened foil onto an empty cardboard tube or fold it into rectangles and "file" it in a box, perhaps a powdered milk carton with its top cut off. Keep the box on the counter where it will be close at hand next time you need to wrap a baked potato or cover a casserole. If you prefer to use virgin foil in cooking, try some of these ideas:

SCOUR POWER. If you have a really dirty piece of foil, match it with a really dirty job like cleaning the barbecue grill or the spill catchers under the stove burners. Wad the foil into a scouring pad—the rough edges will scrape away grease and baked-on dirt.

TIME FOR REFLECTION. Old aluminum foil, carefully cleaned and smoothed, can be used to reflect heat and light. Glue small scraps onto wooden stakes to make reflectors for the end of the driveway. Or tape a piece of foil to a light switch so you can see it when the room is dark. If you have

RECYCLE ► RECYCLE ► RECYCLE

Aluminum is one of the easiest metals to recycle, so aluminum companies and community groups regularly organize collection campaigns. Uncontaminated foil earns as much as aluminum cans—23 cents per pound at last look. Reynolds Aluminum maintains a toll-free number to tell people about the next pickup in their community. To get the current number, call the toll-free operator— (800-555-1212) and ask for Reynolds Recycling Program.

larger amounts of aluminum foil, try making a solar cooker. Find a heavy-duty cardboard carton and cut it off as shown. Line the inside with insulation and paint it black. Build a base for the box and paint it black too. Cut a piece of glass to fit over the cut-out side of the box and hold it in place with duct tape. Make the reflective panels from cardboard, cover them with foil, and attach them to the main box with heavy-duty tape. To cook in this oven, place the food and an oven thermometer on the base, cover it with the box, point it toward the sun, and adjust the reflectors until there is no shadow inside the box. Naturally, you'll have to readjust the position of the oven as the sun moves. This oven may be slow, but it does a respectable job of cooking barbecued chicken, baked beans, and even burgers.

MESSES FOILED. Use secondhand foil to catch the spills at the bottom of the oven. If you don't have a large enough sheet, crimp together the edges of smaller sheets.

CAMPFIRE COOKING. For really delicious outdoor eating, wrap potatoes and ears of corn in double layers of secondhand foil and bury them in the coals of a campfire to cook.

The author built this functioning solar oven from pieces of scrap wood, a cardboard box, window glass, bits of insulation, and aluminum foil.

FOOD, LEFTOVER

Leftovers. To many people the word has an unsavory sound, suggesting something that wasn't good enough to be eaten the first time around, much less the second. Perhaps that's the reason Americans throw out so much food. A recent study in Tucson, Arizona, estimates that 8 percent of our residential garbage is edible food—not spoiled food or scraps, but food that could have been eaten by people.

That statistic is a disgrace. The only way to exempt your household from

blame is to follow three rules: (1) Buy food realistically. Make a week's eating plan that accounts for meals eaten away from home. Buy only the fresh foods called for in the plan, and stock up on canned goods to fill in any gaps. (2) Cook what you buy. If you buy spinach and fish for Friday's dinner, don't suddenly decide you want pizza instead. If you plan to order pizza, don't buy spinach and fish. (3) Make creative use of leftovers. In fact, don't even call the remains from meals leftovers. Think of

them as precooked ingredients for use in new dishes like the ones that follow.

PROCESSED FOOD. If you have a food processor, use it to grind meat and purée precooked vegetables. Add the processed foods to soups and sauces.

MYSTERY MEAT LOAF. Meat loaf doesn't have to be a lump of hamburger. Delicious dinner loaves can be made from fish, pork, and poultry. What's more, adding a little puréed vegetable to your meat loaf recipe will perk up the flavor and make it more nourishing.

SLY PIE. Pop your precooked food into a pie shell and no one will suspect its origins. Make your own crust by following the basic pastry recipe in any cookbook. Fill the shell with meat and vegetables and cover with leftover gravy if you have it. Otherwise, cover with a milk and cheese custard and call your pie a quiche.

IN THE SOUP. Almost any precooked food can go into a pot of savory homemade soup. Start with good stock (*see* BONES) and add bits of meat and vegetable.

ALL-PURPOSE OMELETTE. Precooked meats and vegetables can become positively elegant when they are enfolded in an omelette. Beat two eggs with two teaspoons of cold water. Pour the eggs into a hot omelette pan and spread the leftovers in the center. When the omelette is done, fold it in half and serve.

★ SOUR MILK ★ SECRETS

As a kid, I used to secretly hope that milk would go sour, knowing that if it did my mom would make a Wacky Cake. Here's her recipe: Sift 1½ cups of flour, ¾ cup of sugar, 1 teaspoon of soda, 1 teaspoon of salt, and 3 tablespoons of cocoa into an 8-inch pan. Make three holes in the dry ingredients and put 1 teaspoon of vanilla into one hole, 5 tablespoons of oil into another, and 1 tablespoon of vinegar into the third. Pour 1 cup of sour milk over the top and mix well. Bake for thirty minutes at 350 degrees. This recipe may sound funny, but the cake is delicious!

Sour milk can also be used in pancakes, waffles, and doughnuts—check your favorite cookbook for recipes.

★ SAY CHEESE ★

No matter how careful you try to be about consuming the last crumb of cheese, there always seems to be a nub or two getting hard around the edges at the back of the refrigerator. Hardened cheese can be grated and used in au gratin toppings. Shave it into fine bits and sprinkle it on hot soup. Or spread the gratings on toast and run them under the broiler for a melted cheese sandwich.

SECOND-DAY CREPES. Crêpes are another way to make leftovers seem dashing. Make a simple crêpe recipe from 1 cup flour, 3 eggs, 1½ cups milk, 2 tablespoons of melted butter, and a pinch of salt. Thin the batter with milk if necessary and make large thin pancakes in a heavy skillet. Mix the leftovers into a sauce, spread a line of filling down the center of the crêpe, and fold over the edges. Place the filled crêpes in a casserole dish, cover with extra sauce, and cook in a 350 degree oven for ten minutes.

★ BUTTER UP ★

It's not a big deal but you might as well save your butter or margarine wrappers by folding them in quarters and putting them in the refrigerator. Then next time you need to grease a cookie sheet or a casserole dish, you can pull out a wrapper and smear the butter on the pan without getting your fingers greasy.

STUFFED. Stuff tomatoes, peppers, or summer squash with a mixture of diced meat, vegetables, and stale bread, sautéed in a little fat and seasoned to taste. Sprinkle cheese over the top of the stuffed vegetables and run them under the broiler.

GREAT AMERICAN SANDWICH. No one needs to be told that the meat from last night's dinner can make a super sandwich for today's lunch. Slice the meat if possible or dice it and mix with salad dressing.

SUPER SALAD. Cut precooked meats into narrow slices and scatter them over a giant green salad. Marinate cooked vegetables like beans and beets and add them to the salad too. Garnish with cooked eggs, olives, onion slices, and so on.

★ A SECOND ★ CHANCE FOR LEFTOVERS

If you find yourself faced with a lot of leftovers, you need another cookbook. Three possibilities are *Waste Not, Want Not* by Helen McCully (Random House, 1975), *The Use-It-Up Cookbook* (Consumers Union, 1979), and *Half a Can of Tomato Paste and Other Culinary Dilemmas* by Jean Anderson and Ruth Buchan (Harper & Row, 1980). All are sprightly books about extracting every bit of goodness from food, including plenty of plausible ideas about what to do with sour sour cream, lonely egg yolks, and once-cooked foods of every kind. Many of the recipes sound so appealing you'll find yourself plotting meals just so you can use the leftovers.

SAVED BY A WOK. Chinese stir-frying is an ideal way to handle leftovers that cannot bear much cooking. Use a wok if you have one, otherwise a heavy skillet will do. Heat a little fat in a pan. Cut the ingredients—meats like beef, pork, or chicken and vegetables like peas, beans, onions, peppers, and mushrooms—into slivers and small chunks. When the oil is hot, add all the ingredients and stir lightly until they are hot. Add a generous splash of soy sauce and serve over rice.

★ FLOUR POWER ★

There's always a little flour left at the bottom of an "empty" paper flour bag. Don't throw it away. Add a little salt, a little pepper, a dash of your favorite spice. Next time a recipe calls for a piece of chicken or a pork chop dredged in flour, pop the meat into the bag and shake vigorously until it's coated.

THE SECRET'S IN THE SAUCE. Camouflage precooked meats and vegetables with special sauces. Experiment with mayonnaise sauce for cold fish, garlic sauce for cooked potatoes, cheese sauce for day-old broccoli, or béarnaise sauce for last night's beef. Sauces need not be time consuming. Many can be made quickly in a blender or food processor.

See also BREAD AND OTHER BAKED GOODS; FRUIT.

FORKS

Forks get more abuse than other pieces of silverware. The tines bend and break; the intricate shape makes polishing difficult. When a fork no longer rates a place on your table, find it another job, taking a cue from its highly specialized shape, which is ideal for stabbing, combing, and poking, among other things. Here are four suggestions:

MINI-RAKE. Keep an old fork near the houseplants for loosening the soil at the top of each pot. If you like, bend the tines at right angles to make the fork more like a hoe.

DECORATOR FORKS. A fork is a versatile tool for decoration. Keep an old one in the kitchen for scoring the sides of cucumbers, carrots, and other vegetables so slices look scalloped. In the crafts room, use an old fork to make line designs in clay or to make patterns in leather or wood. In some cases, you

may want to sharpen the point on each tine with a metal file.

MESSAGE FORK. Anchor an old fork in a soup can filled with pebbles and use it to hold recipes in the kitchen or messages by the phone.

FORKED BRACELETS. Old forks make handsome jewelry if you have the patience to shape the silver. Start by annealing the fork to make it less brittle (*see* SILVERWARE). Then curve the tines into a pattern or wrap them around a gemstone. Shape the stem of the fork into a bracelet by hammering it until it curls around a piece of pipe the size of your wrist.

FROZEN FOOD TRAYS, ALUMINUM

The convenience of frozen foods is matched by the usefulness of the aluminum trays they come in. The trays can be recycled along with soda cans and other aluminum items (*see* FOIL, ALUMINUM), but many household recyclers prefer to keep them around because they can be washed and reused in so many ways.

The trays have obvious value in the kitchen, where they can be used for homemade pies and cakes, breads and rolls, even casseroles and cookies. The occasional cook could probably obtain a complete set of baking pans absolutely free by selecting frozen foods in the right containers.

Frozen food trays can also be reused for their original purpose if you fill them with homemade food to be frozen for future use. Compartmentalized trays, for instance, are ideal for leftovers. On days when there's a dab of this and a bit of that, put each item in its own compartment to make up a full meal. Then cover the tray with foil, label, and freeze it. After a few weeks, pull out enough trays for every member of the family and have a potluck supper. Similarly, when you make large quantities of food—a turkey, perhaps, or a vat of chili—freeze the extra food in frozen food trays that can be pulled out easily for a quick meal.

Finally, if your supply of food trays can't be contained in the kitchen, let them spill into other rooms of the house. They make clean and reasonably sturdy containers for all kinds of small objects, and the heavy aluminum has dozens of uses. Here are just a few suggestions:

YOUR NAME IN LIGHTS. The aluminum in frozen food trays can be trimmed into letters or numbers so you can put your address on the mailbox, your name on the door, or the dog's name on the doghouse. Make paper patterns for the letters and numbers you need. Then trace them onto the flat aluminum, using a nail to indent the metal. Cut the letters out with tin snips and hammer them flat on a block of soft wood. Then glue the figures on with epoxy cement.

KOOKIE CUTTERS. To make personalized cookie cutters, cut a 1½-inch strip of flat aluminum from a frozen food tray. Crimp a ¼-inch fold on one edge so the metal won't cut into your hand. Bend the metal into the shape you want and connect the two ends by bending one up ⅛ inch and the other down. Hook the ends together and squeeze the seam flat with pliers.

A GOOD REFLECTION. Pot pie pans make fine reflectors for bicycles (bolt the pan or a disc cut from the pan to the frame of the bike), stakes at the end of the driveway (nail the pan to an old broomstick), or the light at the top of the Christmas tree (trim the pan to look like a star, make a small hole in the

★ FROZEN FREEBIES ★

The metal tins used for packaging frozen food are so useful that stores sell them separately. Why buy an aluminum pan when you can get one free with your next frozen food purchase? Here are several popular frozen foods, the pans they come in, and the price you'd pay if you bought the pan by itself.

FOOD	PAN	PRICE
Pot pie	Burner bib	16 cents
Pound cake	Little loaf pan	16 cents
Sweet rolls	Roll pan	30 cents
Apple pie	Pie pan	16 cents
Turkey roll	Large loaf pan	30 cents
TV dinner	Toaster oven tray	22 cents
Pasta	Cake pan	22 cents

center, and stick the light bulb through it before screwing it into its socket).

BURNER BIB. Put a hole in the center of an aluminum pie pan and press it into the shape of the spill catcher under the burners on the stove.

PROTECTOR. Use strips and patches of aluminum to protect wooden surfaces that get a lot of wear—thresholds, corners of furniture, and so on. Cut the aluminum to the appropriate shape with tin snips and nail it to the surface using small but closely spaced brads.

SPATTER STOPPER. Invert pot pie pans over burgers when you fry them. The burgers cook just as well and the fat doesn't fly all over the stove. Or invert pans over the unused burners so they won't have to be washed.

ORGANIZATION TRAY. Compartmentalized trays are terrific organizers for nails in the shop, notions in the sewing room, and office supplies in the study. Use them to keep beads separated by color, screws sorted by size, and so on.

LAZY PAN. To make a simple lazy Susan that will keep spice tins, spools of thread, and other lightweight objects at your fingertips, nest two large aluminum pie pans of the same size together. Poke a hole through their centers, glue washers above and below the hole, and screw the pans loosely to a shelf.

SHOP SHADE. To make a quick shop shade that concentrates light and keeps it from glaring into your eyes, cut a 1½-inch hole in the center of an aluminum cake pan. Make a slit in the pan from the rim to the center hole. Slip one edge of the pan over the other to make a cone and staple in place. Insert a light bulb through the hole and screw it into a socket.

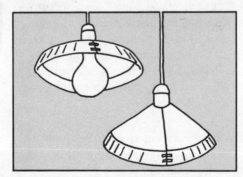

FRUIT

Some people throw fresh fruit away when it starts to get mushy or moldy. What a waste! Really rotten fruit should go into the compost bin (*see* GARBAGE). Fruit that is bruised or decadently ripe can be rescued for a variety of tasty uses. Here are four:

SAUCY IDEA. One easy solution is to cook the fruit into a sweet sauce to use over desserts and ice cream. Peel the fruit; remove cores, pits, and obvious bad spots. Purée in a food processor and add sugar to taste. Serve the topping warm or cold with a dollop of whipped cream.

FRUITY BAKE-OFF. Bananas whose skins have turned black seem to make the best banana bread. You can also substitute other fruits on the verge of spoiling in a basic fruit bread recipe.

COBBLER. An old-fashioned cobbler is another way to use up fruit that's a little past its prime. Peel the fruit, removing the worst spots, and cut it into regular chunks. Spread 3 or 4 cups of fruit at the bottom of a buttered baking dish. Add a dash of cinnamon and dot the fruit with pats of butter. Mix up a basic biscuit dough; spread the dough over the fruit, and bake at 350 degrees for about half an hour. Serve with whipped cream.

FOREVER FRUIT. This idea may seem strange but it's delicious. Find an old crock or jar and wash it thoroughly. Put in 1 quart brandy and set it in a cool place. Whenever you have fruit that's just about to go bad, remove skins, stems, pits, and moldy portions, cut it in chunks, measure it, and put it in the crock with an equal amound of sugar. Almost anything can go into the crock—berries, cherries, apricots, peaches, grapes, apples, plums, nectarines. Cover the crock and stir its contents every day. Gradually, the juice will ferment into a mildly alcoholic potion that is delicious as a dessert topping or as a mixer in homemade punch. Once the crock is full, let the fruit "work" for two months. Then can both fruit and juice for future use.

★ GO BANANAS ★

The juice from banana skins makes a perfectly respectable silver polish. Cut the hard ends off the skins and put the soft parts in the food processor. Rub the banana peel purée on your silver and watch it shine!

FURNITURE

Reviving old furniture is a formidable job. But if you put in imagination, skill, and patience, you'll get out a customized piece of furniture for very little money. And you'll also have the secret satisfaction of knowing that the focal point of the living room was once a monstrosity the trash men wouldn't haul away.

There are no "you have this, you do this" rules for furniture, because there are too many designs and materials. There is one general principle: Stop thinking of that piece of furniture as an albatross and start thinking about it as raw material—for you or someone else. Once you've made that mental adjustment, your choices are these:

THE GREAT FURNITURE GIVE-AWAY.

If a piece of furniture bores you, arrange for someone else to use it. In some cities this happens informally, because the sanitation department collects unwanted furniture on specified days. On the eve of Furniture Day, many people walk the streets looking for unloved end tables and homeless floor lamps.

A more organized way of handling this transaction is to arrange for Goodwill or the Salvation Army to pick up your unwanted items. Call the numbers in the phone book and ask about their pickup arrangements, including receipts that entitle you to a tax deduction for the value of the items. When you think of donating furniture, don't neglect local groups. Churches, senior centers, and other community organizations often need sofas, chairs, tables, and other furniture for lounges, meeting rooms, and so on. Simply call the organization and explain that you'd be glad to donate a piece of furniture if they'll come and take it away. Or put a 3 × 5 card on the local bulletin board describing the items you want to get rid of. Finally, some people have great success getting people to pay them for furniture they don't want anymore by holding lawn or garage sales (*see* TRASH FOR SALE).

R&R FOR FURNITURE.

Often a piece of furniture that seems shabby, dispirited, or hopelessly out of date simply needs a little R&R—repair and restoration. Wood is perhaps the easiest material to repair. Separate broken parts, clean out the break, apply a polyvinyl resin glue to both surfaces, and clamp them together overnight. Burn holes and small tears in upholstered furniture can often be repaired by "borrowing" a patch of fabric from the back of the piece.

In many cases, however, a piece of furniture needs more than repair if it is to become a beloved part of your home. Depending upon your time and skills, you can undertake various forms of renovation. At the simplest, paint a piece of furniture a luscious new color or cover it with adhesive-backed paper, decoupage, or fabric. If you're more ambitious, try reweaving the seat on an old kitchen chair or livening up a tabletop with a hand-painted mural covered with a sheet of glass. Real go-getters might refinish a battered dresser or a set of dining-room chairs or reupholster a favorite sofa.

All these jobs take time, but the results can be spectacular. I still treasure a drop-leaf table that was originally covered with flamingo-colored paint. A solid month of stripping, sanding, and staining restored it to its natural maple. Although many repair and restoration processes are just a matter of common sense, it helps to have a good guide to follow the first time out. Hundreds of detailed how-to books are available; here are several that have sound, step-by-step advice:

How to Restore, Repair and Finish Almost Everything by Lorraine Johnson (Macmillan, 1977).
Do-It-Yourselfers Guide to Furniture Repair and Refinishing (Tab Books, 1977).
Complete Book of Furniture Repair and *Refinishing* by Ralph Kinney (Scribner's, 1971).
Professional Furniture Refinishing for the Amateur by Jessie Savage (Harper & Row, 1975).

Care and Repair of Furniture by Desmond Gatson (Doubleday, 1978).
Reupholstering at Home: A Do-It-Yourself Manual for Turning Old Furniture into New Showpieces by Peter Nesovich (Crown Publishers, 1980).

TRANSFORMATIONS.

Some of the most inspired pieces of furniture are reclaimed from obsolete originals. To accomplish such a transformation, stop looking at old furniture as what it is and ask what it could be if its parts were rearranged. For example:

- Do you have an ugly old buffet? Saw off the legs and use it as a window seat with ready-made storage underneath.
- If you have two extra dining room chairs with square seats and interesting backs, turn them into a love seat by setting the two chairs to face each other and nailing a piece of plywood across their seats. Cover the seat with a foam pad and top with bright upholstery fabric, tacked under the seat.

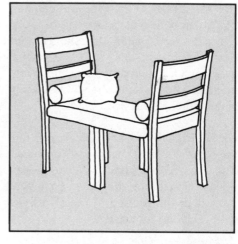

- Turn an unwanted table into a coffee table by shortening the legs, purchasing a sheet of glass the size of the tabletop, and holding the glass in place with stick-on circles of felt from the hardware store.
- Turn an unwanted coffee table into a sitting platform in the corner of the room by shortening its legs even more and covering it with pillows or carpet.
- Do you find your kitchen chairs irksome? Cut off their backs and use them as stools. If the chairs have ladder backs, turn them into towel racks by mounting them on the wall.

- Use a small nightstand as the support for one end of a door desk. Support the other end by nailing a 2 × 4 to the wall at the same height as the top of the nightstand.
- A single drawer from an abandoned buffet or dresser can become an extender for a cramped kitchen cabinet. Stand the drawer on end against the cabinet wall and line it with pegboard spaced out from the back with 1 × 1 strips.

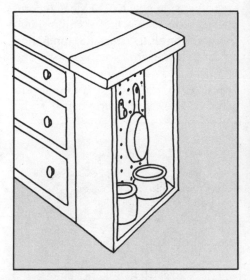

To create this storage unit, the author married the top of a Victorian buffet with the inside of a rolltop desk.

★ STYLE BOOKS ★

The secret to recycling furniture is to do it with style. Don't apologize for the old piece. If you're going to put effort into its restoration, turn it into a one-of-a-kind creation. If you doubt anything good can come of Great-uncle Elmer's armoire or the wash table in the corner of the basement, take a look at *Treasures from Throwaways* by the editors of Better Homes and Gardens (Meredith, 1976) and *New Ideas for Old Furniture* by Leslie Linsley (Lippincott & Crowell, 1980). Both books provide detailed instructions for creating household furnishings out of improbable discards. Far from being slapdash, the results often look like decorator originals. Even if you don't have the same objects available for transformation, both books will inspire you with their ingenuity.

- Do you have a hated dresser? Remove the drawers, take off their hardware, and make them into bookshelves. In the dresser cabinet, use the drawer spacers as supports for plywood shelves. To create a sort of hutch cabinet, set the bookshelves on top of the dresser cabinet.
- Turn an old table into a narrow kitchen desk for paying bills and writing notes by using a circular saw to cut one third off the long side of the table. Cut down the legs on the narrower piece of the tabletop and nail it on top of the wider piece as a shelf. Bracket the desk to the wall.

The list of ideas could go on and on. It is limited only by your ability to see new shapes and functions in furniture. There are, however, a few ground rules to keep in mind: (1) Don't cut up antiques—they are worth more in their natural state, if not to you then to a collector. If you have an old piece of furniture and are uncertain about its value, take it—or a photo of it—to a reputable antiques dealer for an appraisal before you start cutting. (2) Use a circular saw to cut through furniture so you'll get a smooth, straight cut. If you don't have a power saw, rent one and practice on scrap wood until you have a feel for its operation. (3) Spend some time refinishing your new furniture. A bookshelf made from dresser drawers will look like that unless you take the time to sand and refinish. (4) Be bold. Remember that you hated the thing in its old form, and if the new form fails, you can always move on to the next possibility.

SALVAGE. Before consigning a piece of furniture to the dump, take it apart and salvage anything that might be useful in another setting. In general, look for pieces of hardwood, casters, knobs, handles, swatches of undamaged fabric, wood screws and miscellaneous hardware, legs, cushions, mirrors, rungs, and spindles. Before cutting into furniture with a saw, use a magnetic stud finder to locate hidden nails, or you may end up having to get a new saw!

See also WOOD SCRAPS.

GARBAGE

The official definition of garbage is "discarded animal and vegetable matter." In most households, true garbage accounts for 10 to 20 percent of the waste—everything from the leaves on the lawn in the fall to the leftovers that have metamorphosed in the rear of the refrigerator. Left to its own devices, nature would recycle all this by letting it rot back into the soil. People, however, usually interfere by mixing the garbage with cans, bottles, paper, and plastic and then stuffing it into plastic bags.

Lately, our national energy problems have inspired people to take a new look at biomass, aka garbage. Essentially, garbage can be turned into three useful products. One is alcohol, liquid fuel which can be used to run small machines like lawnmowers and chain saws and even automobiles if they are properly converted. The second product is methane, a gas which can be burned to heat homes and cook food. The third product is compost, organic material which goes back into the soil to nourish plants.

Both methane and alcohol production require more than the average family's accumulation of table scraps and vegetable peels. As a result, most of the experiments with these fuels have been conducted on farms, where there is a ready supply of animal waste and crop residue. On the other hand, some people with large gardens or enough ambition to collect waste from supermarkets and restaurants have installed alcohol-producing stills and methane-producing digesters in the suburbs. One man in North Carolina gets enough methane by digesting household scraps, leaves, and sewage to heat his home, cook his food, and fuel his gas lamps. Another man in New York State is producing backyard alcohol from squash and pumpkins.

Both methane and alcohol production are small-scale technologies which hold the promise of energy self-sufficiency for individuals. Although methane can be explosive if it is improperly handled, it can also be a safe and efficient fuel. India, for example, has been producing methane since 1905 and has 6,000 operating digesters. Similarly, moonshiners have been producing backyard alcohol in this country for decades. If anything, making alcohol to drive instead of drink is easier, though fuel makers must still contend with antiquated regulations, which differ from state to state. (For information on alcohol production laws in your state, call the National Alcohol Fuels Information Center, 800-525-5000; 800-332-8339 in Colorado.)

Nonetheless, in households that produce only a pound or two of organic garbage per day per person, composting is the most reasonable way to reuse it. Composting used to be the preserve of organic vegetable gardeners, but there's no reason for them to have a monopoly on this process. Apartment dwellers can use their compost in place of expensive potting soil, and suburbanites can spread it around their shrubs or lawns in place of fertilizer. Properly made, a compost heap improves on nature's decomposition cycle by speeding it up and eliminating unpleasant smells and other side effects. The goal in composting is to create the optimum environment for all the bacteria, fungi, and molds that transform orange peels and eggshells into good earth.

Although compost can be made without one, most people use some

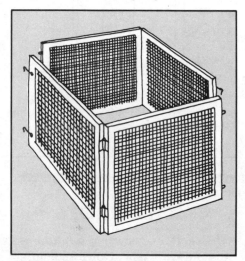

★ THINGS TO PUT IN YOUR ★ COMPOST HEAP

Eggshells	Pea pods
Coffee grounds	Plant stalks
Small amounts of paper	Feathers
(tear it up first)	Leather scraps (even old shoes
Banana peels	if you cut them up)
Orange peels	Fish scraps
Peels of all kinds	Sour milk
Wood chips	Melon rinds
Grass clippings	Tea leaves
Moldy bread	Tomato skins
Spoiled food	Weeds
Peanut shells	Ashes
Apple cores	

kind of bin to hold the organic materials as they decompose. One popular design consists of four old screens, formed into a bottomless box by hinging two corners and attaching hooks and eyes at two corners. This bin can be moved when you want to turn the pile, and folds up for easy winter storage. Fifty-five-gallon drums also make good compost bins. One design, suitable for a basement or garage, calls for punching several drainage holes in the bottom of the drum, setting it on cement blocks, and putting a pan underneath to catch runoff. As the drum begins to fill with organic material, shove a section of perforated pipe through the center to provide extra ventilation and reduce the number of times you need to turn the pile. You can also convert a 55-gallon drum into a rotating composter with about $25 worth of hardware, available as a kit from Sotz Corporation, 13600 North Station Road, Columbia Station, OH 44028. Several other manufacturers produce ready-made composters.

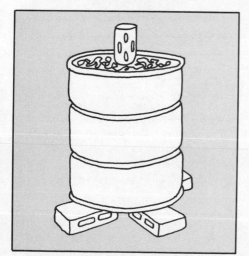

Whether you opt for a plain or fancy bin, fill it with the same materials. In general, variety makes the best compost. Layer as many different types of materials as you can—household garbage, grass clippings, animal manure, and so on. As much as possible, the materials should be shredded or chopped into uniform pieces not much over 2 inches in length. Larger objects will eventually decompose, but they'll slow down the process in the rest of the pile. Layer the materials until the bin is two-thirds full and then stop adding fresh material. If you have a second bin, you can fill it while the first one is working.

The work in a compost bin is done by bacteria of two varieties. Aerobic bacteria are a fastidious, hardworking breed that smell nice and make compost fast. Their anaerobic cousins make compost and methane, but they take more time and produce the noxious odors that most people associate with rotting garbage. For a good supply of aerobic bacteria, oxygen must circulate through your compost heap; aerobic bacteria thrive and anaerobic die in its presence. To improve the ventilation of your pile, provide air vents in the bin, pile the contents of the pile loosely, and turn the pile every three or four weeks. Depending upon the size of your pile, turning may involve forking the entire heap into a new spot or mixing with a shovel. Either way, be sure you do it to keep anaerobic bacteria from taking over. In fact, if your compost heap starts to smell bad, don't cover it up, mix it up.

In addition to air, a compost pile needs water—the standard rule is moist but not soggy. Usually household garbage contains enough moisture, but if you are composting leaves or other dry matter, you may need to douse the pile with a pail of water (*see* GREY WATER). As

★ COLLECTIVE ★ COMPOSTING

Because composting is such a good idea, a few cities separate out their organic waste from the trash and turn it into a useful and potentially profitable soil enricher. Since 1950, the Environmental Protection Agency has started about twenty composting plants. All have been forced to close because agribusiness in this country prefers to enrich soil with chemical fertilizers. In Holland, on the other hand, where the tulip industry demands large quantities of quality soil, nearly one hundred composting plants are operational, devouring almost a sixth of the country's organic wastes.

A few American communities are trying to complete the compost loop for themselves. At the Institute for Local Self-Reliance in Washington, DC, about two hundred people pooled their garbage in community compost heaps for several years. The group collected about 500 pounds of garbage a week and composted it in a space 6 feet by 30 feet. Each month, the system provided 1,000 pounds of compost, which was used to enrich an adjoining garden, also operated by the community. After the initial setup, the only cost was labor—about five person-hours per week. Although the Institute has discontinued this project, they still publish a booklet entitled "Municipal Composting." Copies are available for $4 from the Institute for Local Self-Reliance, 1717 18th Street NW, Washington, DC 20009. For larger efforts, a report entitled *A Compost Strategy for the City of Seattle* is available from the Recycling and Resource Recovery Program, 807 Municipal Building, Seattle, WA 98104. Another good source of information about composting on a large scale is *Bio Cycle*, available from Rodale Press, 33 East Minor Street, Emmaus, PA 18049.

★ MAKING ★ COMPOST IN THE KITCHEN

Yes, you *can* make compost indoors. A kitchen composter will make small quantities of compost for houseplants by using up kitchen scraps. Start with a milk carton or other waterproof container. Close off the pour spout, turn the container on its side, and cut a flap large enough so you can reach inside with a spoon. Cut up all your organic material before putting it in the carton. The pieces should be as thin as possible and no more than 1 inch long. You may even want to whirl some items in the blender or food processor to make the pieces small and even.

If the garbage is unusually gloppy, drain off the excess moisture. Then spread it over the bottom of the container and cover with a fine sprinkle of unsterilized soil. Next day, stir the first layer, add a new layer of organic material, and sprinkle more soil over the top. Keep adding garbage until it comes to within an inch of the container opening, and stir thoroughly once a day.

When the container is full, start a second one and set the first one aside so the bacteria can finish their work. Continue to stir the first container daily, and moisten it if the compost seems to be drying out. Do not add new organic material. At the end of three weeks, the first carton should contain crumbly brown soil. Use the soil for potting plants or sprinkle it around the tops of houseplants as a nutritious pick-me-up.

the composting proceeds, the pile will heat up and may reach temperatures of up to 160 degrees. Don't be alarmed. The heat is beneficial, because it kills off weed seeds and pathogenic bacteria. The pile will also shrink, leaving room for new contributions.

Depending upon the materials you use, the size of the pile, and the frequency with which you turn it, your compost should be done about six weeks after you stop adding new material. You'll recognize the finished product by its fine consistency, brown color, and sweet smell. It looks like good earth. And, of course, that's what it is. Use it to enrich the garden, pot plants, start seedlings. If you have a brown thumb, give it away to your neighborhood gardeners. Perhaps they'll reward you with a basket of home-grown tomatoes.

★ BOOKS THAT WILL HELP YOU ★ TURN YOUR GARBAGE INTO . . .

COMPOST:

Rodale Guide to Composting by Jerry Minich and Marjorie Hunt (Rodale Press, 1979).
Let It Rot: The Gardener's Guide to Composting by Stu Campbell (Garden Way, 1975).
Everyone's Guide to Home Composting by Robyn Behm (Van Nostrand Reinhold, 1978).

METHANE:

Practical Building of Methane Power Plants by L. John Fry (L. John Fry, 1223 North Nopal Street, Santa Barbara, CA 93103).
Methane: Planning a Digester by Peter John Meynell (Schocken, 1978).

ALCOHOL:

Making Fuel in Your Backyard by Jack Bradley (Biomass Resources, P.O. Box 2912, Wenatchee, WA 98801).
Methanol and Other Ways Around the Gas Pump by John Ware Lincoln (Garden Way, 1972).
Alcohol Fuel Packet, National Center for Appropriate Technology, P.O. Box 3838, Butte, MT 59701. The Center also publishes up-to-date bibliographies of materials on alcohol fuels (30 cents) and methane (50 cents).

GARDEN HOSES

Hoses are always getting punctured, slashed, or mashed. Even when it's in damaged condition, a hose is a great household resource. You can lengthen or shorten it, slit it or tie it, use it to cushion one thing and to improve your grip on another. For example:

BLADE GUARD. Cut an old hose into sections as long as the blade on an axe, a saw, or even ice skates. Use a linoleum knife to slit the hose. Slip the split hose around the blade to protect its cutting edge and to prevent injuries. Shorter lengths of hose can be protective holders for screwdrivers, chisels, and other tools.

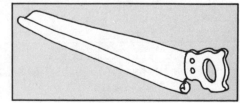

HOLES IN THE HOSE. If the hose has a puncture leak, puncture it some more with a fat nail and use it as a soaker hose on the lawn or in the garden.

SNEAKY SNAKE. Small animals fear snakes, and some people say they'll avoid the vegetable patch if you paint splotches on a short length of hose and leave it coiled snakelike in the garden.

FIT TO BE TIED. Before tying a rope or wire to a tree, slip a small piece of hose over it and position it next to the bark so the tree will be protected. Use the same technique to protect furniture and other objects when you have to lash them to a dolly or a truck.

SHORTIE. If your hose is ruptured near the nozzle, cut it off with a linoleum knife. Use the shorter hose for shorter jobs. Or clamp two short hoses together using a strip of rubber from an inner tube and a worm gear hose clamp. You can also replace the threaded cap that screws onto the faucet, using an inexpensive kit available in any hardware store.

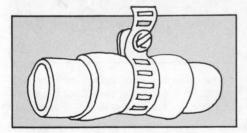

HANDLE IT. To improve your grip on tools, cut short sections of hose and twist them onto the handles. When the grips on a bicycle's handlebars split, replace them with short lengths of old hose. Slit other short pieces of hose with a linoleum knife and slip them around the handles on buckets and bushel baskets to keep the wire from digging into your hands.

•••••••••••••••••••••••••••

GLOVES

Personally, I always lose my gloves before they're worn out. But if I had an old pair, here's what I'd do with them:

DUST GLOVE. Save an old pair of cotton or wool gloves for dusting. Pull them on, run your hands over the furniture, and the job is done. When they're dirty, toss them in the washing machine.

TWO-LINER. Old gloves that have worn thin can be used as liners under regular winter gloves for extra warmth or under rubber gloves to eliminate that clammy feeling.

FIVE-FINGER PUPPETS. To make a fanciful set of finger puppets, stuff the fingertips of an old glove with a wad of cotton and tie off the stuffed tips with bits of yarn. Make faces on the puppets with a marking pen and add a little yarn for hair. Pull on the glove and stage an entire puppet drama with one hand!

AT YOUR FINGERTIPS. Use a single old glove as a belt holder for small tools. Make two slits for the belt and cut off the tips of the fingers. If necessary, hand-stitch around the cuts to keep the glove from raveling.

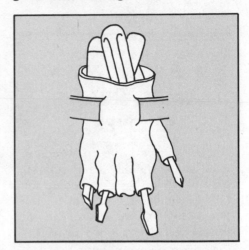

MATCHMAKING. If you have two old gloves for the same hand, turn one inside out and wear it on the other hand. These gloves may look funny but they are fine for work gloves.

The quickest way to make a family of puppets is to tie off the fingertips of an old glove.

FINGER EXERCISES. When your gloves have holes in the fingertips, make a virtue of necessity. Cut out the fingers, stitch around the edges to keep them from raveling, and use the gloves when you hunt, fish, or work with tools in the cold.

★ AND WHAT ★ ABOUT RUBBER GLOVES?

Rubber gloves seem to wear out even more quickly than regular gloves. When they do, slice up the cuff for rubber bands. Cut off the fingers and slip them onto mop or broom handles so they won't fall over when you lean them against a wall. Slip two fingers over the jaws of pliers so they won't mar things. Slip a single fingertip over your index finger when you need to sort through papers quickly. Cut flower shapes out of the beaded part of the glove and glue them to the bathtub with Pliobond glue. The rubber prevents slipping, and the glue can be dissolved with nail polish remover if you want to remove them.

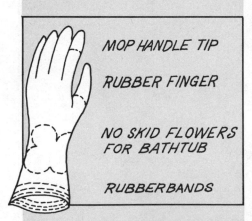

MOP HANDLE TIP

RUBBER FINGER

NO SKID FLOWERS FOR BATHTUB

RUBBERBANDS

GREASE

See FATS AND GREASE

GREETING CARDS

Some people are almost superstitious about not throwing out greeting cards, as if saving them could preserve the moment. Instead of stashing your old cards in shoe boxes, reuse them in ways that extend your pleasure by highlighting their bright illustrations. Here are a few possibilities:

ONE MORE TIME. If a greeting was good the first time, why not send it again? Buy colorful stickers to paste over the original signature. Make a new envelope to fit the old card or open the original carefully by inserting a nail file under all its seams. Fold the envelope inside out, glue the seams, address, and remail.

MAKE A NOTE OF IT. Double-fold cards often have blank panels. To take advantage of that fact, open the card flat and cut off the half that has the writing on it. Refold the half that has the illustration and a blank panel and use it as a note card.

CUTOUTS. Illustrations cut from heavier card paper can be name tags for packages or elements in a mobile. Flimsier pictures can be glued on place cards, collage placemats (glue pictures onto 12 × 18-inch sheets of cardboard and coat with clear acrylic), or homemade cards (fold a fresh piece of paper in four, glue the illustration on the front, and write your own message inside).

DECOUPAGE. Greeting cards make fine cutouts for decoupage, since many are textured as well as colorful. Select, sand, and paint the object to be decorated. Cut out your design using fingernail scissors and glue it to the object with white glue. When the glue is dry, varnish the object. Let the varnish dry, sand lightly, and varnish again. Repeat the process about ten times, or until the illustration from the card seems to be part of the object. For a more detailed description of decoupage and its possibilities, see *Decoupage: A New Look at an Old Craft* by Lesley Linsley (Doubleday, 1972) or *Contemporary Decoupage* by T. R. Newman (Crown Publishers, 1972).

A TISKET, A TASKET. Greeting cards can be laced together to make cheerful, inexpensive baskets and other items. Punch holes through the cards at ½-inch intervals and lace them together with bright yarn or ribbon.

To make baskets and other containers from greeting cards, punch holes along the edges and lace the cards together.

GREY WATER

Grey water is "dirty water"—the water you used today for washing your face, rinsing your vegetables, and cleaning your clothes. In short, it is all the waste water generated in the home that doesn't go through the toilet. Unlike toilet flush water (*see* BODY WASTES), grey water doesn't require extensive treatment before it can be reused in nondrinking situations. Unfortunately, most household water systems mix the grey water with the other sewage, so both require complex and costly treatment.

In a few places people are beginning to think of grey water as a resource to be reclaimed. During the droughts in recent summers, many people routinely left bathwater in the tub and used it to water plants and flush the toilet. More ambitious homeowners have figured out ways to divert the water from sinks and tubs so that it goes straight outdoors to irrigate the garden or the lawn. As water becomes more scarce, grey water is likely to be recognized as the resource it is.

●●●●●●●●●●●●●●●●●●●●●●●●●●●●●

GUM

See CHEWING GUM

HAIR

Do you feel vaguely regretful about throwing out the wad of hair that accumulates in your hairbrush? Hair is organic, so it can go in the compost heap (*see* GARBAGE). It also carries human scent, so a tangle of it on the branch of a young fruit tree or berry bush is supposed to keep away deer and other animals.

If those ideas seem crass, consider the solution of Victorian ladies, who lovingly placed their fallen hairs in hair receivers. When they had accumulated enough, they stuffed it into rats—long, narrow tubes of fabric (you could make one from an old stocking) which were used to add fullness to buns and other hairstyles. Women with a lot of spare hair sometimes stuffed pillows with it, and those with more time than hair braided it into delicate bracelets and rings.

If you'd like to try your hand at these hairy crafts, collect the hair in an old stocking. Tie off the end of the stocking and wash the entire package in mild detergent or shampoo. When your rinse water runs clean, hang the hair-filled stocking up to dry. Once the hair is clean, untangle it for braiding—use two clean brushes and card it as you would sheep's wool—or leave it bunched together for stuffing.

Never in Your Wildest Dreams

Bill Black is a Saint Louis barber who felt bad about throwing out all the clippings from his customers, so he started taking them home and putting them around his philodendrons. The flowers thrived, and Bill decided to study the fertilizer value of hair. He found that 6 pounds of human hair contains the same amount of nitrogen as 100 pounds of cow manure, plus twenty-seven trace minerals and elements that are beneficial for plants. Rather than keeping all this fertilizer to himself, Black now packages his clippings and sells them as Fert-Hair-Lizer.

HAM CANS

See CANS

HANDLES

See PLASTIC HANDLES

HANDBAGS

Handbags come in such a variety of shapes and sizes that it's difficult to devise a one-reuse-fits-all formula. An adaptation that seems natural for one bag will be ridiculous for another. Still, before you toss out a handbag, rethink its use as a carrier. If it's too shabby to hold your wallet and compact, maybe it could carry something else. Here are seven possibilities:

- Bike bag: cut the handle in half and use the straps to tie the bag to the handlebars or behind the seat of your bicycle
- Overnight bag: when you're traveling light, cram an extra set of underwear and a toothbrush into an old handbag
- Picnic pouch: fill with sandwiches, apples, and chocolate chip cookies
- Needlework tote: keep your current sewing project in an old handbag and use compartments and pockets for needles, thread, scissors, etc.
- Tool bag: on Saturdays when you're doing odd jobs around the house, put your most used tools in an old handbag and carry them with you
- Camera bag: keep lenses, extra film, light meter, lens brushes, and other equipment in a tough old handbag
- Organization bag: small, outdated clutch purses can often be used as change purses, make-up kits, or organizers inside larger bags

If a handbag is simply too worn for public use, take it apart and reuse the pieces. Save unworn leather and canvas sections for small craft projects (*see* LEATHER). Save any inside pockets, especially those with zippers, and sew them into homemade bags. Retrieve all rings, clasps, and other hardware. Most of all, keep usable handles and attach them to tool chests, toy boxes, picnic baskets, or other handbags.

If the handbag is being retired for want of a handle, fashion a new handle from an extra belt, a macrame strap or a handle salvaged from some other bag.

HANGERS

The world is divided into people who always have too many hangers and people who never have enough. The people with an overabundance are the lucky ones, since coat hanger wire is one of the most versatile of household resources, stiff enough to poke things out of a clogged vacuum cleaner hose and pliable enough to bend into an instant hook for the paint can that needs to be hung from the top rung of a ladder. Think of using coat hanger wire whenever you're faced with a problem of hanging, supporting, fastening, or probing. Here are a few of the many dozens of uses:

SUPERBUBBLES. To make bubbles that will amaze your children, untwist the neck of a coat hanger, straighten the wire, and recurve it into a large hoop with a handle. Mix a bottle of ordinary blowing bubbles with 2 ounces glycerine (available in drugstores) and a squirt or two of grease-cutting detergent. Stir gently and pour into a cookie sheet with sides. Dip the hanger loop and pull gently through the air to make giant bubbles.

CAMPER CRAFT. Keep a supply of old, unpainted hangers for use around the campfire. A straightened hanger makes a dandy marshmallow cooker. If you need more stability for hot dogs, bend the hanger in half and skewer each dog twice. And if you are ambitious enough to attempt a toasted sandwich, wire the metal ends from a coffee can to the hanger and clamp the sandwich firmly between them. Hold the handles of all camping utensils with a potholder to prevent burns.

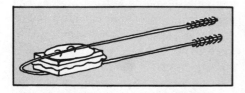

NATURAL NET. To make an impromptu net for catching fish, frogs, and butterflies, stretch the loop of a hanger into a rough circle. Out of lightweight fabric or cheesecloth, make a bag whose mouth is the same size as the circle. Fold the open edge of the bag over the wire and stitch or safety-pin in place. Use the hook as the handle, or, if you wish, drill a deep hole in the end of a broomstick, straighten the hook, coat it with epoxy, and insert it into the hole.

BOOK HOOK. To make a handy support for a book that has directions you're following, squeeze the two arms of a hanger together as shown.

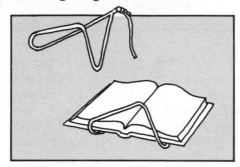

HOOKED ON HANGERS. A hanger comes with a ready-made hook. Snip off the hanger's arms an inch below the twist. Now twist the short ends together to leave a little keyhole that lets you hang the hook on the wall. If that hook doesn't suit your purposes, use pliers to bend pieces of hanger wire into S-hooks, pegboard hooks, screen door hooks, and more. If you need extra strength, twist two pieces of hanger wire together before shaping the hook.

BOOT BOTTOMS UP. To hang boots out of the way during the summer, make a boot hanger by bending a coat hanger as shown.

KING KONG CLIP. Cut the hook off a hanger and use pliers to bend the long piece of leftover wire into an enormous paper clip. Use the clip on *very* important papers.

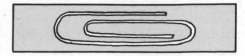

EGG LIFTER. If you've ever burned your fingers retrieving a three-minute egg, consider this nifty contraption. Cut a 2-foot piece of wire from a hanger and straighten it. Make loops at each end of the wire by wrapping it around a broom handle. Then find the center of the wire and make a loop and a half around the broom handle, as shown. To grasp the egg, squeeze the two sides of the lifter, position over the egg, and release.

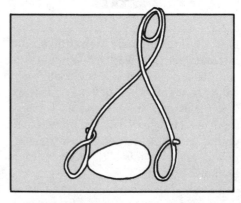

HANGER DUSTER. To make a duster for furniture and walls, cut bits of yarn into 4-inch lengths and loop them securely around an old hanger. Cover the hanging part with the yarn fringe, then bend the two legs together and fashion the hook into a handle.

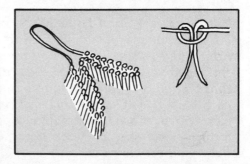

MOBILIZATION. Hangers are natural supports for mobiles. Cut a hanger at the elbows, straighten the shoulders, and turn them up at the end. Cut the extra piece of wire into short sections to make branches in the middle of the mobile. Hang the elements in the mobile from thread, adjusting length and position until everything balances.

RECYCLE→RECYCLE→RECYCLE

If you cannot use up all your extra coat hangers, take a batch back to your cleaner—they'll be glad to get them.

★ ADVANCED HANGERS ★

If your closet is bulging with ordinary wire hangers, retrain some of them so they can be used for special purposes.

Pants Hanger. Slit a long cardboard tube and slip it over the bar of a hanger to make a pants hanger that won't crease your trousers.

Skirt Hanger. Add two spring-clip clothespins to make any hanger into a skirt hanger. Or, if your skirts have hanging loops, use pliers to crimp notches in the shoulders of a wire hanger about 1½ inches from the elbows.

Coat Hanger. Need a heavy-duty hanger? Lash three or four ordinary hangers together with picture wire or twist-'ems from bread bags.

Space-Saver Hanger. Organize a crowded closet by linking several hangers together. Cut the hooks off two hangers and use pliers to untwist the wire. Put an open hanger under a complete hanger and twist the open hanger's ends over the bar of the complete hanger. Repeat with the other open hanger.

No-Slip Hanger. Wrap a hanger with scraps of yarn to make a no-slip hanger for slinky dresses and silk shirts.

Drip-Dry Hanger. Make a rust-free drying hanger by cutting a plastic dry cleaning bag into 2 × 3-inch strips. Bunch each strip at the center and tie it around a hanger until the wire is completely covered. Fluff up the ends of the plastic strips.

metric tons of hazardous waste, over 60 percent of it generated by the chemical industry as they make the drugs, plastics, fibers, and fertilizers that are so much a part of contemporary life. Although new laws are designed to trace toxic materials to make sure that they are disposed of safely, little has been done about the hundreds of dumps around the country containing drums and "ponds" of lethal materials.

The average citizen doesn't have much direct contact with hazardous waste—until it contaminates his or her well or leaks through the basement wall or creates fetid puddles in the backyard. For information about what citizens can do under such circumstances, write for a copy of "Hazardous Waste Primer," available for 75 cents from the League of Women Voters, 1730 M Street NW, Washington, DC 20036.

Although industry produces most of our hazardous waste, remember that homes too can be a source of dangerous waste materials. Aerosol cans explode, used motor oil contains heavy metals, cleaning fluids (particularly drain cleaners) are caustic, and liquids ranging from nail polish remover to turpentine are toxic and flammable. In other words, if you're going to complain about hazardous wastes, don't contribute to the problem. Keep such products in leakproof containers and use them up. If you must dispose of such materials, contact the local sanitation department to find out about proper procedures.

See also BATTERIES; CANS; MOTOR OIL.

HARDWARE

Hardware holds things together, and the true handyperson would never dream of throwing away hinges, nuts, nails, screws, bolts, and other, unnameable odd bits of metal. These treasures should be salvaged whenever possible from appliances, old furniture, and other discards. If you have any doubt about their value, just check the price of brass cup hooks or piano hinges at your local hardware store. If the used hardware is rusty, clean it up by soaking it overnight in naval jelly. Then sort and store in found containers—egg cartons and baby food jars are particularly good.

HAZARDOUS WASTES

Some wastes are annoying, and some are downright dangerous. Every year this country throws away 40 million

HOSES

See GARDEN HOSES

HOT WATER HEATERS

See WATER HEATERS

HOUSES

See BUILDINGS

HUMAN ORGANS

People don't usually think of throwing away their organs, but those who are buried with their bodies intact are doing just that. To recycle your kidneys, eyes, and other organs, request a copy of the Uniform Donor Card from the American Medical Association, 535 North Dearborn, Chicago, IL 60610. If you wish to donate all or part of your body for transplantation, education or research, fill out the card, sign it in front of witnesses, and carry it in your wallet. In some states, you can also note on your driver's license that you are an organ donor.

And while we're on the subject, don't forget to recycle your blood. The average American adult can donate blood five times a year without ill effect. Call the local chapter of the Red Cross to find out where and when to donate.

UNIFORM DONOR CARD

OF _____
Print or Type name of donor
In the hope that I may help others, I hereby make this anatomical gift, if medically acceptable, to take effect upon my death. The words and marks below indicate my desires.
I give   (a) _____ any needed organs or parts
         (b) _____ only the following organs or parts

_____
Specify the organ(s) or part(s)
for the purposes of transplantation, therapy, medical research or education.
         (c) _____ my body for anatomical study if needed.
Limitations or
special wishes, if any _____

UNIFORM DONOR CARD

OF _____
Print or Type name of donor
In the hope that I may help others, I hereby make this anatomical gift, if medically acceptable, to take effect upon my death. The words and marks below indicate my desires.
I give   (a) _____ any needed organs or parts
         (b) _____ only the following organs or parts

_____
Specify the organ(s) or part(s)
for the purposes of transplantation, therapy, medical research or education.
         (c) _____ my body for anatomical study if needed.
Limitations or
special wishes, if any _____

Signed by the donor and the following two witnesses in the presence of each other:

_____   _____
Signature of Donor   Date of Birth of Donor

_____   _____
Date Signed   City & State

_____   _____
Witness   Witness

This is a legal document under the Uniform Anatomical Gift Act or similar laws.

Signed by the donor and the following two witnesses in the presence of each other:

_____   _____
Signature of Donor   Date of Birth of Donor

_____   _____
Date Signed   City & State

_____   _____
Witness   Witness

This is a legal document under the Uniform Anatomical Gift Act or similar laws.

To become an organ donor, simply obtain the Uniform Donor Card, sign it in front of a witness, and carry it in your wallet.

ICE CREAM STICKS

The flat wooden sticks at the center of ice cream bars and Popsicles are coveted by craftspeople, who sometimes buy just the sticks when a project outstrips their appetite for ice cream. People who don't want to build planters can still find uses for an occasional ice cream stick. It is, after all, a simple slat of wood which can be wedged into a window that rattles or used as a spur-of-the-moment straight edge. Here are other possibilities:

SPLINT IN TIME. Use ice cream sticks as splints when you repair broken toys, tool handles, or spindles on chairs.

STIRRING THINGS UP. Ice cream sticks are ideal for stirring small batches of paint and spreading glue.

ON FILE. Have you ever needed to sand the inside of a curlicue or eradicate rust in a tight spot on your car? The job can be a lot less frustrating if you cut out a long, narrow piece of sandpaper and glue it to an ice cream stick. Trim the overlap with a razor blade and use the tiny file for sanding.

APPLE ON A STICK. Caramel apples are a favorite fall treat, and you can make your own if you save ice cream sticks all summer.

ID FOR PLANTS. Use ice cream sticks to help you remember where you planted what in the garden. Write on the sticks with indelible markers so the rain won't wash off your notations.

ICE CREAM STICK CONSTRUCTIONS. If you want to occupy a group of kids some rainy afternoon, teach them to make trinket boxes from ice cream sticks, glued together log-cabin style. Advanced ice cream stick artists also make planters, sewing boxes, lamps, and Buddhist temples. For instructions, consult "Building with Craft Sticks," a $2 publication available from craft stores or Craft Course Publishers, 260 South Paseo Tesoro, P.O. Box 704, Walnut, CA 91789.

INNER TUBES

The tires on most American cars are now tubeless, so an inner tube is a scarce household resource. Salvage them whenever possible from trucks, bicycles, and, occasionally, foreign cars. To distinguish tubed from tubeless tires, check the air valve. If it protrudes through the tire, there's a tube inside; if it's welded right into the tire wall, the tire is tubeless.

For years, intact inner tubes have

been used as inflatable beach toys. Though they may not be as much fun, damaged tubes are just as useful. Cut the rubber with a pair of heavy scissors and use it to solve all kinds of household problems. Here are a few suggestions:

BIG BAND. Cut across an old inner tube to make heavy-duty rubber bands, which can be used to clamp things when you glue them.

PATCH UP. Small pieces of inner tube make fine patches for air mattresses, children's swimming pools, floating toys, and other inflatable objects. Rough up the rubber with a piece of sandpaper and apply rubber cement to the patch and to the area to be patched. Clamp them together until the glue dries.

STRETCHY HINGE. Make a simple hinge for a homemade box and lid from a strip of inner tube rubber. Cut a thick strip of rubber and use two screws to attach one end to the box. Set the top on the box, pull the rubber over it, and fasten the hinge to the lid with two more screws. Use washers so the heads of the screws won't tear through the rubber.

STRAPPED. Strips of inner tube can be used as straps to hold books together, to hold a helmet or hat on your head, or to hold tools against a wall. Cut a strip of rubber of the appropriate width and length and attach snap fasteners to each end. These handy grippers, available in any hardware store, clamp right into the rubber. Matching grippers can be fastened to walls, helmets, and other surfaces.

SLINGSHOT. Inner tube rubber still makes the best slingshots. Find a heavy forked stick and cut a slit in the end of each fork. Cut a strip of inner tube, 1 inch wide, and tie a knot at each end before slipping the rubber into the slits.

HOMEMADE SOLES. If you crochet or knit your own slippers, make them last longer by adding a sole made from inner tube rubber. Just trace the foot of the slipper on the rubber, cut it out, and stitch it on with heavy thread, using a thimble.

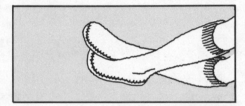

SOFT STUFF. Use pieces of inner tube rubber to cushion and protect fragile objects and surfaces. Glue small pads on the bottoms of trivets that scratch the table or appliances that mar your countertops. Wrap larger pieces around trees when you have to fasten a rope or wire to them. Tack a strip along the sill of a window that's likely to slam.

WEATHER TUBE. Strips of inner tube rubber make crude but effective weatherstripping for windows, doors, and cracks in outbuildings. Cut the rubber into 1-inch strips and tack it over the draft-producing cracks.

SLIP PREVENTION. Stitch or glue small pieces or rubber to the bottom of throw rugs to keep them from slipping out from underfoot. Fasten small patches to the soles of new shoes that are slippery.

LEAKY TUBES. One of the quickest ways to stop a small leak in a pipe or a hose is to wrap a strip of inner tube around the spot with the hole. Then clamp the hose in place with a worm gear clamp.

SOFT TOUCH. Bicycle inner tubes can be cut into sections and slipped onto the handles of garden tools, hammers, hedge clippers, etc. This trick not only improves your grip on the tool but also makes blisters less likely.

JAR LIDS

The primary function of jar lids is protecting the contents of the parent jar, but they can also be used as ashtrays, coasters, cookie cutters, shallow containers for mixing glue or sorting tiny objects, and any of the following:

ROLLER COASTER. Save matching lids of the same size and paint them. Glue circles of felt or cork to the inside of the lids and use them for icy drinks. This is a good made-it-myself present.

BACK TO BASICS. Jar lids make good bases for fat candles, flowerpots, drippy jelly jars, paint pots, and other messy things.

LEG LIDS. Put jar lids of the proper size under the legs of your furniture so the weight will be distributed and won't crush the carpet. If you paint the lids a color that blends with the carpet, no one will suspect their origin.

FRAMED. To use jar lids as crafty little frames for photographs, cover the lids with paint or fabric. Trace the shape of the lid over the photograph. Cut out the circle slightly inside the line you've drawn and glue it into the lid. Glue several photo lids to a strip of wide ribbon.

SAY IT WITH BUTTONS. Have something you want to say to the world? Write it on your own custom-made button. Spray paint a jar lid and let it dry. Stencil or print your message freehand in a contrasting color and let the lettering dry. Cut a circle of heavy cardboard the same size as the jar lid. Make two slits in it to accommodate the head and pin of a large safety pin. Glue the cardboard circle into the button so the pin sticks out. When the glue dries, pin your button on your lapel.

JARS AND BOTTLES

The average American household buys 143 glass containers per year. Fortunately, the characteristics that make glass appealing to manufacturers also make it valuable at home. Glass bottles never leak or absorb odors. And they are, of course, transparent, allowing full view of the contents. These assets have not been overlooked by housewares manufacturers. Every department store carries dozens of canisters, crocks, dishes and organizers that are nothing more than glorified glass jars. With a little ingenuity, you can make many of these objects out of empty jars and bottles, especially if you master the delicate arts of glass cutting and decorating. Of course, many glass containers can be used without modification. Here are suggestions:

MINI WASHER. A glass jar with a wide mouth makes a terrific little washing machine for small objects such as gloves and stockings. Put the washable in the jar and fill it two thirds full with water. Add mild soap, and shake the jar vigorously for several minutes. Rinse the washable and hang it up to dry.

PINNED. Use another plump jar to make a sewer's companion. Fill the jar with pins. Cut a circle of foam rubber the size of the lid, cover it with fabric, and glue it to the top of the lid for a pincushion.

AIR FRESHENER. Find jars with interesting shapes and fill them with homemade potpourri. Punch holes in the lid of the jar or use a jar with a prepunched lid—a Parmesan cheese jar, for example. Fill the jar with dried flowers or spices. For potpourri recipes, consult *Potpourri* by Ann Felner (Workman Publishing, 1977).

BELL JAR. If your hobby is making dried flower arrangements, building miniatures, or collecting natural specimens, use wide-mouthed jars as covers for your creations and collectibles.

ROOTING FOR JARS. Short fat jars make good rooters for houseplants. Just fill with water, add a cutting, and wait for roots.

RAIN GAUGE. Curious about how much rain fell last night? Make your own rain gauge from a tall bottle with parallel sides, perhaps an olive jar, and a funnel. Find a second jar with a diameter the same as the mouth of the funnel and pour exactly one inch of water into it. Pour the water from the large jar into the narrow jar and mark the level it comes to with nail polish. Divide the distance from the bottom of the jar to the mark into ten equal parts. To use the rain gauge, build a stand that will hold the funnel in the narrow jar and leave it outside in a storm.

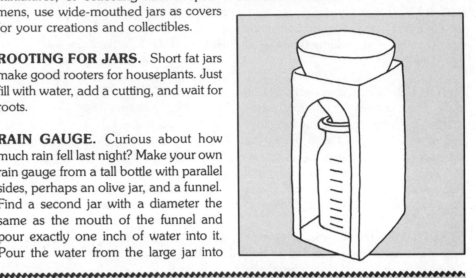

Never in Your Wildest Dreams

Everybody remembers the childhood pastime of blowing over the mouth of a pop bottle to make music. Organ builder Justin Kramer not only remembered but improved on the idea by building a musical instrument as complex as an organ out of soda bottles. In 1973 he patented his "Jugorgel," an 88-bottle instrument that makes haunting, breathy music. Since then, Kramer has produced variations on his theme, including a smaller "six-pack organ."

★ How to Cut ★ a Bottle

The possibilities for reusing empty bottles and jars multiply dramatically if you learn how to cut them. For years people have been cutting bottles, with mixed success, by soaking a string in kerosene, tying it around the bottle, lighting the string, and plunging the bottle into cold water. A second folk method calls for filling the bottle with warm water to just below the cutting line. Then use a funnel to pour ½ cup melted paraffin into the bottle so it forms a cap on the water. Refrigerate until the bottle is ice cold. Now heat more paraffin to the boiling point and use the funnel to pour it onto the hardened wax in the bottle. The bottle should crack on the line where hot and cold paraffin meet.

The problem with both these methods is that they often produce a fairly jagged edge. Still, if you only want to cut an occasional bottle to make a greenhouse top for a plant or a hurricane shade for a candle, try them. All you can lose is an old bottle you were going to pitch out. If you do end up with sharp edges, be sure to cover them with heavy tape.

If you're going to try ambitious projects that require a smooth, finished edge, you'll need a more sophisticated cutter. You can probably find one at your local crafts store or mail-order from American Handicrafts, 8113 Highway 80 W, Fort Worth, TX 76116.

If you can't buy a bottle cutter, you'll have to improvise. All bottle cutters operate on the same principle: Weaken the bottle where you want it to break and then apply stress until the bottle cracks. Most experienced bottle cutters follow four steps: First, clean the bottle, since glue, paper, and dirt will interfere with the cut. Second, score the bottle. To do this, wrap a piece of masking tape around the bottle slightly below the point where you want it to break. Lay the bottle on a cushioned surface, perhaps a thin piece of foam rubber. Hold the glass cutter firmly with one hand or mount it on the work surface. Roll the bottle forward firmly so the cutter makes a thin, continuous scratch all the way around the bottle. The object of scoring is to weaken, not break the bottle.

The third step is the application of stress. This can be done in three ways. You can rotate the bottle over a lighted candle until the score mark is thoroughly heated. Then apply ice to the score mark; the sudden change in temperature will cause the glass to crack. You can also insert a curved metal rod or a glass cutter lengthened with a piece of coat hanger wire into the bottle. Tap the end of the instrument firmly against the inside of the score mark. After you've tapped all the way around the bottle, the stress should cause the glass to fracture. Finally, you can wrap a wire around the bottle and send electric current through it; this applies intense heat to the score mark. A hot-wire cutter can be constructed with a transformer, a nichrome wire, and a toggle switch—if you know what you're doing.

The last step in bottle cutting is polishing, since no matter how carefully you cut the bottle, the edges will be rough. Smooth them with a power sander or by hand, using coarse emery cloth or carbide silica paper. Use finer and finer paper until the edges of the glass are rounded and can't cut anymore.

If all this sounds like a lot of work, it is. Just as important, mastering the process takes time. I cut through a dozen Perrier bottles before I got one that could be turned into a glass, and even that required more sanding and polishing than I wanted to do. Still, if you have the patience, this can be a rewarding craft. And think of all the free glassware you can make!

★ Books for ★ Bottle Cutters

Bottle cutting, like potato chip nibbling, can be an addictive pastime. Fortunately, there's no end to the things that can be made from bottles. If you are short on inspiration, consult *101 Projects for Bottle Cutters* by Walter Fischman (Crowell, 1973) or *Creative Bottle Cutting* by B. Kay Fraser (Crown Publishers, 1972). Fischman's book is serious and workmanlike; Fraser's is more fanciful. Both are very thorough on basic technique.

GIFT JAR. Don't forget that a nicely shaped or decorated jar makes a welcome gift when it's full of homemade cookies, candy, or jam.

LIGHTS ON. A jar makes a good hurricane-lamp for a lit candle. Drip hot wax onto the bottom of the jar and anchor the candle before lighting it. Or cut off the base of a narrow-necked bottle. Hold the bottle by the neck and insert the candle in the neck from the inside. In this portable holder, the candle can't be extinguished by drafts.

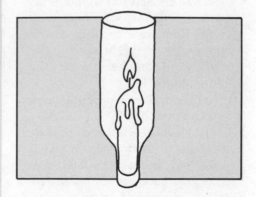

SNOW SCENE. A short, fat jar is just right for making an old-fashioned snow scene that will delight the children. Remove the cap from the jar and create a tableau by glueing little plastic figures to the inside of the cap. Put ¼ teaspoon moth flakes in the jar and fill with water. Screw on the lid and turn the jar upside down to create a blizzard of "snow." If the lid leaks, apply a band of silicone sealer around the lip of the jar.

WINDOWS ON THE WORLD. Bottles that are incorporated into walls create interesting visual patterns and admit light. Some people use only the bottoms of bottles; others build with the entire bottle, as pictured. If you use bottles of different colors, the results resemble stained glass. Think about creating bottle windows in bathrooms, entrance ways, skylights, and interior dividers.

★ A GANG OF ★ JARS

If one glass jar is useful, then several glass jars must be better. The problem is that a group of old jars often looks like just that. To turn your jars into custom-designed storage units, try one of these ideas:

• Select three or four jars of the same size and use epoxy to glue them base down to a refinished piece of hardwood scrap. Paint the lids of the jars.

• Select jars with a large lip or a sharp indentation on the side—half-gallon wine bottles and Smuckers jelly jars are good. Find a piece of shelving a little wider than the jars and use a jigsaw to cut keyhole slots into the wood. Each slot should be as wide as the jar at its narrowest point and twice as deep as the jar is wide. Hang the shelf on the wall with L-brackets and slip the jars into the slots.

• Find a 2 × 2-inch piece of wood and nail the lids from small jars to it. Mount the wood on a pivot or hang it from deep brackets mounted under a cabinet. Fill the jars with spices, nails, or anything else and screw them to their lids.

When students from Renssalaer Polytechnic Institute in Troy, New York, built this "recycled" house, they created a window wall by mortaring together entire bottles of various sizes and colors. The other exterior walls of the building were made from No. 10 cans; interior walls were "paneled" with cardboard tubes. The roof was made from layers of corrugated cardboard coated with cold tar.

RECYCLE→RECYCLE→RECYCLE

On a larger scale, glass containers can be recycled two ways. One is to design them so they can be returned and refilled. The other is to crush the glass into cullet, which can be used to make new glass or as a component in insulation or cement or a paving material called glassphalt.

The debate over returnables has intensified during the last few years. Six states have "bottle bills" that require soft drinks and beer to be sold in returnable bottles. Thirty other state legislatures regularly consider the issue, though the bills are usually defeated by the glass industry lobby, which often outspends its opponents 100 to 1.

Advocates of bottle bills insist that they reduce litter, save energy, and produce jobs for the people who collect and wash the bottles. Indeed, one California business called Eco-Encore recycles a million wine bottles each year and can't keep up with the demand from local wineries. A group in Portland, Oregon, called Bottleworks has been so successful recycling bottles that they would like to see returnable legislation extended to wine bottles, pickle jars, mayonnaise jars, and other large glass containers.

At the bottom of the controversy is the simple fact that beverages in returnable bottles do cost less—if you return the bottles. And therein lies the rub. Glass manufacturers claim that American consumers don't want to bother schlepping bottles back to the store. There's some truth to the argument, since even the conscientious citizens of Oregon misplace one out of every seven returnables. Still, when you figure that the average returnable can be refilled fifteen times if it's a beer bottle and seventeen times if it's a soda bottle, it just doesn't make much sense to buy one-timers. So don't. Even in states which don't have bottle bills, you can usually find a few distributors who sell beverages in returnables. Patronize them.

Aside from beverage bottles, there are many other glass containers that need recycling, so most communities have some kind of collection center that will accept clean glass sorted according to color. Be sure to remove the metal bands that encircle the necks of some bottles.

Cullet doesn't command a very high price, primarily because the raw materials in glass don't cost much. The going rate is about a penny per pound, or $20 per ton. Unfortunately, the cost of shipping the cullet to a glass manufacturing plant often cuts into that price, because regressive federal legislation sets higher freight rates for recycled materials. To find out about the glass recycling plant nearest your community, write to the Glass Packaging Institute, 1800 K Street NW, Washington, DC 20006.

Purchasing a six-pack of soft drinks in returnable bottles saves about one-quarter liter of gasoline and eighteen cents or more.

KEEPING WARM. Make a casserole warmer from a short fat jar with a wide cap. Drill ¼-inch holes around the top of the cap so the candle that goes inside the jar can breathe. Cut off the bottom of the jar and cut a square of window screen to fit over the opening. Put a short, fat candle on the jar lid and screw the jar just so it's secure. Light the candle, lay the screen over the top, and set the casserole on it.

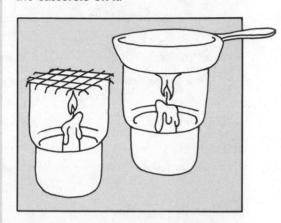

BANK ON IT. Any wide-mouthed jar makes a good bank for loose change. Use a punch can opener to cut a slit in the lid long and wide enough to accommodate a quarter. File down any rough edges and screw the lid on the jar. If everyone deposits loose change, there will be enough for a round of ice cream sundaes in a month or so.

WHAT'S-IT JAR. Make a "bank" for all the odd things that show up in a household—the unidentified key, the screw-that-came-out-of-something-I-can't-remember-what, the button off junior's shirt, and so on. The advantage to keeping all this stuff in a jar is that you'll be able to see at a glance whether a particular lost item is in the bank when you need it.

LET THERE BE LIGHT. If you ever find yourself in need of an emergency lantern, you can make one from any wide-mouthed jar. Fill the jar half full with ordinary cooking oil; do not use kerosene or gasoline! Wire two nails together into an X and tie a piece of cotton string to the nails, slightly longer than the oil is deep. Drop the nails into the oil to anchor the wick. To light, wire a match to a straightened coat hanger so you can reach into the jar with it.

★ A GARDEN OF CUT GLASS ★

If you're accustomed to thinking of bottles as bottles, it will take a little time for you to see all the planters, bowls, and glasses hidden in their shapes. This chart should help.

BOTTLE YOU HAVE	WHAT YOU CAN MAKE	HOW TO DO IT
No-deposit soda bottle	Funnel	Cut the bottle in half and use the long-necked section as a funnel.
No-deposit soda bottle (long neck)	Egg cup	Cut off base of bottle and 4 inches off the top. Invert the top and glue it to the base with epoxy.
Mixed-drink bottle	Iced tea glass	Cut the bottle 6 inches from the base and polish the cut edge very carefully.
Fruit punch bottle	Fishbowl	Cut bottle 8 inches from the base.
Airline liquor bottle	Shot glass	Pour a shot of liquor into the bottle and mark the level of the liquid. Cut the bottle ¼ inch above the mark.
Dill pickle jar	Cereal dish	Cut the jar 4 inches above the base.
Gallon jug	Dinner plate	Cut the bottle ½ inch from the base.
Tall beer bottle	Beer glass	Cut the bottle ½ inch from the base. Invert the top and attach it to the base with epoxy glue.
Champagne bottle	Ashtray	Cut the bottle 3 inches from base. Invert and use dimple as ashtray.
Mayonnaise jar (institutional size)	Cake cover	Cut the jar 10 inches above the base. Invert and use epoxy glue to attach a handle—perhaps a plastic cap or salvaged drawer pull.
Lemon juice bottles	Juice glasses	Save four bottles and cut them 4 inches from base.
Worcester sauce bottle	Napkin rings	Cut 1½-inch slices from the bottle.
Catsup bottle	Dinner bell	Cut the bottle just below the shoulder, where the straight sides start. Use a carpet needle to thread fishing line through a cork. Tie a metal washer to the line and stuff the cork into the mouth of the bottle. Adjust thread so washer hits side of bottle.
Salad oil bottles (large size with straight sides)	Canisters	Collect four bottles and cut each to a different height—4, 5, 6, and 7 inches. To make covers, cut two circles of wood, one that fits inside bottle, one slightly larger. Glue pieces of wood together and varnish.
Grape juice bottle	Blender jar	Grape juice jars with wide mouths fit some electric blenders. If yours is one of them, cut the bottom out of the grape juice jar and cap it with a plastic lid.
Coffee jar	Dessert dish	Cut ½ inch off the base of the jar and 4 inches off the top. Invert the top and glue it to the base with epoxy.
Large wine bottle	Serving bowl	Cut bottle 5 inches from base or just above the pattern in the glass.
Spaghetti sauce jar	Cheese saver	Cut jar 4 inches from base. Invert over circle of wood.
Cooking wine bottle	Goblet	Cut bottle 3 inches from base. Invert base and glue to top.
Fruit juice bottle	Lamp shade	Cut bottom off jar. Decorate with stained glass paint. Cut hole in lid large enough to accept cord from light fixture but not the fixture itself. Slip cord through and screw lid on jar.
Perrier bottle	Mixed-drink glass	Cut bottle 4 inches from base and polish edge carefully.

FISH IN A JAR. Goldfish don't know the difference between a large wide-mouthed jar and an aquarium. If the jar is big enough, plant a few pieces of seaweed in the gravel at the bottom. Although you can't leave the lid on very long, this "aquarium" can be covered briefly if you need to take your fish on a trip.

A goldfish can't tell the difference between a fishbowl and a recycled jar.

SPRINKLE BOTTLE. Five-and-ten-cent stores still sell sprinkler caps for narrow-necked bottles. Use the sprinkle bottle to water plants, moisten clothes that need to be ironed, or dampen adhesive-backed wallpaper.

★ FREEBIE ★ ABOUT BOTTLES

For still more ideas about what to do with empty glass (and plastic) bottles, send for a free copy of "How to Make Useful Articles for the Home from Glass and Plastic Bottles." Published by the Glass Bottle Blowers Association, 608 East Blatimore Pike, Media, PA 19063, the booklet contains prize-winning ideas as well as useful tips about cutting, drilling, and smoothing cut edges of bottles.

SOAP'S ON. You can make a liquid soap dispenser from a tall, narrow-necked bottle. Find a long threaded bolt whose head is larger than the mouth of the bottle and whose shaft is longer than its neck. Now find a thick rubber washer, also larger than the bottle's mouth. Fill the bottle with liquid soap. Screw the washer onto the bolt and shove the washer inside the bottle. Fasten the bottle to the wall above a sink, using metal bands or straps made from inner tube rubber. When you want a bit of soap, press the bolt up so the soap dribbles out of the bottle. When the bolt drops down, so does the washer, blocking the flow of soap.

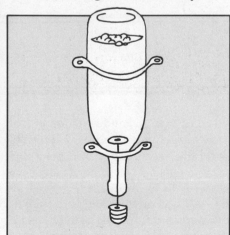

SPRING THING. Use empty jars as individual greenhouses over seedlings in the spring. During the day, prop the rim of the bottle up so air can circulate around the plant.

FLY CATCHER. If you're bothered by a houseful of pesky flies, try making this simple but humane fly catcher from a wide-mouthed jar. Put fly bait (perhaps a piece of raw meat) on a saucer. Set two pencils on the plate on either side of the meat and balance the jar on the pencils. Flies will congregate under the jar, and when you tap on the glass they will instinctively fly upward to escape. Then it's a simple matter for you to slip a piece of paper under the mouth of the jar while it's inverted so you can transport the flies outside for release. This method is especially handy if you have a pet frog that needs a daily supply of fresh flies.

BOTTLE BOOKENDS. Two matched bottles or jars can make quick and inexpensive bookends. Fill the bottles with colored water (use a few drops of food coloring) or layers of colored sand and cap tightly. To keep the bottles from slipping, glue circles of felt or rubber cut from old rubber gloves to their bottoms.

★ GLASS WITH ★ CLASS

Camouflage your found jars and bottles with decorations. Containers that don't need to be washed can be outfitted in raffia, ribbon, lace, yarn, or rickrack. Apply a little silicone glue to the trim and wind it around the jar. Cover the jar completely or make stripes of varying thickness.

To conceal the contents of a jar, cover it with fabric or adhesive-backed paper. Use ready-made decals or cut out your own. Bottles also take well to decoupage. Paste your design on the glass and cover with several coats of acrylic sealer.

Glass can also be painted with special paints, available in craft shops. One type, sold under names like Cryst-L-Glaze and Glas Stain, actually colors the glass, leaving it transparent. Other types of paint coat the glass so you can't see through it.

★ A Bottle for ★ Every Room in the House

When you store the right things in them, old bottles can be decorative as well as functional. Use wide-mouthed jars from spaghetti sauce, pickles, mayonnaise, and peanut butter so it's easy to retrieve the stored objects.

- Kitchen: pasta, beans, oatmeal, dried cereals, crackers, nuts, pretzels
- Bathroom: Q-Tips, cotton balls, bath oil beads, soap balls, rolled washcloths
- Sewing room: thread, pins, snaps, buttons, rickrack
- Study: paper clips, pencils, pushpins, rubber bands, hard candy
- Bedroom: pennies, bobby pins, matches, safety pins, collar stays
- Workshop: nails, screws, string, washers, drill bits, pegboard hooks

CAN DO. Quart mayonnaise jars are just the right size for the metal canning rings, but they are made of thinner glass, so they won't withstand the stress of pressure canning. The jars can be used safely in a boiling water bath.

FOOD CHOPPER. To make a quick but effective food chopper from a mayonnaise jar, find a short dowel rod. Attach a knob to one end and cut a slit in the other. Poke a hole the size of the rod through the lid of the jar and insert the rod. Cut two 2 × 3-inch pieces of flat metal from the lids of a large can. Bend the metal strips at a 90-degree angle and insert the bend in the slot in the dowel, using wire if necessary to hold the blades in place. Put another lid in the bottom of the jar to serve as a platform for the food.

PLANT IN A BOTTLE. As everyone knows, found jars can make charming terrariums. Select a wide- or narrow-mouthed jar, depending upon your skills with long-handled terrarium planting tools. Fill the jar one quarter full with sterile soil and plant little plants. For more ideas read:

Fun with Terrarium Gardening by George and Virginia Elbert (Crown Publishers, 1973).

Terrarium Book by Charles Evans (Random House, 1973).

Complete Book of Terrarium Gardening (Scribner's, 1974).

JEANS

See BLUE JEANS

JUNK MAIL

Is your mailbox overflowing with alluring offers for products you don't want from companies you've never heard of? Stem the flood by requesting a Consumer Application from the Mail Preference Service, 6 East 43rd Street, New York, NY 10017. Once you register with MPS, its members, mostly merchants, will stop sending you mail.

See also ENVELOPES and PAPER.

KEYS

Everyone is nervous about throwing out keys, so they accumulate. Before long you have a dozen unidentified keys. If you file down a tooth or two so they won't fit their own locks, you can feel free to adapt these useful little pieces of metal for other purposes.

TOOL CHAIN. With the use of a power grinder you can turn a bunch of old keys into a handy assortment of small tools to keep on your key chain. Grind the end of a key to a point and use it to punch holes in everything from leather belts to beer cans (A). Even off the ridges on another key and use it as an emergency fish scaler or to scrape ice off a car windshield or mud off your shoes (B). Grind another key off at the end and bevel it into a screwdriver (C). Flatten out the notches in a key and grind a crook into the end to make a bottle opener (D). You'll have many uses for this miniature tool kit.

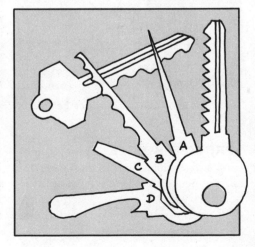

LATCHKEY. Do you need a latch to close a door, hold a storm window in place, or fasten the door on the rabbit hutch? Position an old key so it holds the moving part in place, drill a hole in the wood beneath the keyhole, and screw in a screw, tight enough to hold the key horizontal and loose enough so it can swivel down when necessary.

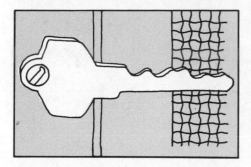

KEY RING. Use old keys as clappers in homemade bells. Start with old bottles of various shapes—the individual wine bottles given out on airplanes are perfect. Remove their bottoms (see JARS AND BOTTLES), then drill a small hole through the cap of the bottle and thread a piece of fishing line through it. Knot the fishing line at one end and tie the key to the other end so it is suspended inside the bottle. Use the bell as a dinner bell, a Christmas ornament, or part of a set of wind chimes.

WEIGHTY MATTERS. Keys are handy weights with predrilled holes. Keep a few in your fishing box for weighting lines. Slip several into the hems of drapes to keep them hanging straight. And so on.

See also HARDWARE.

work surface. Position the knife so people can't bump into it unwittingly, or, better yet, protect the blade when it's not in use with a sheath made by slitting a length of old rubber hose.

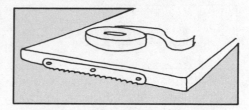

CHOP-CHOP. To make a handy chopper for mincing onions and other vegetables, remove the handle from an old serrated or paring knife and drill two holes in the blade's spine. Cut a slit in a block of wood as long as the knife blade and drill holes that correspond to those in the blade. Slip the blade into the wood, run bolts through the holes, and tighten them down.

See also METAL SCRAP; SILVERWARE.

KNIVES

Buy good sharp knives and take care of them. Then you won't have to worry about what to do with them when they wear out, because they won't. That doesn't mean you won't be plagued by the occasional table knife of unknown origin, the paring knife with a broken handle, or the serrated knife that can't be sharpened. Each of these can be treated as a narrow band of metal that can be used to pry things apart and do some kinds of cutting and carving. Thinking of the knife in that way should suggest transformations like these:

A KNIFE BY MANY OTHER NAMES. An odd table knife is a treasure in the workshop, especially if its edge is serrated. Use it as a spare screwdriver, a saw for Styrofoam and cardboard, and a file for little jobs.

KNIFE APPEAL. Make a quick, clean slicer for potatoes and apples from an old knife blade. Start with a blade about 6 inches long and drill a ¼-inch hole at each end. Insert a screw with a ⅜-inch head through one hole and screw it into a 2-inch wooden peg to serve as a handle. Insert a 2-inch screw that is clean and rustproof through the other

hole and secure it with a drop of solder. Twist the screw into a potato or other vegetable and start turning the slicer with the wooden knob. As you turn, the screw will go deeper into the potatoe and the knife will slice it into one continuous strip.

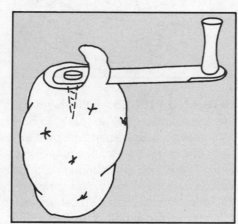

THE CUTTING EDGE. A serrated knife blade too dull to function in the kitchen will still cut string, tape, paper, and other odd things. Remove the blade from its handle and drill three holes in the spine. Using all three holes, screw the knife to the narrow edge of a counter, shelf, or tabletop so that the blade protrudes slightly beyond the

★ **HOW TO MAKE** ★ **GAY BLADES OF YOUR KNIVES**

Knives don't ask for much. They want to be kept clean and in racks where they don't need to jostle with other utensils. If they are fancy kitchen knives, they want to be drawn across a sharpening steel before every use. If they are more plebian knives, they still want to be sharpened now and then on a grindstone. Use a small whetting stone, lubricated with a drop of oil. Hold the blade of the knife so it makes a twenty-degree angle with the stone and move it back and forth across the stone, sharpening first one side and then the other.

LADDERS

If you find yourself with a broken wooden ladder, cut off the section with the broken rungs and even out the legs. Refinish the wood, screw pot hooks along the sides, and hang the ladder from your kitchen ceiling with chains or rope and toggle bolts. Use the ladder for hanging utensils, pots, and pans.

See also WOOD SCRAPS.

LAWN MOWERS

Lawn mowers have limited usefulness when they can't cut grass anymore. For that reason, if no other, take care of your mower. Be especially meticulous about cleaning it in the fall and tuning it up in the spring. When your mower finally fails you, chances are good you can still use the blades for shredding things or the frame for moving things. Here are details:

SHREDDERS. Both power and push mowers can be converted into useful shredders for leaves, weeds, and other materials destined for the compost heap. To convert a manual mower, remove and mount the blade mechanism on a fixed frame so it can turn freely. Extend the central shaft, and hook the shaft to a ¼-horsepower motor with a V-belt. For more explicit instructions, consult *Cloudburst, A Handbook of Rural Skills and Technology* (Cloudburst Press, 1717 North 45th Street, Seattle, WA 98103; 1973). To convert a power mower, locate a piece of lightweight pipe, 3 inches in diameter and 3 feet long. Use L-hooks to fasten the tube to the opening at the front of the power mower platform, keeping the bottom of the pipe even with the platform. Turn the mower on and have one person hold it while another feeds organic material through the pipe, being careful, of course, not to stick their hands into the pipe or under the machine while it's in operation.

BITS AND PIECES. If you begrudge the space taken up by an unemployable lawn mower, take it apart and keep any parts that might be useful in future projects. Promising possibilities include wheels, the motor on a power mower, the wooden roller from a push mower, tubing from the handle, nuts, bolts, and gears.

CADDIES AND DOLLIES. Turn a push mower into a hand truck for heavy objects simply by turning the mower over so the blades don't touch the ground and using the wooden roller to support the load. As long as you push it forward, the blades won't spin. Turn your power mower into a lawn caddy by removing the engine. Then bolt an old trash can to the platform and use it to carry tools, leaves, and other things.

LEATHER

Leather shoes, belts, wallets, briefcases, purses, and luggage can all be taken apart so the leather can be reused in new projects. Even if the original object is badly torn, scuffed, or discolored, good pieces of leather can probably be salvaged.

Cut the leather apart at the seams with a utility knife and flatten all the pieces. Clean them by rubbing saddle soap into the leather with a damp rag. Rinse with a damp sponge and allow the leather to dry. Then rub in a conditioner like neat's-foot oil to replenish the natural oils in the leather.

Odd bits of leather can be turned into all sorts of useful projects. For ideas and instructions on working with scraps of leather, see one of these books:

The New Book of Leatherwork: Projects for Today by Joseph Delano (Arco, 1976).
Leathercraft by Sid Latham (Follett, 1978).
Leather by Nicky Hayden (Scribner's, 1979).

Complete Book of Leathercrafting by Jane E. Garnes (Tab, 1979).

See also BELTS; BOOTS; HANDBAGS; SHOES.

★ LITTLE THINGS ★ TO MAKE FROM LEATHER

- Buttons
- Buckles
- Handles
- Innersoles
- Book covers
- Picture frames
- Change purses
- Eyeglass cases
- Dog collars
- Linings for pockets
- Key tags
- Clothing patches for elbows and knees
- Sheaths for tools
- Luggage tags

LEAVES

If you rake the leaves off your lawn in the fall, don't just pack them away into garbage bags. The sight of all that rich soil nourishment trapped uselessly in plastic should distress anyone with the slightest idea about how our planet works. Instead, try these ideas:

LEAF PACK. Leaves make fine insulation for plants during the winter, so rake piles of them over the strawberry patch and up around the shrubs. Loosen the leaves in the spring so they don't mat down and stifle new growth.

A MATTER OF MULCH. Chopped leaves can be used as mulch, that heavy layer of organic matter gardeners spread around their plants to inhibit weeds.

QUICK COMPOST. Leaves can, of course, be added to your compost heap; they will decompose more quickly if they are chopped first. If you'd like all that leafy nutrition to stay on your lawn, run your power mower back and forth through the leaves until they are chopped up into little pieces. Over the winter, the pieces will decompose and fertilize the grass.

Leaf composting can also be done by communities. In Maplewood, New Jersey, for example, the city has been composting leaves ever since a 1965 ordinance banned burning. Bagging leaves is also prohibited. Instead, citizens rake their leaves into the gutter, where vacuum trucks collect them. The leaves are dumped in a central location, sprayed with water, and allowed to sit undisturbed for fourteen months. At the end of that time, the compost is sold to city residents at minimal cost.

BASKET CASE. Leaves and other plant materials can be woven into charming baskets if you know the techniques for preparing and joining them. For detailed directions, consult *Basketry Today with Materials from Nature* by Dona Z. Meilach (Crown Publishers, 1980).

LEFTOVERS

See FOOD, LEFTOVER

L'EGGS EGGS

Most manufacturers don't seem to care what happens to the packages for their products. One big exception is L'Eggs Products, Inc., the company that thought of packaging pantyhose in plastic eggs. The *L'Eggs Idea Book* is a 96-page paean to Eggs and their many uses as sachets, candle molds, stamp holders, string dispensers, Christmas ornaments, planters, banks, and much more. Although you might want to argue about whether it makes sense to buy a product whose unusual package contributes to its cost, still it is refreshing to find a manufacturer who cares about the ultimate fate of what it produces. For a copy of this book, send $1.25 to L'Eggs Products, Inc., P.O. Box 2495, Winston-Salem, NC 27102.

See also PLASTIC CONTAINERS.

These marbleized desk accessories are among the projects suggested in the L'Eggs Idea Book.

LIDS

See BOTTLE CAPS; JAR LIDS; PLASTIC LIDS; PULL TABS

LIGHT BULBS

Light bulb companies have been working to extend the life span of light bulbs with new expensive models that are supposed to burn for ten years. The life of an ordinary bulb can be tripled by using a little gadget called Bulb Miser, available in many hardware stores for about $3. Of course, such devices simply delay the inevitable. Burned-out light bulbs should be used with care because they are made of thin glass that breaks rather easily.

Light bulbs can be cut with a hot-wire cutter that heats a thin band around the bulb, causing just enough stress to crack the fragile glass. If you only want to cut a few light bulbs, your television repairer may be willing to do the job with a TV tube cutter. The cut edges of a light bulb should always be covered with a narrow band of plastic tape to prevent cuts. If you master the art of cutting light bulbs, you'll be able to make all kinds of interesting flasks and containers. If you don't, you'll have to exploit the bulb's sensuous shape. Here are a few ideas:

DARN IT. A whole light bulb makes a dandy darning egg (*see* SOCKS). Keep a burned-out one in the sewing basket and insert it into the toes and heels of derelict socks. Use a 25-watt bulb in children's socks.

CHRISTMAS BULBS. Almost any small object can become a Christmas ornament if you cover it with enough glitter. Light bulbs, however, have a frankly ornamental shape. Collect a set of bulbs and dip them into metallic paint. Glue on glitter, rickrack, or cutouts from Christmas cards. Make a hook for each bulb by winding a piece of fine wire around the metal grooves. Hook the ends of a second piece of wire around the first piece on either side and tighten the first piece by twisting its ends together. Cover the top of the bulb with a small piece of aluminum foil, slit in the center so the wire loop can protrude.

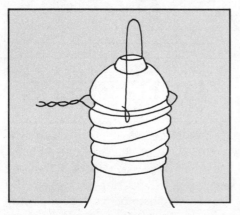

PLANTING BULBS. To make a striking terrarium for a single miniature plant, cut a light bulb just beneath the metal with a hot-wire cutter. Remove the filament and other innards and clean the bulb with soapy water and a toothbrush. Find a 35-mm film canister or a plastic pill bottle to fit the base of the

Never in Your Wildest Dreams

Before you throw out your next burned-out light bulb, think of Hugh Hicks, a Baltimore dentist who collects light bulbs. Admittedly, Hicks has gone beyond the ordinary 75-watt variety that you just pulled out of your lamp. His collection of 60,000 bulbs includes the largest light bulb ever built—a 50,000-watter constructed for the Paramount Theater when it ran The Edison Story—and the smallest—a NASA bulb that can't be seen without a 50-power microscope.

light bulb. Weight the container with a little sand, fill with soil, and pot the plant in it. If tiny hothouses don't appeal, turn the cut light bulb upside down and use it as a rooter, supported in a sling made from six-pack plastic circles. Use two circles for strength and thread fishing line through the circles at three equidistant points. Hang the rooter in a sunny window.

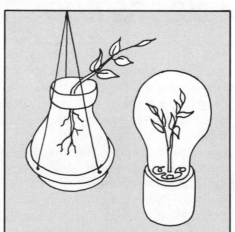

SHAKE THOSE BULBS. To make a pair of maracas for your household band, start with two burned-out light bulbs and a pile of newspapers torn into

1-inch strips. Dip the strips of paper into wallpaper paste and wrap them around the light bulbs until you have a ¼-inch layer of paper covering the entire bulb. When the paper is thoroughly dry, tap the maracas on a countertop until the glass inside breaks and rattles. Paint with poster paints.

LINENS

See BLANKETS AND OLD QUILTS;
SHEETS; TOWELS

LINGERIE

Women's slips and sleepwear are often a source of sheer fabrics and lovely lace. Salvage straps and fasteners to be used on other garments. Then use the fabric for projects like these:

SWEET SNIFFING. Make little pillows from lingerie fabrics and stuff them with rose petals or other sweet-smelling mixes (*see* JARS AND BOTTLES). Trim the sachets with lace from the original garment.

LAUNDRY BAG. If you hate to wash fine washables by hand, make yourself a laundry bag from an old slip. Cut the slip off at the waist and sew shut. You can sew snaps on the bag to keep it shut or tie it closed with a piece of string. Fill the bag with stockings or other lingerie and toss it into the washing machine with the rest of your laundry. Its contents will come out effortlessly clean.

SLIPUP. Full slips can often be cut apart into two garments—a half slip (simply thread elastic through the top of the bottom half of the slip) and a camisole (hem the bottom of the top half).

See also CLOTHES; FABRIC SCRAPS.

MAGAZINES

The first rule about magazines is: Read 'em or cancel your subscription. There is nothing more depressing than two months of unread newsmagazines on the coffee table. The second rule is: Reuse 'em, either by having someone else read them or by using the paper in special projects.

READY REFERENCE. Many magazines include how-to articles that would undoubtedly be valuable in the future—if you could find them. You can, of course, cut out the articles and file them. Or store the entire set of magazines in an empty detergent box—the 32-ounce size is fine for 8½ × 11 magazines. Cut off two corners of the box on a diagonal and stand it on end on a bookshelf. As you read an issue, make notes about the articles you might want again and glue them on the spine of the box.

SIT UPON. Have you ever sat on the cold hard ground, singing camp songs or watching touch football? A magazine could have cushioned and warmed your posterior. Find several thick magazines and make a pouch for them out of heavy plastic, perhaps an old shower curtain or rain slicker. Whipstitch the edges of the pouch together with heavy thread. Take your Sit Upon to the next picnic or outdoor concert and sit upon it.

PASS-ALONG READERS. Many institutions are eager to have used copies of magazines. Contact local nursing homes, hospitals, prisons, and schools. The local library may want your cast-off copies, particularly if you can offer a complete year. If all else fails, bundle up a dozen old magazines and drop them off in the next waiting room you encounter—perhaps at the dentist or the auto repair shop. When you donate magazines to a charitable organization, you may be entitled to a tax deduction, so ask for a receipt estimating their value.

BEADS AND BAUBLES. Bulky beads made out of wood or ceramics are expensive, but those made out of magazines are free. Tear out the brightest, most colorful pages you can find. Draw long thin triangles on the pages and cut them out. The base of the triangle determines the width of the bead; the height determines its bulk. Now find thin throwaways—toothpicks, the empty refills from ballpoint pens, bobby pins without their tips, etc. Spread white glue on the triangle, leaving the bottom inch uncoated. Starting from the bottom, wrap the triangle around the toothpick. When you get to

the top, add an extra dab of glue to be sure the tip is fastened down securely. Let the bead dry, cover with clear varnish, and remove the toothpick. To make cylindrical beads, roll up rectangles instead of triangles and slice them

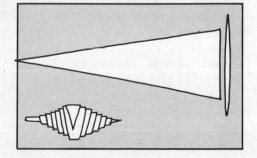

into appropriate lengths with a razor blade. Kids love to make these beads, and when they are rolled carefully they look good enough for grown-up uses like macramé, jewelry, or room dividers.

FOLDOUTS. Remember those accordion paper bells and jack-o'-lanterns that people used to hang up at kids' parties? You can make the same decorations for nothing out of old magazines. Start with a fat magazine—*Reader's Digest* is good—or try glueing two magazines together. Remove the heavy covers and start folding the pages. Although the possibilities for shapes are almost unlimited, for your first try make something simple like a cone, which can be used as a Christmas tree. Fold each page in three steps as shown in the illustration, creasing each fold with your thumbnail. When all the pages of the magazine are folded, form them into a circle around the magazine's spine. Spray-paint and add ornaments. If this kind of craftwork appeals to you, detailed instructions for other projects are in "Folded Magazine Novelties," a pamphlet available for $2 from Craft Course Publishers, 250 South Paseo Tesoro, P.O. Box 704, Walnut, CA 91789.

See also PAPER.

SPROUT OFF. Many containers can be used as sprouters, but margarine tubs are uniquely suited because they are covered, opaque, and the right size for a family-sized serving of sprouts. Use seeds labeled "for sprouting." Place seeds in the bottom of the margarine tub, cover with warm water, and let them soak overnight. Next morning drain the seeds, cover the container, and let the seeds sit. Rinse and drain the sprouts twice a day until they are long enough to eat. For more information on sprouting, look for *The Sprouter's Cookbook* by Marjorie Blanchard (Garden Way, 1975).

HAVE BOWL, WILL TRAVEL. Margarine tubs are perfect for carrying condiments, relishes, and dips to picnics. When you're traveling in the car, package surprise snacks for the kids in the little tubs, so each can have his or her own.

See PLASTIC CONTAINERS.

MARGARINE TUBS

If you only have enough space to save one type of plastic container, collect margarine tubs. The size is convenient and the snap-on lid means that these freebies can be used in place of Tupperware and other expensive storage containers. Stack the tubs in the corner of the cupboard and grab one when you need a bathtub toy for junior, a no-spill container for nails, or a place to put that half cup of leftover spaghetti. Here are other ideas:

HOOP HOOP HOORAY. If you want to do a spot of embroidery, perhaps to repair a rip (*see* CLOTHES), make a quick embroidery hoop out of a margarine tub. Use a pair of scissors to cut the center from the tub's lid, leaving ½ inch around the rim. Now cut off the bottom of the tub, leaving an inch around its rim. Hold the fabric taut between these two pieces and snap them together.

MATCHBOOKS

Throwing out an empty matchbook may seem inconsequential. Still, you'll be surprised at how much satisfaction there is in reusing one of the little devils.

MINI BOOK. Always jotting little notes to yourself? Then you need a covered mini pad made from a matchbook. Take out the staple that goes through the bottom of the book and remove the match stubs. Now cut bits of scrap paper into pieces 1½ × 1¾ inches. When you have a stack of paper about ¼ inch tall, insert it into the short flap of the matchbook and staple.

MATCH POUCH. Turn a matchbook into a handy pouch that will hold a razor blade for your shaving kit, a couple of paper clips in your briefcase, or a needle and pins for your purse. Remove the staple at the bottom of the matchbook and take out the bit of cardboard the matches were attached to. Flatten the top of the book and close the sides with tape. Pull up the top flap to fill the pouch, and fold it down to protect the contents.

••••••••••••••••••••••••••••••••••••

MATTRESSES

Throwing out a mushy mattress is such a difficult chore that it may be easier to find a new use for the thing. If you start thinking of the mattress as a giant cushion, ideas like these will probably occur to you:

TRAMPOLINE. Children love nothing more than bouncing up and down on a mattress, so why not indulge them? Put the old mattress in the basement and let them jump and tumble.

TRUNDLE BED. If the old mattress is still sleepable, cover it with dry cleaner

bags and store it under the bed. When you have more company than beds, pull it out, make it up, and let a couple of guests sleep on it instead of on the floor.

COMFORTABLE CAR. If you travel in a station wagon, install an old mattress in the back. It won't take up much luggage space and will make a big difference for passengers who want to sleep or play in the back of the car.

MINI MATTRESSES. An old mattress stuffed with fiber or a newer mattress filled with foam rubber can be cut up and re-covered to make floor cushions, a mattress for the dog's bed, or a bolster for your own bed. Starting from one corner of the mattress, mark the dimensions of the cushion you want to make. Use heavy scissors to cut through the ticking, not the filling, on one side of the mattress. Use your hands to separate fiber filling or a knife to cut through foam rubber. Remember to take a little extra out for a cushion so the edges of the ticking will meet. Now cut through the second layer of ticking and join both layers with a whipstitch. Cover your new cushion with heavy-duty fabric like corduroy or denim salvaged from old clothes.

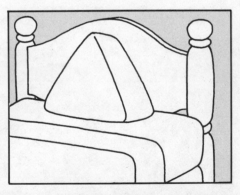

••••••••••••••••••••••••••••••••••••

MEAT TRAYS

Supermarkets sell meat perched on little trays made of paperboard, polystyrene, or clear plastic. Think of the trays whenever you need a "disposable" plate or a thin, waterproof shield. Here are a few suggestions:

PICNIC TIP. Save meat trays of the same size and use them instead of paper plates at picnics. If you are carrying flat food to the picnic—carrot sticks, cold cuts, etc.—pack them in a meat tray and invert a second tray over the first as a cover. Hold the trays together with rubber bands.

BAKE OFF. If you like to give baked goods as gifts, put them on clean meat trays so the recipient doesn't have to bother returning your plate.

DRIP CATCHER. Plastic meat trays can be used to minimize mess all over the house. Put them under flowerpots to catch the overflow when you water. Leave one on the kitchen counter as a spoon rest and another near the sink for sponges and scouring pads. Set them under paint cans, glue pots, and other mess makers.

LETTER PERFECT. Styrofoam meat trays are easily cut with a razor blade, and the flat bottom makes a perfect background for stencil patterns. Cut out stencils for your children to color, for your Christmas cards, or for decorating wood and fabric creations. Pin the meat tray stencil to the material to be decorated and trace around the lines or fill in the spaces with paint.

FOOT TRAY. Believe it or not, the flat pieces of Styrofoam from meat trays can be used as cushions in uncomfortable shoes or insulators in winter boots. Trace the shape of each foot on the tray, cut out the shapes, and insert them into your shoes or boots.

ARTIST'S TRAY. A Styrofoam meat tray makes a quick palette for the budding artist. Just cut a thumbhole and mix the colors right on the tray.

NO SLIPUPS. Fasten small squares of the flat Styrofoam from meat trays to the underside of rugs to keep them from slipping or to the bottoms of bookends, figurines, and lamps to keep them from scratching tables.

See also FAST FOOD CONTAINERS; STYROFOAM.

MESH PRODUCE BAGS

Whenever you find onions or grapefruits packaged in woven mesh bags, save those bags! The coarse mesh can be cut up for all kinds of jobs. For example, a square fastened over a gutter spout will keep out leaves; a piece tacked to a wooden frame can be used to sift ashes and compost. Whole bags have uses, too. Consider these ideas:

NET WORTHY. Mesh bags are the perfect material for homemade fish and butterfly nets. Make a circle as large as the mouth of the bag out of coat hanger wire and stitch the open edge of the bag to it. Use the extra wire as a handle, or make a longer handle from a broomstick.

DRY STORAGE. Large mesh bags are excellent storage for home-grown goodies like onions, apples, and gladiolus bulbs. The smaller bags can be used to dry herbs. Just fill the bag loosely with leaves and hang it in a warm and airy place.

SCRUB-A-DUB. Mesh bags make tough scrubbers for pots, pans, and the charcoal grill. Cut the bag into 6-inch squares and lay one on top of another. Weave a string through the center holes in all the squares and pull it tightly so the squares gather at the center. Wrap the string around the center several times and tie securely. If you're in a hurry, just wad up a bag and scrub away.

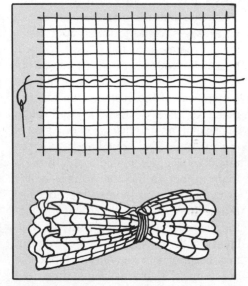

BAGS FOR ALL REASONS. Mesh bags can be converted into fold-up shopping totes, like those used by European shoppers. Soak off any labels and cut large bags down to a convenient size. Fold the upper edge of the bag under and weave a drawstring through the double layer. If you wish, use ribbon or macramé cord to weave decorative rings around other sections of the bag. Fold up the bag and take it shopping so you can put small purchases directly into it without collecting a lot of little paper bags.

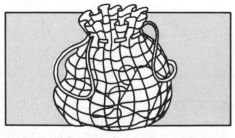

SUET IN A BAG. For many birds, suet in a mesh bag is a favorite fast food. Make a suet ball (*see* FATS AND GREASE), pack it into a mesh bag, and hang it from a sturdy branch.

METAL SCRAP

Many of the things people are most reluctant to throw away are made of metal. If you've always suspected that the dump was not the best resting place for old typewriters, plumbing fixtures, and lawn chairs, you're right. Metals of all kinds can be rerefined, so in a world with declining supplies of natural resources, the junk heap becomes an important "mine above ground."

An entire industry exists just to reprocess the secondhand metal in old cars, appliances, and other objects. At the personal level, your scrap dealer (look in the Yellow Pages under "Metal Scrap") may be a modest source of cash. The aluminum frame from that worn-out lawn chair is worth about 23 cents a pound, and the copper fixtures in an old refrigerator may be worth as

If every landfill had high graders to inspect trash as it arrived, metal scrap like this would not be wasted.

★ TESTING YOUR METAL ★

TYPE OF METAL	IDENTIFYING CHARACTERISTICS	COMMON SOURCES	APPROXIMATE MARKET VALUE
Copper and brass	Reddish or golden color. May be green from tarnish.	Pipes, wires, pots, refrigerator tubing, car radiators	25–75 cents per lb.
Aluminum	Lightweight metal with silver color. Can often be bent with bare hands.	Beverage containers, cookware, appliance housings, storm windows, screens, ladders, lawn furniture	20 cents per lb.
Lead	Very heavy. Can often be scratched with a fingernail.	Automobile batteries, ammunition, printing type, fishing sinkers	12 cents per lb.
Steel	Dark gray, often rusty. Attracts a magnet.	Automobile bodies, housings for most large appliances, swing sets, pipes, bumpers	1–2 cents per 100 lbs.
Die-cast (zinc and aluminum)	Brittle metal, often chrome-plated.	Handles, knobs, trophies	5 cents per lb.
Stainless steel	Shiny metal. Will not attract a magnet.	Sinks, beer kegs	5 cents per lb.
Cast iron	Very hard metal. Often black or gray. Will attract a magnet. May rust.	Wood stoves, automobile engine blocks, pumps	2 cents per 100 lbs.

much as 40 cents a pound. Some people with access to a pickup truck collect stray metal objects from garages, neighbors, and farms and turn them in once a month or so to earn a little extra.

Although your contribution to our metal scrap reserves may seem insignificant, the role of the scrap dealer is likely to take on new importance in the future. America's per capita consumption of metals is more than four times the world average. In order to satisfy that voracious appetite, we import large quantities of aluminum, nickel, and other metals. Those imports could be reduced if we recycled more of the metal we already have. Just as important, the use of reprocessed metal usually results in a tremendous savings in energy. For example, it takes four times the energy to make steel from iron ore as to make steel from scrap. Unfortunately, regressive legislation concerning freight rates and depletion allowances handicaps the scrap industry. The Institute of Scrap Iron and Steel is lobbying to change these laws. A list of publications and films explaining the role of the scrap dealer is available from Institute of Scrap Iron and Steel, Inc., 1729 H Street NW, Washington, DC 20006.

Never in Your Wildest Dreams

At first glance, you might mistake it for a typical Southern home with a gracious front porch and landscaped grounds. Closer inspection reveals why Pope's Mansion is a landmark in Pelham, Georgia. The house is embellished, inside and out, with intricate sculptures built from concrete and scrap metal. Laura Pope, owner of the house, worked on it from 1917 until she died, in 1952. Her materials included wheels, machine parts, sewing machines, tin cans, iron beds, car parts, and hundreds of other metal objects. Why did she do it? "It's up to us," she said, "to do something in life that is worthwhile."

MILK CONTAINERS

As with other beverages, milk should—and could—come in returnable containers. In most parts of the country, it doesn't, so consumers, especially those with children, face an avalanche of waxed cartons and plastic jugs and have to reuse as best they can. When you empty a milk container, rinse it with a baking soda and water solution to keep it from smelling sour. Store plastic jugs by threading string through the handles and hanging them from a hook in the pantry, garage, or basement.

Turn to your cache of cartons whenever you need a container of any kind. Instead of buying an oil drainage "kit" in the store, drain your motor oil into an old milk carton. Instead of buying blocks of ice, make your own by filling empty milk cartons with water and freezing them at home. Once you start thinking this way, you'll be using milk cartons to solve problems that would have cost money in the past. Here are more ideas:

WAX CARTONS

UNBREAKABLE BLOCKS. Milk cartons make large, lightweight blocks for kids. Just cut off the top of the carton and cut 5-inch slits at each corner to make 4 flaps. Fold in the flaps and tape them in place. Decorate the blocks yourself or get a set of Fun Covers, bright paper wrappers that transform simple milk cartons into lively toys. Fun Covers are available in six patterns—words, numbers, bricks, trucks, big city, and downtown. Each set costs $4 from Playper Corp, P.O. Box 312, Teaneck, NJ 07666.

FLAT CARTON. To make small and inexpensive flats for seedlings, tape shut the opening of a milk carton, turn it on its side, and cut it in half lengthwise. Fill both halves with dirt and plant.

Fun Covers transform milk cartons into attractive building blocks and trucks.

PLASTIC JUGS

HALF A JUG. The small spout on milk jugs makes it tough to use them for anything but liquids—unless you enlarge the opening. Slice off your milk jugs at an angle so the container has a handle and can be used for toting anything.

SHOUT IT OUT. Cut out the bottom of a milk jug to make a megaphone. Use it to call the kids to supper.

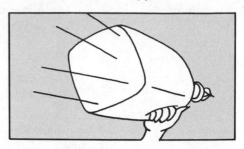

GLOP POT. Cut another plastic jug off straight across the middle. Punch six holes in the bottom with a nutpick. Set the container in the sink and use it for draining peelings and leavings before they go into the compost.

GET THE SCOOP. To make a handy scoop for dog food, potting soil, and other loose items, lay a milk jug on its side and slice it on a diagonal that runs from a point just below the handle to the base edge on the opposite side of the jug.

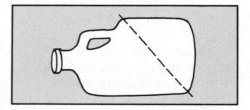

SHAPE UP. If you're trying to get into shape but don't have a set of weights, improvise by filling two milk jugs with water. Hang the jugs by their handles from either end of a broomstick and hoist away.

FILL 'ER UP. Plastic jugs can, of course, hold beverages other than milk. Fill them with iced tea, lemonade, and fruit punch for the kids. In the fall, find a neglected apple tree, collect the windfalls, and cart them to the local cider press, where they'll fill your extra plastic jugs with cheap, sweet cider. If the cider starts to turn before you can drink it, freeze it right in the plastic jugs, leaving 4 inches of air space for expansion. You might also use plastic jugs for collecting maple sap in the spring, keeping a supply of cold drinking water in the refrigerator, and holding company-size batches of juice or lemonade.

PLASTIC JUGS AND WAX CARTONS

PAINT POT. When two people are trying to paint from the same bucket, cut off a milk carton and pour some of the paint into it. Cutoff cartons are also convenient working containers for turpentine and other cleaning fluids.

TWICE THE ICE. Blocks of ice made in milk containers can be used to cool freezer chests on picnics or trips. Or make crushed ice by wrapping the frozen milk container in an old pillowcase, taking it to a cement floor, and walloping it with a hammer.

HOT CAPS. Cut the bottoms out of milk cartons to make convenient and inexpensive hot caps for plants on chilly spring nights. The plastic jugs can be left in place all day if you remove the cap to allow air circulation.

BATTER UP. When you mix batter for waffles or pancakes, pour it into a milk carton. Then just pour the amount you want onto the griddle, and if there is any left over, store it right in the carton.

QUICK CLEANUP. If you need an extra dustpan for the shop or the garage, slice off the bottom and front of a milk carton. Cut the sides at an angle so you can sweep debris into the carton easily.

See also PLASTIC CONTAINERS.

RECYCLE → RECYCLE → RECYCLE

Plastic milk jugs can be recycled. The Golden Arrow Dairy in San Diego, California, proved that. As part of an experimental program, the dairy collected polyethylene milk jugs from customers on its delivery routes. The jugs were ground up and the scrap was used in the production of lawn sprinklers and drainage tiles for farmers. Although this particular program was eventually discontinued, the Society of the Plastics Industry called it "potentially commercially viable." That means there's money to be made by anyone who can figure out how to gather up this nation's milk jugs and use them as the raw material in some other product.

MIRRORS, BROKEN

A broken mirror is supposed to mean seven years' bad luck. Surely the curse is mitigated if you recycle the fragments. In general, the best thing to do with a broken mirror is to salvage the larger pieces and cut them to fit into new situations. Mirror can be cut with an ordinary glass cutter, available in most hardware stores for under $2. Simply mark the cut line on the mirror with grease pencil, oil the cutting wheel, and pull it firmly along a straight edge. The cutter makes a score mark and the mirror should crack smoothly along the line when you tap it. I say "should" because this technique takes practice. Once you've mastered it, you can make any or all of the following:

- A small rectangular mirror for the sun visor in the car. Hold it in place with two heavy rubber bands.
- A smaller rectangular mirror to fit inside the top of an aspirin tin. Presto! The world's smallest compact!
- A mirror for the top of a jewelry box.
- Mirror tiles to be pasted almost anywhere—on a table, on a wall. Cut mirror squares of the same size and glue them down with tile cement.
- A mirror mat for a photograph. Cut the mirror to fit into a picture frame and center the photograph right on top of the mirror.
- Large squares of mirror for looking up chimneys and down laundry chutes to check for impediments.

If you find yourself with a lot of odd bits left over after all this cutting, use a splash of mirror in the mosaics you make out of your broken dishes (*see* DISHES).

★ LOOK FOR ★ THE SILVER LINING

If you are about to pitch a mirror because it has flecks and dull spots, try this trick: Turn the mirror over and tape flat pieces of aluminum foil over the problem spots. In many cases, the foil will correct the flaw.

MOTOR OIL

About half the automobile owners in this country change their own oil. If you're one of them, don't dump the oil down a sewer or on the ground. Used motor oil contains many contaminants, including lead, which can pollute water and kill plants. It's no good dumping the oil in a container and setting it out with the trash, either. The compactor on most garbage trucks will crush the container and oil will dribble out, causing more pollution. Instead, try one of these ideas:

DUST CONTROL. Highway departments sprinkle oil on dirt roads to keep dust down during the summer. You can

RECYCLE → RECYCLE → RECYCLE

Dirty motor oil can be rerefined and used again as motor oil. We've known how to rerefine motor oil since the turn of the century, and during the World Wars, it was a patriotic obligation to save used oil for the boys on the front. Unfortunately, the Federal Trade Commission undermined the rerefining industry in the 1950s by insisting that they label their product "previously used." In a society where new means good, that was the kiss of death, and the industry dwindled to a fraction of its former size.

Today, Americans waste 70,000 barrels of used lubrication oil per day. Although there are efforts afoot to change labeling requirements and to sell motor oil in deposit containers, the government has moved very slowly. In the meantime, your best bet is to pour used motor oil into a leakproof container (perhaps an empty milk jug) and cart it to your local service station. Many stations have arrangements with waste oil collectors, who pay around 15 cents a gallon for the dirty oil. If your station won't take your oil, ask around for one that will. If you can't find anyone recycling oil in your community, you may want to start your own program. For information and advice, write for a copy of "Recycle Used Motor Oil," available from the American Petroleum Institute, Marketing Department, 2101 L Street NW, Washington, DC 20037.

do the same thing for a driveway, but use the oil sparingly, because heavy runoff will kill the adjoining lawn.

TOOL TREATMENT. To clean and protect your tools, fill a bucket with sand and dribble used motor oil over the top. When the oil has soaked in, plunge the metal parts of the tools into the sand several times. This is a good treatment for garden tools at the end of the season and for scissors, screwdrivers, and saws anytime.

NOXIOUS PLANTS. Since oil will kill plants, use it as a selective herbicide to get rid of grass in the cracks on a sidewalk or poison ivy at the base of a tree.

QUICK STARTS. Keep a coffee can of motor oil and soak kindling in it before trying to light a fire. Don't let the soaked kindling sit around, and be careful when you apply the match, because the fire will flare up fast.

STOP ROT. Fence posts, tomato stakes, and other wooden poles become impervious to water if you soak them in motor oil for twenty-four hours before pounding them into the ground.

CHEAP HEAT. Used motor oil can be burned as fuel if you use a special burner to filter out contaminants. The *Mother Earth News* has developed a build-it-yourself waste oil heater that's made from an old hot water heater. Plans are available for $10 from Mother's Plans, P.O. Box A, East Flat Rock, NC 28726. If you aren't handy enough to tackle that sort of job, investigate the Burnzall Heater made by Burnzall, Box 189, Route 422, New Castle, PA 16103.

MOWERS

See LAWN MOWERS

NAILS

An old nursery rhyme concludes, "For want of a nail, the kingdom was lost." The moral is simple: Save nails. Keep the leftovers from do-it-yourself projects and salvage old nails from crates, buildings, or furniture you dismantle. The benefits are obvious. Next time you need a nail for hanging a picture, building a bookcase, or repairing the woodwork, you won't need to buy it.

You'll also be happy to have nails around for other, less conventional uses. Think of a nail as a short metal rod with a pointed end and suddenly new possibilities spring to mind. Here are a few of them:

PULLING PUNCHES. A sharp nail is a perfect punch for leather, plastic, metal, and other materials. Position a block of wood under the material to be punched, place the tip of the nail where you want the hole, and deliver one sharp blow with a hammer.

HOT POTATO. Long clean nails can be inserted into baking potatoes to make them cook quicker.

SIMPLE SECURITY. To make a simple "lock" for a double-hung window, close the window and drill a single hole going through the bottom of the upper sash and the top of the lower sash. Insert a long nail into the hole. The hole-with-a-nail-in-it technique can also be used to hold windows open, to secure modular storage units, and to keep gates shut.

SPIKED MEMOS. To make an old-fashioned memo holder, drive a large nail all the way through a ½-inch piece of wood. Paint the wood and set the holder, nail up, on the desk.

HANG-UPS. Extra nails can always be used as hooks in the basement or garage. You can even use them in the clothes closet if you use epoxy to glue a plastic toothpaste cap to the end so the head doesn't rip through fabric. Pound the nail hooks into studs at a slight angle for extra strength.

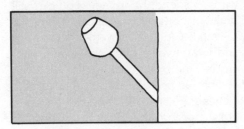

S-HOOKS. Use S-hooks to hang everything from plants to mobiles, hammocks to porch swings. To make a simple S-hook from a thin nail, hold the nail with one pair of pliers and bend it into an S shape with a second pair of pliers. The force you have to apply to bend the nail indicates the amount of weight it will hold without giving. For a larger nail, clamp it in a vise to bend it.

SCULPTED NAILS. With a little solder, nails can be joined into rugged-looking candleholders, paperweights, trivets, nameplates, and ornaments. For detailed instructions about how to bend and solder nails, see *Nail Sculpture* by Elmer Grumber (Sterling Publishing, 1968).

See also HARDWARE.

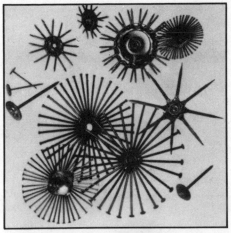

Medallions like these are quickly created by soldering nails together.

★ NAILED AGAIN ★

Removing nails so they are straight enough to be reused takes practice and patience. Use the claw of the hammer or the notch in the pry bar to loosen the nail by pulling from one side and then the other. When the nail is loose, withdraw it by pulling straight up.

Obviously, this method won't work all the time. Yet even bent nails can be reused as "staples" for holding wires and ropes in place. Grasp one end of the nail with pliers and use a second pair of pliers to bend the nail into a right angle. Hammering on the angle, pound the point of the nail into the wood beside the wire to be secured. When the other leg of the nail is almost flat against the wood, swivel it around to cover the wire and pound its head into the wood.

NECKTIES

There may not be much fabric in an old necktie, but what there is will probably be richly colored and worth saving, if only so it can be used as an appliqué patch on another garment. Think of ties

as narrow tubes of fabric that can be stuffed, wrapped, or tied in a knot. Here are a few samples of things you can do with them:

A CASE FOR TIES. Since ties are tubes, they are easily converted into handsome cases for umbrellas, glasses, cigarettes, and other narrow objects. Measure the object, add 4 inches, and cut the tie to that length, measuring from its wide end. Turn the tie inside out and stitch the narrow end shut. Now turn it right side out and sew a snap on the tip of the point so it will fold down and close over the top of the case.

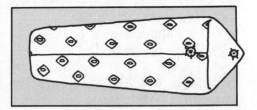

ALL WRAPPED UP. Tie fabric can be a sumptuous covering for small objects, such as a simple picture frame made from a piece of heavy cardboard. Remove the stitching from several ties, take out the lining, and flatten the fabric. Now cut a piece of cardboard into the shape of the frame you want to make. Pad the frame by stapling on a triple thickness of terry cloth, cut from an old towel. Cover the back of the frame with glue and wrap the tie fabric around the cardboard, keeping the fabric taut. When you come to the corners, draw the fabric straight across them. After the glue dries, snip the excess corner fabric and glue down the edges.

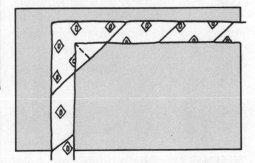

STRAPPED. Ties make strong, attractive shoulder straps for cameras, purses, knapsacks, and other carriers. Cut off the widest part of the tie and simply knot or sew the ends around the metal rings on the object to be carried.

FIT TO BE TIED. People with flamboyant taste have joined ties into skirts, capes, and even café curtains. Remove the stitching from the ties and press them flat. Sew the ties together at their edges, starting from the wide end. When the necessary number of ties have been stitched together, trim the narrow ends off evenly and add a waistband, a collar, or a tube (for the curtain rod).

STUFFED SNAKE. Kids will adore a stuffed snake made from an old tie. Close off the narrow end of the tie and stuff the tube with stockings. Turn down the point of the tie to close off the wide end and whipstitch the edges shut. Sew bits of felt onto the wide end to make the snake's eyes, nose, and tongue.

NARROW ESCAPES. Even if the wide part of the tie is stained, the narrow part can be used as a tie-on headband, a wrap belt, or a choker necklace. Cut off the wide section, trim the end into a matching point, and hem the cut edges.

See also FABRIC SCRAPS.

It takes about twelve ties to make a skirt.

NEWSPAPERS

Everyone agrees that newspapers should and can be recycled. The only question is why more municipalities don't have source separation programs. Until separate pickup for newspapers becomes a routine part of garbage collection, individuals will simply have to schlep their old papers to a community recycling center. Try to make regular trips, so the recycling doesn't seem like such a burden. Another way to minimize the number of papers you have to haul to the recycling center is to use some of them in projects like these:

SHINE ON. Crumpled-up newspapers make terrific lintless polishing cloths for windows and mirrors.

MORE MULCH. Newspapers are a fine mulch for garden vegetables. Wet the newspapers so they don't blow around and spread several layers between the row vegetables. Weeds can't penetrate the papers, and when the papers finally do decompose, they enrich the soil.

PET PAPERS. Pet owners know that torn strips of newspaper make good bedding for hamsters and litter for cats. Use pads of paper to line the bird cage and train the puppy.

PACK IT IN. Strips of newspaper make great packing material when you are mailing or moving breakables. Tear several sheets into 2-inch strips. Then separate the strips and crumple them up to cushion the breakables.

SAVING HEAT. Cellulose insulation is made primarily from shredded newspaper, but you won't be able to convert the Sunday paper into insulation unless you have access to a shredder. The finely shredded particles of paper must be mixed with borax (about 12 pounds per 100 pounds of paper) to make them fire-resistant and aluminum sulfate (25 pounds per 100 pounds of paper) to make them unattractive to rodents. Then the treated newspaper particles can be spread between joists in the attic and will function effectively as long as they don't get wet. Warning: Do not under any circumstances spread untreated newspapers in the attic, because they can be a serious fire hazard.

NEWS LOGS. For $15 or so, you can buy a contraption for rolling newspapers into "logs" from a mail-order company like NASCO, 901 Janesville Avenue, Fort Atkinson, WI 53538. If you don't want to spend the money, you can still make the logs with a piece of broomstick 18 inches long. Open the newspaper and wrap two or three sheets at a time around the broomstick, making the roll as tight as possible. When the roll is 2 inches thick, tie with thin wire and pull out the broomstick. Soak the skinny log in kerosene or used motor oil for several hours. When the log has absorbed some of the oil, wrap more newspapers around it, and keep wrapping until the log is 5 inches thick. Secure the bundle with light wire and store outdoors in a well-ventilated place.

This useful contraption rolls newspapers into compact logs for woodstove or fireplace.

DOWEL HOUSE. Many designers have used dowels and tubes in furniture. You can get the same effect by making dowels from old newspaper. Mix up a batch of very runny wallpaper paste and put it in a large washtub. Dip pieces of newspaper into the paste until they are wet and wrap them around lengths of coat hanger wire. Wrap each sheet as tightly as you can, smoothing out all wrinkles as you go. When the dowel is as thick as you want it, set it aside to dry for twenty-four hours. Once these dowels are dry, you can paint, cut, or drill them as you would wood.

RECYCLE ➤ RECYCLE ➤ RECYCLE

If your community doesn't have a source separation program, you can still organize the traditional newspaper collection drive, or you can include newspaper collection in the program of your local recycling center. Of all waste materials, newspaper is one of the easiest to sell—there are over 1,500 waste paper dealers in the United States. In addition, newspaper recycling can be highly profitable to the sponsoring group. Each year individuals and organizations earn $50 million recycling newspapers. For more information about setting up a newspaper recycling program, write for a free copy of "How to Recycle Waste Paper," from the American Paper Institute, Box CJ, 260 Madison Avenue, New York, NY 10016.

TRACING PAPER. Newspaper can be used to transfer patterns and designs onto wood, fabric, and other sheets of paper. The classified section is particularly good because the print is dense. Put your material under the newspaper and your design on top. Go over the lines in the design with a blunt instrument, pressing firmly, until the ink on the newsprint is transferred to the material underneath.

★ NOW THERE'S ★ NO EXCUSE

If you don't recycle your newspapers because you hate the chore of stacking and tying them, try using scrap wood to build this time-saving contraption. Make the base the size of a newspaper and the side supports 2 feet tall. Screw simple eye hooks into the top of each post and thread twine through them so it runs down one post, across the base, and up the other post. Then just stack the newspapers in the frame, and when it's full, pull the string out of the eye hooks and tie it neatly around the papers.

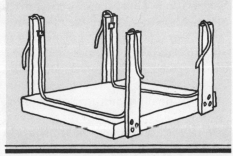

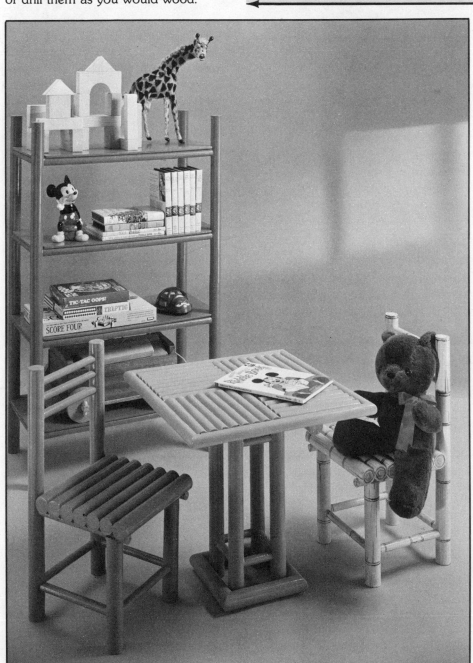

All this furniture was built from "dowels," which are made by rolling pasted newspaper into tight tubes and coating them with acrylic.

★ SOURCE SEPARATION: AN IDEA WHOSE TIME HAS COME ★

Although the technology for recycling newspaper has been available for one hundred years, the only mechanism for collecting paper has been the occasional paper drive by churches, schools, scout troops, and, more recently, private recycling centers. In all these cases, the burden of hauling the paper falls upon the citizen. Within the last fifteen years, about two hundred municipalities, prompted by the rising price of waste paper and the shrinking space in landfill sites, have begun collecting newspapers separately from other garbage.

Some programs are voluntary; others are mandated by local government. In all of them, citizens bundle their newspapers and put them out separately from their other garbage. That's not much inconvenience because most people stack newspapers separately anyway. The city collects the newspapers either with a special truck or with a rack attached to the regular garbage truck. According to the Environmental Protection Agency,

cities break even when the cost of waste newspaper is about $25 a ton, and they usually make a profit when it rises above that price.

If the idea of government making instead of spending money appeals to you, read more about source separation of newspapers. Send for

two free pamphlets—"Residential Paper Recovery, A Community Action Program" and "Residential Paper Recovery, A Municipal Implementation Guide," both available through your congressperson or the Superintendent of Documents, Washington, DC 20402.

By adding racks to ordinary garbage trucks, any community can start collecting newspapers for recycling.

OATMEAL BOXES AND OTHER LARGE CYLINDERS

Schools can always use your empty oatmeal boxes—the kids turn them into tom-toms, totem poles, and dozens of other useful things. On the other hand, you may want to keep a few at home for your own purposes. The round boxes make appealing storage containers, especially if you cut them off at varying heights with a serrated knife. You can paint them, cover them with adhesive-

backed paper, decoupage them, or leave them *au naturel* with the genial Quaker Oats graphic. Protect the outside of the box with a clear coat of acrylic and use it for projects like these:

FAT TUBE. Use an empty oatmeal box to store maps, certificates, and other papers which should not be

folded. If the papers are too large for the box, slice off its end and slip it around the papers, napkin-ring style, to hold them in place.

GIFT BOX. Sometimes a round gift just won't fit into a square box. That's when you pull out your oatmeal box, drop in the gift, cushion it with shredded newspaper, and wrap. The unusual shape is sure to start the recipient guessing.

ONE-HAT STAND. Decorate an empty oatmeal box, put it on a closet shelf, and perch your hat on top to keep it from being crushed or stretched. If you have gloves or a scarf to match the hat, keep them inside the box.

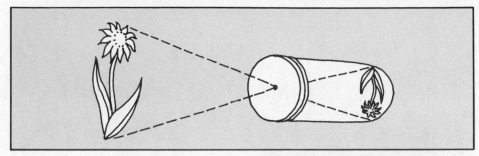

BOX CAMERA. Even in an age of instant pictures, pinhole cameras continue to fascinate kids. You can make one with a clean oatmeal box and free directions from the Photo Information Department, Eastman Kodak, 343 State St., Rochester, NY 14650. Enclose a self-addressed, stamped envelope and request publication A-55.

DISENTANGLED. An empty oatmeal box makes an ideal container for string or knitting yarn. Slice 3 inches off the box with a serrated knife. Put the ball of string in the box, punch a ½-inch hole in the top, and thread the end of the string through the hole before taping the top back on the box. The box is easy to find when you need it, and the string won't get tangled.

★ A BOX FOR ★ EVERY TASTE

So you hate oatmeal? You can still keep yourself in cylinders if you save boxes from salt, cornmeal, and bread crumbs.

OIL

See MOTOR OIL

PACKAGING

Keep track of your trash for one week and you'll find that the largest single portion is packaging—boxes, cans, bags, bottles, and plastic containers that are supposed to be secondary to the product they enclose. Packaging is so firmly entrenched in our culture because it meets needs all along the economic chain. Manufacturers benefit from it because it maximizes shelf life and helps distinguish one product from its competitors. Retailers appreciate it because it allows self-service and helps sell some products. Consumers want packaging because, in many cases, it keeps products fresh, clean, and undamaged. And, needless to say, companies that make packaging think it's just great.

The other side of the story is that packaging consumes enormous amounts of raw materials—half our paper production, three quarters of our glass, 40 percent of our aluminum, and 30 percent of our plastic. Most of these resources go into packages designed for a single use—90 percent of all packaging is thrown out within one year after it is made. Most packages go into the trash (one third of our municipal garbage is packaging), but a lot of it turns into litter (two thirds of a roadside litter sample is likely to be empty packages). Either way, the raw material in most packaging is not reclaimed because it is contaminated by being mixed into the waste stream or because more and more packages are made from two or more inseparable materials.

All this makes packaging expensive.

Part of the cost is, of course, tacked onto the product when you buy it. In the case of elaborate packages like aerosol cans, a full 20 percent of the cost is for a container that cannot be reused. Similarly, the container represents 33 percent of the price of baby food in a jar, 26 percent of motor oil in a can, and 36 percent of beer in a nonreturnable bottle. All together, the average family of four pays about $400 a year for packaging! Added to this is the cost of disposal—an estimated $4 billion per year just to collect packaging—and the cost for one-time use of finite resources, which cannot even be calculated.

Can the benefits of packaging outweigh the costs? Yes, but only if manufacturers use restraint and imagination in packaging their products and if consumers reinforce their efforts by taking packaging into account when making buying decisions. Here are some specific suggestions:

Avoid excess packaging. Instead of having the bottle inside the box, the oranges wrapped in plastic, or the tube inside a blister pack, manufacturers should use the single most efficient packaging layer for enclosing their products, and consumers should avoid overwrapped items. When possible, buy products that have no packaging—cereal from bins, cheese cut from wheels—and bring your own containers to cart them home in.

Buy large packages whenever possible. Large packages use up fewer materials per ounce of product, so they cost less. Also, large packages are easier to recycle. You're more likely to flatten and save a single large cereal box than twelve individual serving packages.

Buy returnable containers when available. At this point, bottles are the only returnable containers (see JARS AND BOTTLES), though a few companies are experimenting with heavy-duty plastic containers that could be returned (see MILK CONTAINERS)

Support standardized packages. More packages could become returnables if they were standardized. Pickle jars, mayonnaise bottles, wine bottles, and others can be collected, washed, refilled, and resold—it's already being done by entrepreneurs around the country—but the job would be easier if more containers came in standard shapes and sizes.

Support package redesign. Several companies have been successful in redesigning packages to consume less materials. The International Paper Company, for example, took on the standard school milk carton and figured out a way to use 31 percent less paper in its construction.

Favor recyclable containers. Bottles, boxes, and cans can be recycled; plastic can't. Until someone thinks up an alternative to throwing away plastic, try to buy products in other kinds of containers. Similarly, avoid two-material packages whenever possible—paper that's laminated with plastic or foil can't be recycled.

(*See also* BOXES, CARDBOARD; CANS; JARS AND BOTTLES; PLASTIC CONTAINERS.)

★ PACKAGE TAX ★

For years some people have argued that the manufacturers who produce packaging should help pay for its disposal. Several states have passed "litter taxes" requiring manufacturers of disposable products like bottles, plastic wrappings, and other packaging to pay a disposal fee to the state when the product is produced. Although such taxes may ease the burden of paying for waste disposal, they do nothing to solve the more fundamental problem of waste proliferation.

★ MAKING BOTTLES INTO BRICKS ★

What if every piece of packaging had two roles, its primary one and another to take over when it was empty? We're not simply talking about jelly jars that become juice glasses or margarine tubs that become leftover dishes. What if empty cereal boxes were made to interlock so they could be used to build furniture? What if cans were manufactured to have a second life as cooking utensils? What if bottles were designed to be reused as bricks?

Those revolutionary "what ifs" are at the heart of the remarkable book *Garbage Housing* (John Wiley, 1975) by Martin Pawley. The book solves two problems—the worldwide housing shortage and the solid waste crisis—by building shelter out of trash. Why, Pawley asks, can't houses be built of the metal, plastic, glass, and paper that gets thrown away every day? Mr. Pawley's book is a detailed, scholarly analysis of the social, political, and economic forces that thwart such constructions. Yet once you've asked the "what if" question, you'll never be able to toss out a plastic bottle, tin can, or cardboard box without a twinge of "is that all there is?"

These bottles, designed for Heineken beer, become interlocking bricks when empty.

PAINTBRUSHES

Paintbrushes usually get thrown away when the bristles are stiff and matted. That's not a good enough reason. Brushes with bristles can be reconditioned by soaking them in Red Devil's Save-a-Brush. Even brushes that are losing their bristles can be put to work on other projects like these:

DUST BRUSH. An old paintbrush can be a great help in dusting off a workbench or getting lint out of machinery parts.

STIPULATIONS. Use a stiff old brush to create a stucco effect in new paint jobs. Spread the paint thickly with a good brush and then slap the old brush against the wall to give the paint texture.

GETTING ALL THE ANGLES. Trim a ragged brush at a 45-degree angle and use it for painting corners and the tight spots around woodwork.

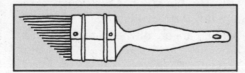

SPOT JOB. Keep a clean old paintbrush with your laundry supplies and use it to daub stain remover onto spots. You'll get better results and waste less cleaning liquid.

PLANT CLEANER. Use a moistened paintbrush to dust off the leaves of your houseplants.

PANS

See DISHES AND COOKWARE

PANTS

A pair of pants is nothing more than two tubes of fabric, some fasteners, and a waistband. As long as you remember that, you'll have no trouble reusing pants that are "out" or worn out.

SKIRTING THE ISSUE. Blue jeans inspired the first pants-to-skirt routine, but there's no reason why other pants can't join the act. Remove the inseam of the pants and flatten the fabric. Add a V of a different fabric to fill the gap, front and back. Cut to desired length and hem.

PANTS POUCH. With a snip here and a stitch there, pant legs can be converted into pouches for everything from shoes to gym clothes, marbles to laundry. Cut off the leg to the desired length and turn it inside out. Stitch across the cut end. Make two slits in the hem at the other end, thread a double drawstring through the hem, and pull it tight to close the pouch.

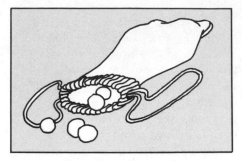

TOP IT OFF. One of the most surprising ways to reuse a pair of pants that's out of fashion is to convert it into a blouse. Cut open the crotch seam, slip the pants over your head, and pull the "legs" over your arms. The waistband still goes around your waist. Mark a wide neckline, cut it out, and hem around the edges. Make darts as necessary to fit the bodice to your body and adjust the pant legs to the length of your arms. This garment may sound outlandish, but it can look great, especially when it's made from soft cotton bell bottoms.

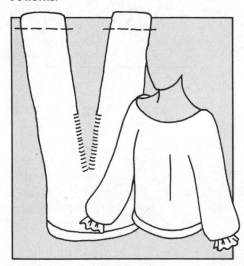

BITS AND PIECES. Pants that have passed beyond wearability should be dismantled for parts. Save buttons, zippers, snaps, and swatches of good fabric.

APPLE SACK. The two tubes in a pair of pants make a tough carrier that leaves your hands free. Turn the pants inside out and close off each leg. Turn them right side out and cut through the waistband and down each side seam about 12 inches. Cut across the front of the leg and up the inseam to remove the front panel. Trim the cut edges with bias tape. To use the carryall, drape one leg over each shoulder and fill the pouches with apples, firewood, bricks you're salvaging from a demolition site, and other bulky loads. You'll be surprised to see how much you can carry.

•••••••••••••••••••••••••••••••

PANTYHOSE

See STOCKINGS

PAPER

In most communities, paper accounts for 50 to 60 percent of all solid waste. That adds up to 65.7 million tons of paper consumed annually in the United States. To bring these figures home, think of them this way: Every year, *you* consume *two* Douglas fir trees. If you'd like to spare one of those trees, try cutting down on the paper that comes into your life. Wipe up spills with sponges instead of paper towels. Use cloth napkins instead of paper. Don't buy the newspaper unless you're going to read it. After you read it, share it with a friend. No matter how conscientious you are, you won't eliminate paper from your life, but you can cut down on the amount that goes into the trash. Some paper can be officially recycled (see box, page 109); some kinds of paper— ENVELOPES, GREETING CARDS, JUNK MAIL, MAGAZINES, NEWSPAPERS, PAPER BAGS— have specific uses that you'll find under those headings. For everyday scrap paper, try ideas like these:

TWO SIDES TO EVERY SHEET. Every piece of paper has two sides. Write on both of them. Remember that Abraham Lincoln drafted the Gettysburg Address on the back of

BLOOMERS. Pants of all kinds can be converted into shorts or pedal pushers by cutting off the tubes and hemming them. For a more tailored look, try making bloomers. Cut off the pant legs below the knee. Slash the outside seam 3 inches up and add a cuff that fits snugly around your leg. Finish the cuff with a buttonhole and button or two Velcro patches and wear the bloomers fastened just above the knee, so the fabric billows a little.

See also BLUE JEANS; CLOTHES; FABRIC SCRAPS.

•••••••••••••••••••••••••••••••

an envelope. You can stash your scrap paper in a box, or you can make your

The paper you use in one year consumes two of these magnificent trees.

scrap into pads and save the expense of memo pads at the five-and-dime.

To make a scrap pad, cut your paper into uniform pieces, stack them neatly, and staple them to a piece of cardboard slightly larger than the pages. Or use a heavy-duty needle and thread to stitch across the top of the pad. Or punch holes in the corners of all the pieces of paper and string ribbon, yarn, or wire through them. Or use a spring clip. Or find a piece of scrap wood the size of your paper pieces, stack the paper neatly on top of it, and screw two wood screws straight through the paper and into the wood. However you put it together, use your new pad for a date-book, a notebook, recipes, or doodling.

UNDER WRAPS. Papers of all kind can be used to wrap packages, cover walls, and decorate found containers. Experiment! Wrap birthday packages in colorful magazine pages. Paper a wall with newsprint protected with clear acrylic. Decorate a pencil can by covering it with glue and rolling it in confetti-size pieces of scrap paper.

FLYING PAPER. Paper of all kinds is the primary component in kites and paper airplanes. The simplest designs in both categories might be for kids, but the more advanced creations can keep adults entertained for weeks. For ideas, take a look at *Create a Kite* by the editors of Consumer Guide (Simon & Schuster, 1977) and *The Paper Air Force Training Manual* by Felix Rosenthal (Celestial Arts, 1979).

This symbol, created by the American Paper Institute, indicates that a paper product is made of recycled fibers.

Never in Your Wildest Dreams

Are you a saver of greeting cards, menus, posters, parking tickets, travel brochures, ticket stubs, laundry lists, business cards, time-tables, certificates, bills of lading, and other bits of paper? No, I can't tell you what to do with them, but I can give you a name for your addiction. Ephemerology, also known as wastebasket arche-ology, is the collection of printed or handwritten materials that would ordinarily be thrown away. What's more, there's actually an organization for ephemerists, which publishes the inevitable jour-nal, which in turn becomes grist for the ephemera mill. To join, contact the Ephemera Society of America at 124 Elm Street, Ben-nington, VT 05201.

RECYCLE → RECYCLE → RECYCLE

Eighty percent of the paper thrown away in this country could be recycled into products as diverse as new paper, egg cartons, and insulation. The dismal fact is that only about 20 percent of the available paper is actually recycled, largely because the instability of the paper market makes it difficult for anyone to make a consistent profit from collecting and selling the stuff. It doesn't have to be that way. In Japan, 46 percent of the wastepaper gets recycled.

In the U.S., most communities recycle at least some of the paper some of the time. In most households, three types of paper could be collected for recycling: newspapers, corrugated cardboard and paper bags, and scrap paper such as thin cardboard, egg cartons, paper with writing on it, junk mail, envelopes, catalogues, magazines, and so on. To be recycled, all paper must be free from contaminants such as food scraps, dirt, wax coatings, cellophane, photographic chemicals, and paper clips.

Actually, recycling paper takes only a few minutes per consumer. Newspapers are so bulky that most people store them in a special place to begin with. Cardboard boxes take up very little space if they are flattened. And everyone can establish a Clean Scrap Box for all the miscellaneous paper. Once you have a system for storing paper, all you need is a center to take it to. To find out about the recycling center in your community or about upcoming paper drives, call your local paper dealer, listed in the Yellow Pages under "Paper, Scrap."

After turning in your old paper, your part in recycling still isn't done. Paper manufacturers claim that one reason the demand for used paper is so erratic is that the public won't buy recycled products. If you have a back-of-your-mind idea that recycled paper is inferior, change it. Most recycled products are indistinguishable from their virgin counterparts. Paper towels, napkins, bags, tissues, stationery, greeting cards, and most cardboard packaging can be made from recycled fibers. Incidentally, don't confuse "recycled" with "recyclable." "Recyclable" means only that the product *can* be recycled, not that it has been. Check to see that the product is labeled "recycled paper," or look for the official American Paper Institute symbol.

★ GIVE AT THE OFFICE ★

Homes may generate a lot of wastepaper, but offices beat them hands down. The average office worker discards 1.6 pounds of paper per day, much of it high-grade paper that could be sold at good prices to scrap dealers. Gradually, companies are beginning to see that it is in their interest to sell scrap paper rather than pay money to have it hauled away. If you think your company might benefit from such a program, order one or all of these how-to-do-it publications:

"Garbage Guide: Paper Profits," Environmental Action Foundation, Suite 724, Dupont Circle Building, Washington, DC 20036.

"Office Paper Recovery: An Implementation Manual," U.S. Environmental Protection Agency, 26 West St. Clair Street, Cincinnati, OH 43268.

"How to Recycle Waste Paper," American Paper Institute, Box CJ, 260 Madison Avenue, New York, NY 10016.

Recycling office paper is easy—and economical.

itself in little mounds. Cool and form into blocks, boxes, planters, and free-standing sculpture. Dry in the oven. Small papier-mâché objects can be coated with clear lacquer or acrylic.

For more information on papier-mâché, consult

Papier-Mâché Crafts by Mildred Anderson (Sterling, 1975).
Papier-Mâché by Robin Capon (Davis Publications, 50 Portland Street, Worcester, MA 01608; 1977).
Papier-Mâché Artistry by Dona Z. Meilach (Crown Publishers, 1971).

HOMEMADE STATIONERY. Like expensive-looking, textured writing paper? You can make your own out of scrap paper such as tissue, wrapping paper, magazine pages, and junk mail. Start by constructing a mold from four narrow strips of wood. Tack them together to make a 5 × 7-inch rectangle (after you've practiced a couple of times, you may want to move up to a larger sheet). Snip a 5 × 7-inch piece out of an old window screen and staple it to the frame.

Now make a paper mush. Start with strips of paper—you can control the color of the stationery by paying attention to the primary color on the pages. Pack the strips loosely into a blender and add 2 cups water. Blend until the paper mush is the consistency of wet tissue. Then pour the mush into a dishpan full of water and stir until the fibers are suspended throughout the water.

Set a stack of newspapers beside the dishpan and cover it with a blotter. Now, dip your mold sideways into the water. Underwater, turn the mold parallel with the bottom of the pan and pull it straight up through the water, collecting pulp as you go. Hold the mold steady over the pan for a minute or so until most of the water drains through the screen. Then flip the mold over onto the blotter. Remove the mold and sop up extra water with an old towel. Cover the wet paper with another blotter and press with an iron set on its lowest setting. When the blotter seems dry, try to peel it away from your paper. If it doesn't come easily, the paper isn't dry—keep ironing. Paper making isn't the easiest thing to do, but handmade paper adds a very

THE ANCIENT ART OF PAPIER-MÂCHÉ. Most adults think of papier-mâché as kid stuff, and it is a good, albeit goopy, way to occupy a roomful of children on a rainy day. On the other hand, a coat of liquid epoxy or acrylic can transform papier-mâché into a durable and respectable medium for adults. With a little effort, you can make wastebaskets, room dividers, furniture, planters, and boxes out of last week's junk mail.

There are two techniques for making papier-mâché. For the first, mix up a batch of wallpaper paste following the instructions on the box. Tear sheets of paper into 1-inch strips and spread glue on them with an old paintbrush. Apply the strips to a mold—a dish, a box, a flowerpot, a balloon. Build up an even layer of paper by overlapping the strips

and spreading them in every direction. Be careful to smooth out each strip to eliminate air bubbles and major wrinkles. When the layer of paper is thick enough, remove the mold, set your masterpiece on an oiled baking sheet, and dry for about ten minutes in a 250-degree oven.

The second papier-mâché recipe produces objects with smoother surfaces. Fill a large pot with water and bring it to a boil. While it's heating up, tear the paper into 2-inch squares. Add the bits of paper to the water, a few at a time, and stir until the paper has broken down into fibers. Drain the mash in a colander and measure. For every 4 cups of mash, add 1 cup white flour. Put the mixture back on the stove and cook at the lowest heat, stirring constantly, until the mash is thick enough to stand by intimate touch to invitations, Christmas cards, announcements, and letters. For more information, consult *Hand Papermaking Manual* by Peter T. Sarjeant (available through Mother's Bookshelf, Box 70, Hendersonville, NC 28739).

PAPER ARTS. Odd pieces of paper can be cut, crumpled, folded, and torn to make mobiles, sculptures, and graphic designs. Often paper which already has printing or writing on it makes these creations more interesting. For example, silhouettes cut from newsprint look dramatic mounted on black construction paper. Snowflakes cut from tissue paper make delightful window decorations. And thin strips from magazines can be fashioned into intricate coiled pictures. For more ideas about making decorations from scrap paper, consult the following books:

Papercrafts by John Portchmouth (Viking, 1973).
Papercrafts by Ian Adair (Arco, 1975).
Paperworks by Florence Temko (Bobbs-Merrill, 1980).
Paper as Art and Craft by Thelma Newman (Crown Publishers, 1973).

See also BOOKS; CALENDAR, LAST YEAR'S; ENVELOPES; MAGAZINES; NEWSPAPERS; PHONE BOOKS.

●●●●●●●●●●●●●●●●●●●●●

PAPERBACKS

See BOOKS

●●●●●●●●●●●●●●●●●●●●●

PAPER BAGS

Minimize the number of bags you need to recycle by carrying a tote and putting small purchases directly into it without benefit of extra bags. The bags you do bring home can, of course, be used both as containers and as a source of heavy brown paper. Many households use up bags without thinking about it, if only by employing large supermarket bags for trash and smaller bags for sack lunches.

If that simple sort of recycling won't suffice, try ideas like these:

DECORATOR BAGS. A few years ago, decorators noticed that brown paper bags had a warm color and earthy texture. After that, bags started showing up in unexpected places—as wallpaper above the wainscoting in a restored farmhouse, as the mat paper under photographs and prints, as placemats woven from folded strips of bag paper. To pull off these effects, treat the bag as carefully as you would a more expensive material. Press out creases with a warm iron and damp pressing cloth, and use a straight edge and a sharp utility knife to get smooth cuts.

TIDY BAGS. Use paper bags to contain and dispose of items that are gooey, germy, or otherwise untouchable. Keep one beside the sickbed for tissues; keep another next to you during a dirty job like refinishing furniture. When you need to pick up something messy—the fragments of a broken jelly jar or a pet's mistake—pull a small paper bag over your hand, pick up the offensive thing, and drop it, bag and all, into a larger bag.

TURKEY IN A BAG. To keep turkey and other meats moist and tasty, cook them in paper bags. Stuff the turkey as usual and butter the top of the bird. Put the turkey in a clean supermarket bag and twist the end closed. Put the bag in your roasting pan and set in a 325-degree oven. Don't turn the oven any higher; allow fifteen minutes per pound. When the turkey is done, tear the top of the bag, lift out the turkey, and pour the drippings into a separate pot.

KID STUFF. Kids find it very satisfying to puff up an old paper bag and smash it. They also get pleasure from making masks out of paper bags. Cut eyeholes in the bag for them and allow the kids to color fearsome faces.

DUST BAGS. Use paper bags to neatly dispose of dust and dirt. To empty a vacuum cleaner, cover the open end with a paper bag and dump. When you remove stovepipe for cleaning, cover both ends with paper bags

until you get the pipe outdoors. If you don't have a suitable place for shaking your dust mop, secure a bag around its neck with a rubber band and shake into the bag.

GREASE BAGS. You have to pay for paper towels—why not use pieces of bag instead for draining the grease from bacon, french fries, and other fried foods? Indeed, some foods, like fritters, stick to paper towels, but they won't to bags.

NEWSPAPER BAG. Large supermarket bags turned on their sides are just the right size for holding newspapers waiting to go to the recycling center.

MAILING PAPER. The post office requires that all packages be wrapped. Instead of buying kraft paper, salvage it from old bags.

COVERED. Brown bag paper is a good protective covering for many things, including books. To make a book cover, cut a flat piece of paper 2 inches taller than the book and 4 inches longer than the length of the book opened flat. Fold a 1-inch flap along the top and bottom of the paper. Open the book and lay it down centered on the paper. Fold one end of the paper over the book's cover and slip the cover into the pocket you've formed. Close the book, pull the paper around the spine, and fold the other end to fit the cover. Open the book and slip the other side of the cover into its pocket. Tape the paper cover to the inside of the book cover.

PAPER LANTERNS. If you don't have outdoor lights to extend a summer's evening, try making lanterns from paper grocery bags. Open the bag and fold down the top twice so it will stay open. Put 3 inches of sand in the bottom of the bag to hold it steady and stick a stubby candle in the sand. Set the bags wherever you need a warm glow.

●●●●●●●●●●●●●●●●●●●●●

PEELINGS

See GARBAGE

PENCIL STUBS

Even a lowly pencil stub can be a resource. Here are possible uses:

STUCK UP. Graphite is a lubricant that can extricate you from sticky situations. Rub the pencil point up and down a stubborn zipper to restore its zip. Or loosen a reluctant lock by first rubbing the key with a pencil.

TOOL IN ONE. A pencil too short for writing may still be okay for making marks. Drill a hole in the end of a ruler and tie a stubby pencil to it, so you'll have to locate only one tool to mark measurements.

PAGE TURNER. If there's an eraser on your pencil stub, cut off the point with a coping saw and use the eraser end for turning pages when looking through a phone book, a catalog, or a stack of checks.

ENCOMPASSING. Make a quick compass out of a stubby pencil, a nail, and a string slightly longer than the radius of the circle you want to draw. Tie one end of the string to the pencil and make a loop at the other end. Tap the nail into wood, paper, or cardboard and put the loop around it. Draw the circle with the pencil, holding the string taut all the way around.

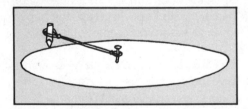

PARALLEL LINES NEVER MEET. Use stubby pencils to draw parallel lines for music, graphs, scale drawings, etc. Find a small block of 1-inch wood. Mark the points where the lines should be on the wood and drill ¼-inch holes centered precisely over each mark. Remove the erasers from several pencils, saw them off to the same length, and sharpen. Put a drop of glue in each hole and screw in the metal heads of the pencils. Place one pencil against a straight edge and draw perfect parallels.

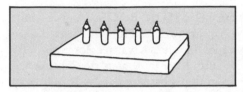

PENS, BALLPOINT

What's the best way to reuse an empty ballpoint pen? Start with the kind that accepts refills and refill it. If you can't resist "disposable" pens, there's still no reason to dispose of them. Simply remove the empty ink tube (see box). Now you have a hollow plastic tube that can be used for dozens of things. Here's a sampler:

DRAWSTRING PEN. Threading a drawstring through a narrow hem can be a frustrating job—unless you use an empty ballpoint pen. Thread the string through the empty plastic tube and tie a knot at the end. If the string is too fine for a knot, tie it in a big loop around the pen. Work the pen through the hem and the string will follow obediently.

ALL STIRRED UP. Use empty pens to stir paint, plant food, and anything

---

★ A PEN ★ DECTOMY

Removing the ink tube from a "disposable" ballpoint pen can be a delicate operation. Sometimes you can loosen the ink tube by prying out the little cap in the top and inserting a fat nail. Press gently on the tube and it may pop out. If that doesn't work, heat the writing end of the pen with a match. The plastic tip that holds the ink tube in place will melt and you can pull the tube free with pliers. This method can be messy if there's ink left in the tube, so work over newspaper.

---

you hesitate to use kitchen utensils in.

BALL AND CHAIN. Empty ballpoint pens are ideal cases for keeping fine jewelry chains from getting tangled. Hold the chain by its pendant and slip it through the tube. Secure the end of the chain by replacing the plastic cap.

ELECTRIFYING. You can make a simple device for testing electrical circuits from a light fixture and two old ballpoint pens with metal tips. Remove the ink tube from one pen and pull off the tip. Insert one wire of a double-strand electrical wire through the pen, strip the end of the wire, and stick the wire into the tip so it makes contact with the metal point. Use liquid solder to hold the wire in place. Press the tip into the end of the pen, and repeat the process with the second pen and the other half of the wire. Now hook up the other ends of the wires to the terminals of the light socket, and screw in a 15-watt bulb. Use the tester to discover whether current is flowing through circuits in appliances that don't work.

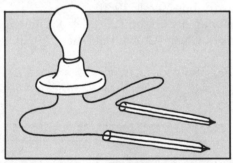

WIRED. If you have a large collection of old ballpoint pens, thread stiff wire through them. By bending the wire, you can shape the pens into such lively items as a trellis for houseplants, a whimsical hanger for scarves or ties, or a trapeze for your parakeet.

PENS, FELT-TIP

Sometimes you can squeeze a few more words out of a felt-tip pen by soaking its point in water for five minutes, then capping the pen and letting it sit for about an hour. If that treatment doesn't help, salvage the plastic parts of the pen.

★ PLEA FOR AN ★ ENDANGERED SPECIES

If throwing out all those felt-tip pens irks you, revive the fountain pen. A well-balanced fountain pen feels good in your hand, lends elegance to your handwriting, and can, of course, be refilled. Admittedly, a fountain pen is more expensive at the outset, but instead of a fast, cheap fling, you'll form a lifelong relationship with your writing implement.

First remove the cap and set it aside. Use a coping saw to cut through the barrel of the pen about ½ inch above the felt point. Pull out the felt core of the pen, using tweezers if necessary, and rinse out the empty tube. Now you have a plastic tube with a pry-off cap on one end and a clip-on cap for the other. These plastic pieces have a surprising number of uses once you start to think about it. Here are a few examples:

HANDLE IT. Both parts from a felt-tip pen can be used to make handy handles. If you make campfire implements from hangers (see HANGERS), use the tube from a felt-tip pen as a heatproof handle. Or, if you have a small tool that you use regularly—perhaps a magnifying glass or a little screwdriver—dab some glue on its handle and jam it into the top of a felt-tip pen so it will clip right onto your pocket or belt loop. Or slip the plastic tube from a pen over a piece of string and use it as the handle on a string-bound package.

SECRET KIT. An empty felt-tip pen combined with its snap-on top makes an inconspicuous carrying case for narrow objects. Those who are electronically talented may be able to figure out how to fit a transmitter or a camera in the pen. If you aren't into spy games, fill the holder with two needles and several colors of thread wrapped around toothpicks to make a sewing kit. If sewing isn't your style, use the case for fishhooks, small nails, hairpins, and so on.

AT YOUR FINGERTIPS. Need a pencil by the phone, on the bedside table, near your workbench? Mount the top of a felt-tip pen on any flat surface with a drop of superglue and stick a pencil in it.

BIG BEADS. Felt-tip pen tubes can be sliced up with an ordinary kitchen knife, so it's easy to turn them into beads. The big holes make it possible for small children to string them on shoestrings or yarn whose tip has been dipped in nail polish.

CLIP IT. The top of a felt-tip pen makes a quick clip for holding messages, bills, and other papers together.

PEA PEN. The tube from a felt-tip pen makes a first-class peashooter. Just be sure to rinse it carefully before use.

PHONE BOOKS

Old phone books can and should be recycled into new phone books. Call your phone company and ask whether you can turn in your old one. If they say no, ask why not. If they hang up, try one of these ideas:

NEATNESS COUNTS. When doing a small but messy job of cleaning, painting, or glueing, just turn back the cover of an old phone book, do your work on the top page, and tear off whatever's gloppy when you're done.

BLOTTER BOOK. To preserve wild flowers and leaves, press them between the pages of an old phone book. The weight of a big city book will keep the flower flat, the newsprint will absorb moisture, and you won't care if the pages get stained.

TRANSFER THIS CALL. The tiny type in the phone book rubs off easily, so the pages can be used to transfer large and simple designs to wood, paper, fabric, and other materials. Put a page from the phone book between the design and the object to be decorated and tack the layers in place. Then trace the lines of the design several times with a blunt instrument until the design has been transferred.

CONFETTI. Slice up an old phone book to make confetti for weddings and other special occasions. Use a paper cutter to make the job go faster, and add some Yellow Pages for color.

NUMBER, PLEASE. Personalize your phone book by circling every number you call regularly with a brightly colored pen. At the end of the year, tear out all the marked pages, staple them together, and keep them by the phone as a quick and cheap reference to your most often called numbers.

See also BOOKS; PAPER.

PICTURE FRAMES

Don't throw out the picture frame just because you're tired of the picture. By removing the little nails at the back of the frame, you can evict the current occupant and install a picture that pleases you more.

Picture frames can also find happiness doing many other jobs, since they are, after all, just framed pieces of glass that can be used to cover and protect other things. As a last resort, carefully take the frame apart and use the wood and glass separately. Before taking such drastic measures, consider projects like these:

LITTLE LOOM. Convert a picture frame into a loom by removing the glass and pound finishing nails into the wood at equal intervals. Wrap yarn or thread back and forth around one set of nails and use the other set to secure the yarn when you go under and over. Use your loom to make potholders, scarves, placemats, and other small items.

DISPLAY FRAME. If you collect mineral specimens, thimbles, or other small collectibles, build display boxes the size of your old picture frames and use the framed glass as a cover.

JEWELRY FRAME. Instead of hiding jewelry in a box, display it in a frame. Remove everything from an old picture frame, including the glass. Cut two pieces of cardboard to fit into the frame and a piece of foam rubber as large as the front opening. Glue one piece of cardboard to the back of the foam rubber and cover the front with a swatch of velvet. Glue the edges of the fabric to the back of the first cardboard and cover with the second cardboard. Put the sandwich in the frame and hold it in place with tiny brads. Hang the frame near your mirror and pin brooches to it. Use pins to hang up brooches, necklaces, and bracelets.

TRADE-IN TRAY. A picture frame is just a tray without backing. To convert it into a tray, cut a piece of wood to the same dimensions as the frame. Remove the contents from the frame and cut a piece of mat board to fit behind the glass. If the mat board is not flush with the back of the frame, cut out extra layers of cardboard until it is. Center the stack of cardboard, topped by the mat board, on the piece of wood. Arrange pictures, dried flowers, or a piece of fabric on the mat board and center the glass over the design. Remove all nails from the back of the frame and spread white glue on it. Press the frame into the base, being careful to align the edges. When the glue has dried, turn the tray over and drive short finishing nails through the backboard into the frame. Add handles and finish all wood to the same color.

MOLDINGS. The wood in a picture frame is really flat molding with mitered corners. Use all four pieces as a rim around an end table. Or tack a single piece of molding along the bottom of a lap desk to keep pencils from rolling off. Or nail the molding on a wall and paint it the same color as the wall to create an elegant paneled effect.

See also WOOD SCRAPS.

PILL BOTTLES

If your pills come in little glass bottles, see JARS AND BOTTLES. If they come in plastic cylinders with kidproof lids, save the empty containers for storing all kinds of little things from thumbtacks to BB's. When your supply of small objects gets smaller than your supply of pill bottles, try ideas like these:

FLOATS. Most prescription bottles are airtight, so they float. To make an instant fishing bobber, open a bottle, slip your fishing line between cap and container, and snap together. Or mark a place in a stream or lake by tying a weight to one end of a string and a prescription bottle to the other. The weight will sit on the bottom and the bottle will float above it.

HAVE BOTTLE, WILL TRAVEL. Leakproof pill bottles (fill with water and check) are just the right size for taking a little shampoo, detergent for hand washing, and other creams and liquids when you travel. To make a traveling toothbrush holder, cut a V-notch in the cap of a pill container. Put the brush in the container and snap on the lid so the handle protrudes through the hole.

HUMMINGBIRD BOTTLE. If you are lucky enough to have hummingbirds, make a feeder for them by using a heated ice pick or nail to punch two holes in a prescription bottle near the cap. Tape a wire loop to the bottom of the feeder so it will hang upside down. Now mix up some sugar water—about 5 teaspoons of sugar per cup of water—and add a drop of red food coloring to attract the hummingbirds. Put the water in the bottle, hang it upside down, and wait for the hummingbirds to discover it.

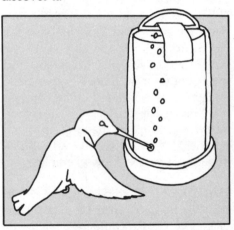

PARTS WHEEL. To make an organizer for tiny parts, nail the tops from four pill bottles to a cube of wood. Drill a hole through the cube and bolt it to the wall above your workbench.

★ EQUAL TIME ★ FOR TINS

What about those little metal tins that aspirins come in? Well, you can always refill them with aspirins from a bigger—and cheaper—bottle and carry them in your purse or pocket. You can also carry an empty tin for those awkward moments when you light up a cigarette and can't find an ashtray anywhere.

★ PILL BOTTLE ★ COTTON

The cotton stuffed in the top of pill bottles can also be reused. Tear it into little puffs for applying make-up or baby oil. Wrap a bit of cotton around the end of a toothpick for an instant swab or a tiny paint-brush. Or soak two clean bits of cotton in cool water and put them on your eyelids when you want a quick refresher.

EMERGENCY BOTTLE. If you have children who like to roam in the summertime, make each one an emergency necklace from an old pill bottle. Use a hot nail to punch two small holes in the cap of the bottle and loop a chain through it. Put a Band-Aid, two telephone dimes, a safety pin, and a tube of first aid cream in the bottle and attach the cap. Your youngsters can wear the bottles around their necks.

MELT A BOTTLE. Plastic pill bottles melt into weird shapes at high temperatures, so kids and adults with kidlike sensibilities like to "bake" them. Put bits of crayon into pill bottles and set them on a cookie sheet covered with foil. Turn the oven to 500 degrees and put the cookie sheet inside. If you have a glass door in the oven, watch while the pill bottles collapse into little puddles. When the puddles harden, drill holes in them and use them as shade pulls, buttons, pendants, and parts for mobiles.

PROFESSIONAL BOTTLE. To make a thermometer holder like they use in hospitals, punch a hole the size of your thermometer in the plastic cap of a pill bottle. Then fill the bottle with cotton soaked in alcohol, cap, and insert the thermometer through the hole. This keeps the thermometer sterile and available.

See also JARS AND BOTTLES; PLASTIC CONTAINERS.

PILLOWS

If you have an old pillow that cannot be saved, let it go out with a flourish. Have an old-fashioned pillow fight and wallop away with that pillow until the seams burst. Of course, before you destroy the pillow, you might consider reuses like these:

HALF A PILLOW IS BETTER THAN NONE. If your pillow has gotten too flat for comfort, shake all the stuffing into one end and stitch across the pillow about an inch above where the stuffing ends. Cut off the extra fabric and cover your new throw pillow.

IT'S WHAT'S INSIDE THAT COUNTS. Most modern pillows are filled with synthetic fibers that don't have much use outside of pillows. Old-fashioned pillows, however, are filled with down, the fine feathers from geese that are so desirable in comforters and outerwear. If you are lucky enough to have several of these pillows, open them up and reuse the down in a vest, a comforter or a pair of booties for winter lounging. Remember that the down will settle if you stuff it into one large space, so quilt your garment or comforter to keep the down spread more evenly.

STUFFED. If the covering on your pillow tears, make a new cover and stuff the old filling into it. If the stuffing gets lumpy, take it out, pour it into a cardboard box, and fluff it up by hand. Then use it to stuff throw pillows, cloth animals, and other small items.

PLASTIC BAGS

Plastic bags are a great household resource, because they can be filled, tied, cut up, flattened, washed, doubled up, sewn, folded, and stuffed. To clean a bag, turn it inside out and toss it in with your laundry. But don't put it in the dryer—just hang it up to drip dry.

FREE BAGGIES. Why buy little bags for leftovers and sandwiches when you can have them for free? Cut down old bread and vegetable bags to about 7 inches long and close the bag with spare bread wrapper tags.

PLASTIC-BACK BOOK. If you want to protect a paperback book without hiding the cover, make a plastic cover from an old bag. Follow the instructions for book covers under PAPER BAGS and use extra tape.

DRIP RUGS. Plastic bags spread on the floor just inside the door on rainy or snowy days provide a waterproof place to leave boots. If plastic bags look tacky to you, turn them into a braided rug. Any lightweight bag can be used, but dry cleaner bags make the job go faster. Cut the bags into strips 6 inches wide and braid them as you would a rag rug. Join strips to each other with plenty of rubber cement.

WATERPROOF IT. When you make tablecloths, bibs, scarves, or other items from scrap fabric (*see* FABRIC SCRAPS), waterproof them with a lining from a plastic bag. Find a bag larger than the item and trace the shape of the part to be lined. Cut out the plastic shape and match it to the original, wrong side to wrong side. Take a ¼-inch seam around the outline of the object on three sides and turn it inside out. Close the fourth side by hand.

PLANT SITTER. If you have to be away and have no one to take care of your plants, put them all in the bathtub and water thoroughly. Then cover the plants with a dry cleaner bag taped to the sides of the tub, to create a mini greenhouse that will keep the plants moist until you return.

STUFF IT. Plastic strips cut from bags can be used to stuff boat cushions, plastic bathtub toys, beach pillows, and other objects that get wet.

★ BAGGED FOR ★ STORAGE

Plastic bags make good storage containers because you can see where everything is and because they conform to the shape of the item, conserving precious storage space. To exploit these features fully, use recycled bags to store
- **Sweaters and other winter woolens**
- **Shoes and boots**
- **Blankets**
- **Balls of yarn**
- **Home-frozen foods**
- **Fabric scraps**
- **Extra pillows, lamp shades, and other bulky items**

RAIN GEAR. Use plastic bags to make impromptu rain gear. Cut a triangle of plastic, 18 inches on its long side, and use it as a rain kerchief. Cut a hole in the top of a dry cleaner bag and pull it over your body as a quick raincoat. (Be sure to cut the hole *before* pulling on the bag, since the plastic is thin enough to cause suffocation.) In an emergency, you can even slip your feet into plastic bags and hold your "boots" on by slipping rubber bands around your ankles. This rain wear isn't exactly fashionable, but it will keep you from getting soaked in an unexpected shower, so carry a set in your car, backpack, or picnic basket.

ONE-LINER. Flat pieces of plastic, cut from bags, can be used to line shelves, picnic baskets, paint trays, and even boots with holes in them. Fasten the liner in place with plastic tape.

PLASTIC ARMOR. Use plastic bags to protect you during a messy job. Wrap a dry cleaner bag around you as an apron and tie the top two corners in a knot. Protect your arms from drips when you paint by pulling on bottomless plastic bags and fastening them with rubber bands. Do the same thing for your pants when you need to kneel in the garden.

COVERED DISH. To make a cover for a refrigerator dish, cut out a circle of plastic 4 inches wider than the mouth of the dish. Hold the cover in place with a rubber band, or sew a ½-inch hem around the edge, thread elastic through the hem, pull it tight enough so the cover will hug the bowl's sides, and tie off the elastic.

PLASTIC CONTAINERS

Plastic containers are a real challenge because they can't be recycled like papers, boxes, bottles, and cans. When you run out of things to do with them, you have to send them to the landfill where they take up precious space because they don't decompose or the incinerator where they give off corrosive gases or melt, clogging grates and vents.

Fortunately, plastic containers are relatively easy to reuse around the house. They don't break like bottles or rust like cans, and plastic is easy to work with. An ordinary kitchen knife or scissors will cut through almost any bottle. For painting and glueing, use cement and paints designed for plastic model building. Both are available in most variety stores and won't rub or wash off the plastic. Indelible felt-tip markers can also be used on plastic—just let the ink dry thoroughly before handling. New reuses for plastic containers seem to appear every day. Here are some favorites:

SUPER-DUPER SCOOPER. Any plastic bottle can be a scoop, but the best ones are made from large bottles with molded handles. Hold the handle up and slice through on a diagonal that begins 3 inches below the handle and ends at the bottom of the opposite side. Use a large scoop made from a bleach bottle or milk jug for pet food, potting soil, rock salt, sand, and compost. Use small scoops cut from syrup bottles for cereal, flour, pasta, and other foods.

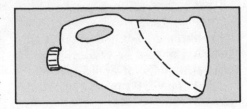

BUOY OH BUOY. Plastic bottles float when tightly capped, so use them as buoys to mark channels, fishing spots, and swimming areas. You can even make an impromptu lifesaver by knotting rope around the handles of four empty gallon jugs and tying them around a little person's waist.

DROUGHT RELIEF. Save a supply of plastic containers to be used in the garden next time rain is scarce. Simply cut off the top of a plastic container and punch several holes in the bottom. When you plant water-loving plants like tomatoes, cucumbers, and melons, sink a container halfway into the soil right next to the plant. Next time you need to water, fill the container with water. Instead of running off, the water will seep slowly into the soil around the roots, where it's most needed.

LOST WAX. Sculptors and others who use the lost wax method can use plastic containers as forms. The plastic disappears when the work is fired.

BANK ON IT. Many plastic containers practically fall over and beg to be piggy banks. To oblige them, cut a slit in one side of the container and glue cork legs to the other side so the bank will stand up. Decorate with felt ears, eyes, and tail.

RECYCLE→RECYCLE→RECYCLE

Plastics have the recyclers stumped. So far, they make up only 4 percent of our solid waste, but the percentage is growing as plastic gobbles up the packaging industry. In 1958, plastic packaging amounted to 736 million pounds; by 1980, that figure had increased to approximately 7.8 billion pounds.

Unlike other forms of packaging, plastic cannot be recycled. Researchers working on the problem haven't come up with an economical reuse partly because the chemical composition of plastic varies. To obtain high-quality recycled materials, the plastic waste must be sorted, creating obvious collection problems. On a small scale, a few companies have successfully collected and recycled easily recognizable containers like milk jugs, fruit trays, and egg cartons. Researchers have also investigated systems for sorting one type of plastic from another.

Still other groups are experimenting with using mixed plastic waste for insulation, packing material, soil conditioners, and low-stress building materials. Another promising possibility is the use of plastic waste to produce fuel through pyrolysis, a thermal decomposition process. For more information about this research, obtain a copy of "Recycling Plastics" from the Society of the Plastics Industry, Inc., 250 Park Avenue, New York, NY 10017.

Plastic recycling may be economically feasible in the future, but it's not workable now so there are virtually no markets for scrap plastic. As a result, most recycling centers will not accept it, and the consumer has no choice but to mix it in with other trash. The only way to be ecologically responsible about plastic is to buy as little as possible and reuse as much as possible of what you must buy.

and containers for all the other supplies you need to store in the bathroom. If you're really ambitious, make yourself a waterproof shower caddy by cutting three containers to the same size, punching holes in their sides, and lacing them together as shown.

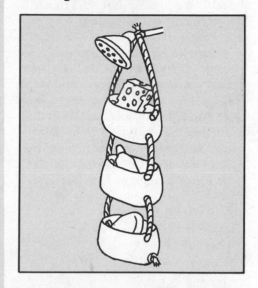

TRAVELING CANDLE. Turn the top of a plastic bottle with a handle into a portable candleholder by slicing off the jug just beneath the handle. Weight the base with clay or plaster and twist the end of the candlestick into the mouth. Don't let the candle burn down to nothing, because the plastic will melt.

STIFFENER. When you need a stiffener for a canvas tote bag, a cloth wallet, or a cap visor, cut a piece of plastic the proper shape from the side panel of a plastic bottle and sew it into the object. The plastic will last longer than cardboard and can even be washed.

SHEET WARMERS. In the nineteenth century, every well-equipped household had ceramic foot warmers, jugs that were filled with hot water and slipped into bed to warm up icy sheets. This is an idea worth reviving, but you don't have to buy an antique warmer. Simply find a large plastic jug with a waterproof cap, fill it with hot—not boiling—water, and pop it into bed ten minutes before you're ready to retire.

PRETTY AS A PITCHER. Most plastic bottles look rather coarse, but with a little skillful trimming you can turn the handled ones into nice-looking pitchers

for picnics, camping, or watering plants. First slice straight across the top, removing the small opening. Then shape the sides and lip of the pitcher into a graceful curve.

BATHROOM PLASTICS. Plastic is an ideal material in the bathroom because it can't rust and won't break. Cut off plastic containers of various sizes to make soap dishes, toothbrush holders,

★ MELT A ★ BOTTLE

Plastic bottles melt when they are exposed to heat, a property that could make them an exciting crafts material. So far no one has exploited the possibilities. All I can tell you is a plastic container placed on a foil-covered cookie sheet and put in a 350 degree oven will melt into a one-of-a-kind blob. Try adding chips of crayon or beads or other small objects to a bottle before melting it to make a paperweight. Or drill holes in your melted bottles and use them as key rings and Christmas ornaments.

★ PLASTIC FOR KIDS ★

Plastic bottles make good kids' toys because they are lightweight, free of sharp edges, and virtually indestructible. Just be sure to wash the container thoroughly.

Pinwheels. Kids never get tired of pinwheels, and you can make an endless supply from old plastic bottles. Cut out the largest square of flat plastic you can from the side of an empty bottle. Cut as shown. Pull every other point into the center and secure with a brad. Pound the brad into a dowel, leaving the plastic loose enough to spin freely.

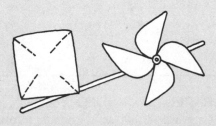

Scoop Balls. You can buy these toys in the store or you can make them from plastic bottles with handles. Just cut the bottom of two bottles off at a slight angle. Give one scoop to each player and let them toss a rubber ball back and forth, throwing and catching it with the scoops.

Solo Scoop. To play scoop ball alone, cut out the bottom of a plastic bottle. Thread a length of fishing line through a cork, tie a knot in the end, and stick the cork in the mouth of the bottle. Attach the other end of the line to a foam rubber ball. Swing the ball into the air and try to catch it in the scoop.

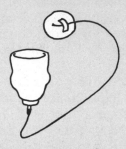

Bowling. Put an inch of sand or water in the bottom of ten plastic bottles and cap them. Arrange them in a bowling triangle and let the kids try to knock them down by rolling a large rubber ball at them.

Critters. A free folder explaining how to make everything from eagles to moose from empty plastic bottles is available from the Consumer Relations Department, Texize, P.O. Box 368, Greenville, SC 29602. Ask for "The Crafty Critters Folder."

PATCHWORK PLASTIC. Some people cut the side panels on plastic bottles into geometric shapes to be used in durable patchwork projects. Use an ordinary paper punch to make holes along the edges of the shape at ½-inch intervals. Then lace or crochet the pieces together with yarn or cord. Admittedly, this technique is not going to produce family heirlooms, but it is useful in making things that ought to be waterproof, such as beach tote bags, picnic placemats, and bathroom window curtains.

APPLE PICKER'S PAL. The best fruit always seems to be at the top of the tree, but that won't bother you if you make a fruit picker from a broomstick and a plastic jug, perhaps a small bleach

container. Poke one end of the broomstick into the mouth of the jug and trim the other end as shown. Then reach up so the picker is directly under a luscious apple, and pull it toward you so the top lip breaks the stem and the fruit drops into the container.

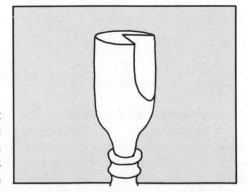

LABELED. The plastic from plastic bottles makes great waterproof labels. Cut out long, narrow triangles for garden markers, rectangles for luggage tags, thin strips for mailbox labels, and so on. Write on the plastic with an indelible felt-tip marker.

★ PLASTIC ★ ARRANGEMENTS

The housewares department of every department store is full of plastic containers for organizing and storing things. You can get the same results for much less money by making your own organizers from empty plastic containers.

Wall Pocket. Make a convenient catchall from a plastic bottle of any size by cutting straight across the front and sides of the bottle with a kitchen knife. Then cut across the back of the bottle, leaving a little tab for tacking it to the wall. Use various-size pockets for matches, keys, coupons, stamps, bills, and other small items.

Paper Holder. To make a simple holder for letters, napkins, receipts, or other papers, cut off the top half of a square-bottomed bottle. Then cut straight down the corners of the bottom half and remove both end panels.

Best Bins. Make bins for vegetables, small toys, and hardware by cutting the tops off large plastic bottles just beneath the handle. Bottles with square or rectangular bases can be further organized in little homemade cabinets. Make the cabinet tall enough to accommodate three or four bins and put furring strips on either side to support the bins as if they were drawers.

★ PORTABLE PLASTIC ★

Plastic containers are so light-weight that they make natural take-along containers. To make your totes look less like plastic bottles, try these ideas.

Basket. Cut across a plastic bottle at a point where the sides are straight. Cut the sides of the lower half into strips of any width. There must be an odd number of strips. Starting at the bottom of the container, weave yarn, ribbon, raffia, strips of fabric, or even plastic bags in and out of the strips. Tuck the ends of the material into the weaving and secure with a dab of white glue. Add a handle made of wire wrapped with the same material.

Caddy. For the simplest tote, cut a plastic bottle to the shape shown and use it to carry cleaning supplies, tools, and so on.

Bucket. Cut across a large plastic bottle at a point where both sides are straight. Use a nail to punch holes just under the rim of the bucket on opposite sides and reinforce them with heavy plastic tape. Make a loop from a piece of coat hanger wire and stick one end through each hole. Bend the ends up to hold the handle in place. Use the bucket for picking berries, painting, shoveling sand on the beach, and so on.

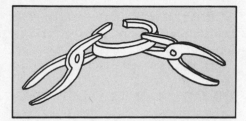

and folding plastic handles, you'll be able to convert toothbrush handles into rings and bangles, needles for crocheting, or shuttles for weaving. File a long, thin handle into a letter opener. Use the curved plastic handles from umbrellas as colorful coat hooks. Make toggle buttons from 2-inch lengths of toothbrush handle, or slice an umbrella handle to make a matched set of buttons for a blouse or skirt. To make button holes, clamp the button in a vise, drill straight through, and run a rat-tail file through the holes to smooth the edges.

PLASTIC LIDS

The plastic snap-on lids that show up on cans for everything from coffee to macadamia nuts are one of the packaging industry's brightest ideas because they make their cans reusable. Even when the can has been appropriated for other purposes, the thin plastic lids have dozens of uses like those that follow:

STACK 'EM. If you buy hamburger in bulk and shape it into patties for freezing, slip a plastic lid between each patty so you can pry off what you need without defrosting the entire package.

SAVE IT. The plastic lids from 1-pound coffee cans fit on motor oil cans so you can save the extra oil next time you have to add half a can to your car or lawn mower.

SINK STOPPER. Lost the stopper for your sink? Set a plastic lid over the drain with its rim down.

KEY THING. If you are always misplacing your keys, make a tag you can't lose by punching a hole in one edge of a plastic lid and stringing it onto your key chain.

CANDLE CONTAINER. Small plastic bottles for toiletries often have pleasing shapes and make fine molds for candles. Cut off the narrow neck of the container, dangle a string wick through the container, and fill with wax (see CANDLE STUBS). When the candle is cool, slit the side of the container and peel away the plastic. Shave off any irregularities with a razor blade.

See also CLEANSER CANS; DETERGENT SQUEEZE BOTTLES; EGG CARTONS; FAST FOOD CONTAINERS; L'EGGS EGGS; MARGARINE TUBS; MEAT TRAYS; MILK CONTAINERS; SODA BOTTLES.

PLASTIC HANDLES

Handles from hairbrushes, kitchen utensils, toothbrushes, umbrellas, and other objects are usually made of thermoplastics, so they can be reshaped. Heat the plastic by placing it in very hot water for three to six minutes, depending upon its thickness. Retrieve the plastic with tongs and shape it with pliers. Plastic handles can also be fastened in a vise and cut with a coping saw. File rough edges with a fine file, smooth with emery paper, and polish with buffing compound.

Once you have the knack of cutting

SCRAPE AWAY. Cut a plastic lid in half with scissors and use the flat edge for scraping cold fat out of pans, leftovers off plates, and batter out of bowls.

INSTANT WASHER. To make a plastic washer, cut a circle of the proper size from a plastic lid. Make the center hole with a paper punch or poke a scissors point through the center and twist to enlarge the hole to the right size.

STENCIL. Plastic lids make fine stencils for letters, numbers, and greeting card designs. Draw the design on the lid with a marking pen and cut out the shapes with a utility knife. Hold the stencil firmly over the object to be marked and paint over it.

★ PUT A LID ★ UNDER IT

Plastic lids can be used to catch spills and drips all over the house. Try using them as coasters for kids' drinks, saucers under plants, spoon rests, drip catchers under paint cans, and mess preventers under soap pads, cleanser cans, cans with bottoms that rust, and sticky bottles.

PLASTIC POUCHES

In the eternal quest for more convenient foods, the packaging industry invented sealed plastic pouches for food. These tough, square bags can be reused if you open them by cutting straight across one edge and then wash them in sudsy water. Use the pouches for home lamination jobs. Slip your driver's license, ID tags for luggage, or other papers that need protection into one corner of the pouch. Trim the two open edges so that they are one inch longer than the card. Press the edges with a warm iron until they melt shut, and then use scissors to trim a quarter-inch border around the card.

PLASTIC TABS

The little plastic tabs that close bread wrappers make wonderful markers if you use an indelible felt marker to write on them. Use scissors to cut two deep slits into the tab at the keyhole end. Then slip a tab over your page in a magazine or on a key folder in a file. Slip the tab keyholes around electrical cords so you don't make toast when you meant to plug in the Cuisinart. The tags can even function as miniature clothespins, so take some along when you travel so you can hang up hand washables.

PLASTIC WRAP

The typical supermarket uses 2,800 pounds of plastic wrap in a year. If you are clever about salvaging their wrappings from vegetables and meat, you won't have to buy the stuff. Remove the plastic wrap by cutting through the seals and seams with scissors. Wash in sudsy water, rinse and hang over a coat hanger to dry. To store the wrap in an orderly way, salvage two aluminum foil boxes with their cardboard rollers. Label one box "small" and the other "large." Store pieces of plastic wrap by rolling them around the roller in the appropriate box. Use small scraps for wrapping cut onions, packing sandwiches, or covering leftover dishes. Large scraps are right for wrapping meat to be frozen, protecting the potato salad at the picnic, and covering the cake pan.

POP TOPS

See PULL TABS

PULL TABS

Pull tabs, the little openers on top of beverage cans, are a particularly pernicious form of litter. Birds and fish try to eat them; bare feet get cut on them. In some states pull tabs have already been replaced with tops that stay attached to their cans, and in others they've been eliminated by returnable-bottle laws. If you live in a state that still tolerates the tabs, turn them in with your aluminum cans (*see* SODA AND BEER CANS) or try reusing a few around the house.

JELLY TAB. If you make your own jelly, embed the flat part of a pop top in the paraffin. When you want to remove the seal, simply pull gently on the ring.

BLOWING BUBBLES. Remember how much fun it was to blow bubbles when you were a kid? You can make those iridescent spheres by dipping a pull tab into a glassful of thick dishwashing detergent. Then pucker up and blow!

PULL CHAIN. To make a lightweight chain out of pull tabs, fold the tab of one top around the ring of the next top and clamp with pliers. Continue until you run out of tops. What use are these chains? Heavy soda drinkers have been known to use them as belts, bracelets, room-dividing curtains, and Christmas tree garlands.

Aluminum pop-tops can become the basis for Christmas ornaments.

Never in Your Wildest Dreams

Several years ago, there was a short-lived craze for making clothes out of pull tabs. If you drink a lot of soda, you can revive the fashion with this simple vest, a classic example of the style. Make chains of rings and link them together with jump rings, available at craft supply stores. This vest is not terrifically comfortable, but it does inspire plenty of conversation.

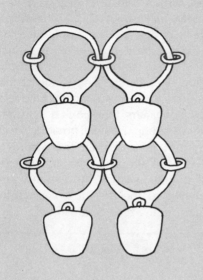

PICTURE THIS. Use the ring from the pull tab as a picture hanger by flattening the tab and tacking it to the picture frame. These little hangers can't be used for really heavy weights, but in our informal test, a single ring did support ten pounds.

PROP TOP. To prop up place cards, frequently used phone numbers, recipes, project directions, and other things, glue the paper to a 3×5-inch card. Flatten a pull tab and glue it to the back of the card so the tab is centered at the bottom of the card. Fold the ring back at a 90-degree angle and set the card on your desk, workbench, or kitchen counter.

PUMP CONTAINERS

Pump containers are preferable to aerosol cans if only because they can be refilled. With what? Here are a few ideas:

QUICK CLEANING. Refill one pump container with a solution of half ammonia and half water and use it for cleaning windows, appliances, and sink fixtures. Fill a second with disinfectant and spray a little on your sponge when you clean sinks and tubs. When you need to clean up pet hair, use a pump container to spray a little water on the carpet or upholstery. The hair will vacuum up more easily.

OILED AGAIN. Keep a pump container filled with cooking oil beside the stove so you can squirt it into your skillet when you need just a drop to keep things from sticking.

WATER PUMP. A pump container filled with water can be used for misting plants, moistening tape or stamps, cleaning small hands on picnics, sprinkling clothes, dampening hair to be curled, cleaning upholstery, and dozens of other chores.

DEATH TO BUGS. Use an old pump container to spray insecticide on your plants. To make your own organic bug repellent, catch two dozen of the offending bugs and put them in 2 cups water. Dump the solution into your blender, whir briefly, and spray on the infected plants.

DYE IT. If you want to dye a small piece of fabric or clothing, spread it on top of a pile of newspapers. Mix up enough dye to fill a pump bottle and spray it onto the fabric. You'll get a unique spatter effect without the bother of dunking and rinsing.

R

RAZOR BLADES

A razor blade too dull to shave your face may still be sharp enough for other tasks, like removing paint from windows, ripping out stitches in clothes, and cutting materials like wallpaper, cork, leather, plastic, and cardboard.

If you use single-edge blades, get a holder from your hardware store. For safety, some models retract the blade when it's not in use. A double-edge blade can be reused safely if you clamp it into a metal spring clip, available in office-supply stores. Alas, there doesn't seem to be any way to reuse cartridge blades, but you may be able to coax a few extra shaves from them if you brush out the stubble with a toothbrush.

RECORDS

When your record collection needs weeding remember records are made from thermoplastics, so they can be reshaped into practical and whimsical objects. To reshape a record, put it on a foil-covered cookie sheet in a 350 degree oven or plunge it into a pan of very hot water. Either way, be ready with a pair of tongs. When the record plastic is pliable, fold it down the center to make a bookend. Or crease two off-center

folds to make a letter rack. Or shape the disc into a gracefully scalloped bowl for fruit or chips at your next disco party!

Once the shape pleases you, hold the record in position until it cools. You can soak off the label and paint your creation, though there's no harm in being frank about the object's origins.

If heating and shaping an old record sounds like loony tunes to you, you can still reuse some of your old platters if you think of them as just that—flat plates of plastic. Here are a few suggestions:

PLATTERS. Wrap an old record in foil and use it as a disposable platter or cake plate when you take food to a potluck dinner or a bake sale.

FRAMED. Make fast and funny frames out of old phonograph records. Draw an 8-inch circle on the picture you

want to frame and cut it out. Spread glue in a 2-inch band around the edge of the picture and center it on the record. When the glue dries, hang the picture from the center hole, slipping the head of a nail through the hole and under the picture.

TURNTABLE. Turn an old record into a lazy Susan that will keep your desk supplies, make-up, tools, or whatever at your fingertips. Use an empty tuna fish can as the base and punch a ¼-inch hole through its bottom. Cut a 1-inch section off a fat spool to sandwich between the can and the record. Find four ¼-inch washers that you've salvaged from an old appliance. Thread a 2-inch bolt through a washer, the record, a washer, the spool, a washer, the can, and a final washer. Add a nut and tighten it so the assemblage stays together but the record turns freely.

REFRIGERATORS

Of all the appliances, refrigerators have inspired the best reuses. It's easy to see why. A refrigerator is, first of all, a big box with a good, tight lid that protects its contents against moisture, insects, and rodents. Also, the box is insulated so temperatures inside can be kept fairly constant. Finally, a refrigerator is full of parts which can be adapted to new jobs: motors, condensers, compressors, freon cylinders, thermostatic switches, copper coils, and more, not to mention the insulation that's between the walls of the box. Think twice before sentencing a refrigerator to the dump. Here are a few specific things to think about.

COOL STORAGE. An old refrigerator makes perfect storage for root vegetables, potatoes, apples, and other winter foods. Remove the latch on the door and the hardware on the back of the refrigerator. Dig a hole in the ground large enough to fit the refrigerator when it's lying down. Lower the refrigerator into the hole by looping a strong rope around one end. Station one person on each end of the rope and two people at the end of the refrigerator. Let the two people at the end shove the refrigerator into the hole while the other two people use the rope to guide the front end. When the refrigerator is in position, fill the cracks around it with dirt. Put your edibles inside, close the door, and cover with hay.

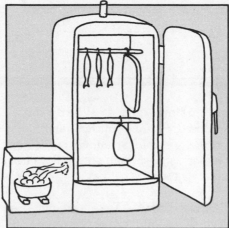

SOLAR MIRACLE. Converting an old refrigerator into a solar collector is a truly satisfying reuse. Several remarkably simple designs have been devised. In one, you simply remove the coils from the back of the refrigerator, embed them in the refrigerator door, and cover the whole with glass. For technical information about building such a collector and hooking it to a hot water or other system, get Issue 48 of *Mother Earth News* by sending $3 to MEN, P.O. Box 70, Hendersonville, NC 28739.

SHOP LOCKER. Use a refrigerator as an extra closet for storing coveralls, heavy tools, and other shop equipment. Drill holes in the metal walls and use toggle bolts to support extra shelves or hangers.

UP IN SMOKE. There's nothing quite like the flavor of home-smoked food, made in your own refrigerator turned smoker. First, remove the compressor at the bottom of the refrigerator. Inside, take out racks, plastic compartments, and the freezer compartment. Stuff mineral wool insulation into vents and ducts. Using a saber saw, cut two 6-inch holes in the walls of the refrigerator, one just above the floor and the other in the

ceiling. Install a vent in the top hole. Rest broomsticks in the supports that held the original shelves, or install closet pole supports. Outside the bottom hole, build a small metal box (an old bread box will do just fine) and make a 6-inch hole to match the hole in the refrigerator. If necessary, connect the two

holes with stovepipe. Build a small fire in the metal box, place a pan of wood chips on the fire, and close the refrigerator door. For information about preparing food for smoking, consult *The Easy Art of Smoking Food* by Chris Dubbs and Dave Heberie (Winchester Press, 1978).

★ DEATH TRAP ★

It's been said many times before, but it deserves repeating. If you have an old refrigerator that's waiting to be reused, be sure to remove the door. Refrigerators are a terrible temptation to children, who can climb inside and suffocate if the door slams.

★ RACKING UP POINTS ★

Those who are intimidated by the thought of turning a refrigerator into a solar collector should take heart. Anyone can reuse a refrigerator rack. Here's how:

- Campfire grill: support the rack on firebricks or stones piled on either side of the coals
- Drying rack: suspend the rack from the ceiling with rope and use it for drying food or hand washables
- Portable cage: wire five racks together at their corners and use the construction as a movable outdoor cage for small animals—kittens, ducklings, rabbits, etc.
- Trellis: fasten a refrigerator rack to a stake with wire and train sweet peas or other vine plants to climb up it
- Window guard: if you have one window that is always getting broken by stray baseballs, tack a refrigerator rack in front of it for the season

RUBBER BANDS

Think of a broken rubber band as a string with stretch. Multiply its length by tying several end to end; increase its strength by braiding three together. Then use your custom-made elastic as an emergency button loop, a snappy drawstring, or a lightweight clamp for things that have been glued together. Here are two other tricks for using up

broken rubber bands:

HOLD THAT LID! To keep pot lids from banging every time you open the cupboard door, screw cup hooks on either side of the lid and stretch a broken rubber band across the bottom of the lid to hold it in place.

TIGHT FIT. If you're trying to replace a screw in a hole that's too loose for it, tie a broken rubber band to the tip of the screw and wrap it around the grooves before screwing it in.

SEEDS

Seeds usually get tossed out with the trimmings from produce, but you don't get maximum benefit from them in the compost heap. Seeds are beautiful as a crafts material, nourishing as food, and, of course, have the miraculous ability to turn into new plants. Here are suggestions for using seeds all three ways:

CHEAP PLANTS. If you love greenery in your home, grow your own from the seeds of avocados, citrus fruits, apples, peppers. For detailed advice on growing throwaway seeds, *see The After Dinner Gardening Book* by Richard Langer (Macmillan, 1971).

FREE VEGGIES. Leftover seeds can also be the basis of a backyard crop of beans or melons if you rescue the seeds before the vegetable is cooked. Wash gently, let them dry, and store in a tight container. There's no guarantee these seeds will produce vegetables—many vegetables are now hybrids. On the other hand, they didn't cost anything, either.

SNACKING SEEDS. Melon, squash, and pumpkin seeds are edible in their own right. Remove the seeds from the parent and rinse. Spread the seeds on a cookie sheet and, while they're still wet, sprinkle with salt and other seasonings. Then pop the seeds into an oven set on its lowest temperature. Check the seeds every hour, mixing them up, until they are thoroughly dry.

SPROUT OFF. Nearly all seeds will sprout under the right conditions, and all sprouts (except tomato and potato) are edible. What's more, sprouts are very nourishing and fun to grow. Try sprouting leftover seeds from peppers, squash, and so on. For directions, *see* MARGARINE TUBS.

SEEDY CHIC. Take advantage of seed shapes and textures by using them in natural jewelry. String the seeds—before they dry, if possible—with a heavy-duty needle and fishing line. A thimble will help you poke the needle through some seeds; others will need a hole made with a hammer and a thin nail. Make necklaces out of watermelon seeds and throw in a few pumpkin seeds for contrast. Or try stringing the kernels from a leftover ear of corn. Or make dangling earrings from citrus seeds with an allspice pod added for texture and scent. Attach the jewelry to clasps salvaged from old costume jewelry and let it dry for several days before wearing.

A FERTILE IMAGINATION. Seeds are also a marvelous material for mosaics and collages. Wash the seeds and allow them to dry for several days. Then glue them in place on a board and protect your composition with clear acrylic when the glue is dry. For inspiration, *see Seed Picture Making* by R. & G. Marsh (Sterling, 1973).

....

SHEETS

Sheets almost always wear out in the center, leaving plenty of flat, no-iron fabric to be turned into scarves, bandannas, aprons, and much more (*see* FABRIC SCRAPS). At the same time, the size and seamlessness of sheets make them especially suited to a variety of large projects. A few ideas follow.

PILLOW TALK. An old sheet will yield at least one and perhaps two pillowcases. Using the edge with the wide hem as the open end of the pillow-case, cut out a piece 42 × 30 inches for a regular pillow. Fold with wrong sides together and stitch up the sides and bottom. Presto! A free pillowcase.

IT'S CURTAINS FOR THAT SHEET. A quick set of café curtains can easily be made out of an old sheet. Use the wide hem as the lower edge of the curtain. Cut the fabric to the desired length, plus 2 inches for the hem at the top. Turn the top edge under and topstitch or hem by hand.

TABLE TRIMMINGS. Convert gaily colored sheets into attractive tablecloths. If you can't find a good piece large enough to cover the entire table, cut a runner from one side of the sheet and make napkins from the other side. Hem the cut edges or finish them with pinking sheers.

ROOM DIVIDERS. If you need a quick divider to create privacy in a bedroom or to make two rooms out of one, make one in short order with old sheet and corrugated cardboard. Fold a double sheet in half, right side to right side, and stitch up each end. Turn right side out. Divide this giant pocket into thirds by stitching two long lines from top to bottom. Measure the pockets and subtract 1 inch from the width. Make three cardboard panels of that dimension by glueing together three sheets of corrugated cardboard for each. Slip the panels into the pockets, trimming if necessary to make them fit smoothly.

RUFFLED. A sheet that is thin at the center but okay on the edges makes a fine dust ruffle for a studio bed. Remove the mattress from the bed and lay the sheet over the box spring. Cut out squares at the corners so the ruffle will hang smoothly and hem the cut edges. Replace the mattress. If this "ruffle" is too plain for your taste, use the sheet as a base and sew on frills.

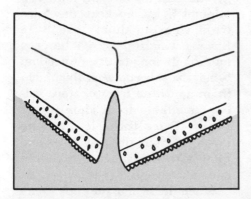

BANNER HEADLINES. An old sheet is often just the thing for making a banner to attract attention to a garage sale, announce a rent strike, or introduce a marching band in a parade. Lay the sheet out flat on a pad of newspapers and paint your message directly onto the fabric.

BLANKET PROTECTION. Old sheets make the best throw covers for protecting things from dust when they are in storage or paint when you're redecorating.

DECORATOR SHEETS. In the last several years, many decorators have noticed that designer sheets look good enough to be used as wall coverings. For such creations, a staple gun is your best ally. Depending upon the composition of your walls, you may need to install thin furring strips so you can tack the fabric to them. Start by stapling the center of the top edge of the fabric where it ought to be. Then straighten the pattern and staple the center of the bottom edge. Stretch out the two sides, pulling the sheet taut, and staple each of them at the center. Now, go back and staple the loose parts, placing the staples every 6 inches and smoothing as you go. When you're finished, mist the sheet with water. It will shrink just slightly as it dries, smoothing out any imperfections.

BED SHEET HAMMOCKS. Need extra beds or chairs in a new apartment, a country place, or a weekend retreat? Make them easily with old sheets, rocks, pieces of rope, and molly-bolted hooks. To make the hammock, fasten hooks securely in two walls that are about 6 feet apart. Gather the sheet together at one end and tie with a cord about 8 inches from the edge of the sheet. Fold the end of the sheet over a rock and tie a knot around the sheet just below the rock. Tie another rope under the rock and use it to suspend the hammock from a hook. Repeat the procedure at the other end of the sheet. To convert the hammock into a hanging chair, fold the sheet in half. Wrap one rock at the end of the sheet and one at each of the two remaining corners and hang the sheet from three ceiling hooks, arranged in a triangle.

What could be simpler than this sling seat, made from an old sheet?

IN THE BAG. To keep the inside of your sleeping bag clean, make a liner from an old sheet. Fold a twin sheet in half and stitch across the bottom and halfway up the side. Cut six pieces of bias tape and sew them to the sheet at all four corners and halfway up both sides. Sew six more pieces of tape to corresponding spots on the inside of the sleeping bag. Tie the tabs on the liner to the tabs in the bag. When the liner gets grimy, just untie the tabs, pull it out, and wash.

GIANT LEAF BAG. The easiest way to scoop up old leaves in the fall is to spread an old sheet on the ground and rake the leaves right onto it. Then gather the four corners of the sheet and haul the leaves to the compost heap.

SHOE BOXES

Shoe boxes have to be the world's most reusable boxes, thanks to their convenient size, compact shape, sturdy construction, and tight-fitting lids. Here's a sampling of potential projects:

REINFORCEMENTS. When you want to carry something heavy in a grocery bag, slip an empty shoe box into the bottom to strengthen it.

THE TRAVELING BOX. Turn an old shoe box into a lunch box, a tackle box, or a portable sewing kit. Paint the box and seal it with acrylic. Cut a slit just wide enough for an old belt in the top of the box at each end. Slip a belt through both slits and around the box. Buckle it at one end. To fill the box, unbuckle the belt and lift the lid.

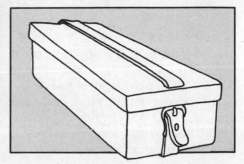

PROJECTOR PROJECT. If you have a camera but no slide projector, you can make a workable substitute from a shoe box. Cut a round hole at each end of the box, one to accommodate a flashlight and one to hold a camera lens. Mount the lens and flashlight, using tape and cardboard supports as necessary. Put the lid on the box, turn on the flashlight, and point the lens at a wall about 5 feet away. Move the box nearer and farther from the wall until the image is sharp. Mark the spot where the image is best and set a table there. Now hold a slide inside the box and move it until you get the best image on the wall. Mark the spot on the floor of the box. To build a slide carrier, cut out four strips of heavy cardboard, 3 inches tall and 4 inches wider than the shoe box. Cut notches centered on the strips. In two strips, the notches should be 1¾ × 1¾ inches. In the third strip, the notch should be 2 × 2 inches. Sandwich the three strips together with the 2 × 2 notch in the center and glue. Cut a slot in each side of the shoe box at the point where you made your mark so the slide carrier will slip in and out easily. Now put a slide in the carrier, turn on the flashlight, and project it on the wall. This projector is frankly primitive, but it works well enough for the once-a-year slide show or for the person who wants to project a slide as the basis of a wall painting.

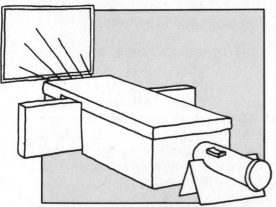

KRAZY KITS. If you can't think of a gift for a friend, make up a customized kit and package it in a shoe box. A kitchen kit for newlyweds would contain a can opener, a wire whisk, and other utensils. A kit for an indoor gardener could hold all the things necessary to make a terrarium, and so on.

LIFETIME FILE. A shoe box is just the right size for holding canceled checks, note cards, recipes, receipts, and other small pieces of paper that need to be kept in order.

★ THE BASIC BOX ★

You can put almost anything in a shoe box, but it seems made to order for:

- **Dominoes and other game pieces**
- **Silverware for picnics**
- **Spools of thread, wire, fishing line**
- **Keepsakes**
- **Hardware salvaged from old appliances**
- **Sets of wrenches, ratchets, and screwdrivers**
- **Photographs**
- **Attachments for drills, sewing machines, food processors, etc.**
- **Cookies**

SHOES

Shoes are among the hardest things to throw away. Sometimes they just didn't fit right in the first place, so you haven't worn them and they sit in the closet accusing you of bad judgment. Other times they've taken on the shape of your feet and are so comfortable that you wear them every day even though there's a quarter-sized hole in one sole.

Unfortunately, there isn't much to be done with old shoes, except salvaging the leather (*see* LEATHER) or using the soles to extend the life of other shoes. Other choices are more whimsical.

BURY MY SHOE. Leather is an organic material, so leather shoes—not plastic imitations—will eventually decompose. To make the most of this fact, try burying old shoes in the garden.

SHOE FLY. Leather makes a dandy flyswatter. Cut the tongue out of a large shoe and staple it to a slat of wood.

★ BE YOUR ★ OWN COBBLER

When you fall in love with a pair of shoes, delay the inevitable as long as possible. If the uppers come unstitched, use a heavy needle to thread fishing line through the original holes. To keep the soles from wearing down, use Sole Saver, a wonder paste that hardens into tough, long-lasting protection. When the soles do wear thin, build them up with a layer of crepe soling, available from shoe repair shops. Trace the sole onto the crepe, cut out the new sole, and glue it to the shoe with rubber cement.

When the heel of the shoe wears down, replace it with tread from an old tire. Cut through the sidewalls of the tire to get a flat section of tread. Pry off the old heel with a screwdriver, trace its shape on the tire tread, and use a utility knife to cut out the shape. Put the shoe upside down on the end of a 2 × 4 so you'll have a surface to pound against, and find some wide-headed nails long enough to go through the tread and into the shoe but not through it. Position the heel on the shoe and pound in nails at ½-inch intervals all the way around. Use the utility knife to trim off any tire tread that protrudes from the side of the heel.

THE WELL-SHOD PLANT. Some people find it amusing to use old shoes as cachepots for plants. If you are one of them, seal the shoe with a coat of acrylic. Cut off a plastic container so it fits inside the shoe. Pot the plant in the container and conceal it in the shoe.

SENTIMENTAL SHOE. If an old pair of shoes has sentimental value because you met your lover, ran for public office, or won the Boston Marathon while wearing them, fill the toes with plaster of paris, cover the shoes with clear acrylic, and use them as bookends.

SOLES GO SOLO. Produce a pair of slipper socks by marrying a pair of old shoes to a pair of heavy wool socks. Use a razor blade to cut through the stitching that attaches the soles to the shoes. Stitch the soles to the sock bottoms with carpet thread and a heavy needle, using the holes from the original stitching. These cozy socks will last for ages.

★ IF THE SHOE ★ DOESN'T FIT . . .

Don't toss out a pair of shoes because they cramp your feet. First try these remedies:

- If the shoe is too tight on your toes, wad up several pieces of newspaper and moisten them with water. Stuff the balls of newspaper as tightly as you can into the toes of the shoe and let them sit until the paper dries out.
- If the heel scrapes the skin off the back of your foot, moisten the inside of the back of the shoe. Heat a piece of flat metal (perhaps an old knife) over the stove and rub it over the inside of the heel, smoothing out the stiffness and stretching it slightly.
- If home remedies don't work, take the shoes to a shoe repair store, where they'll have special machines for adjusting tight shoes.

SHOWER CURTAINS

When you replace your shower curtain, keep the old one. Where else are you going to find a free sheet of heavy-duty plastic that can be used to protect anything and everything? If the shower curtain is mildewed, disinfect it by soaking it for a couple of hours in a bathtub filled with warm water and vinegar. Scrub away the stains with mild detergent and hang the curtain in the sun to dry. Then store it until you need a spatter cloth for furniture in a room that's being painted, a ground cloth for your sleeping bag, a tablecloth for the picnic table, or a cover-up like those that follow:

PRIVACY, PLEASE. If you need a dressing room at the beach or on a camping trip, hook an old shower curtain to a Hula Hoop, using the original shower curtain hooks. Hang the screen from a tree branch with clothesline.

SHOWER CAPER. Looking for cheap rain gear? Make a cape out of an old shower curtain. Drape the shower curtain over your head so that the top edge, with the hook holes, forms the front opening of the cape, and have someone cut the bottom off to the right length. Find two jar lids that just fit through the hook holes. Punch holes through their centers, thread a short piece of cord through the holes, and knot it. Use the lids as fasteners at the top of the cape, and add extras if you need them.

DEFROSTER. If you hate the task of scraping ice off your windshield on winter mornings, outwit Mother Nature with the help of your old shower curtain. Cut a section of plastic that covers the windshield and hangs down on each side. Hem the plastic and slip strong magnets into the hems. Then spread the plastic over the windshield in the evening, using the magnets to anchor it on the car. The magnets won't hold in a gale, but on calmer nights they'll keep the windshield free of frost and snow.

DRAFT DODGER. Hang an old shower curtain behind lightweight draperies in the winter. The extra layer creates a pocket of dead air that helps insulate the room from the cold air outside the window.

NECK-TO-KNEES APRON. To make a full-length apron for really messy jobs, cut a cobbler pattern from your shower curtain and attach ties at the top and the middle so you can tie the apron around your neck and waist. If you like, add a plastic pocket or two.

SUMMER SHOWER. Keep an old shower curtain handy to cover outdoor equipment—bicycles, barbecue grill, lounge chairs—during sudden summer showers.

BIG BAG. Turn a shower curtain into a bag for beachware, laundry, diapers, or storage. Fold the curtain in half and cut it off to the desired length. Stitch up the bottom and side. Turn the bag inside out and thread a cord through the holes at the top.

SILVERWARE

After a few years of housekeeping, everyone ends up with extra pieces of battered silver (or stainless) that don't match the main set. The best reuses of these items exploit their specific forms, but there are more general possibilities. For example:

HANDLE WITH CARE. The handles from old pieces of sterling silverware can be fashioned into elegant rings for fingers, napkins, or curtains. Cut the handles from the silverware with a hacksaw and pound the ends flat with a ball peen hammer. Anneal the silver by heating it with a small blowtorch until it is red hot. When the silver is cool, bend it at a right angle and shape it into a ring by pounding it with a rubber mallet around a pipe of the right size. If making a ring seems too difficult, cut the handle off shorter, smooth the cut edge, drill a small hole through the top, and use the piece as a pendant on a silver chain.

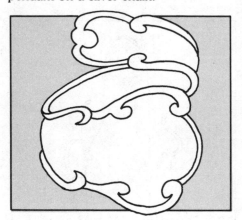

WINDWARE. Old silver makes a lovely tinkling sound when it swings freely. To make a set of wind chimes, use a power drill to make small holes in the handles of forks and spoons. Hang the utensils from the tines of a serving fork with monofilament fishing line.

IT'S CURTAINS. The handles from old forks and spoons make elegant tiebacks for curtains. Cut off the bowl or tines of the implement and hand drill a hole through the handle near the cut. Bend the handle so the leg with the hole is longer than the other leg and you'll have room to insert a screw through the hole and into the window frame.

An odd spoon becomes a unique curtain tieback.

CAMPING WARE. Pull out those extra pieces of silver and divide them into knife, fork, and spoon sets. Slip each set into an empty toothpaste box and put it in the picnic basket. Next time you head for the great outdoors, everyone will have a boxed set of silver at mealtime.

See also FORKS; KNIVES; SPOONS.

SIX-PACK PLASTIC

The plastic rings from six-packs of soda or beer are remarkably strong. If you use mostly returnable bottles, you'll only have a few and can use them to support small hanging planters (*see* LIGHT BULBS), or to hang signs from doorknobs—staple a ring to the top because the plastic is less likely to tear.

If you consume many six-packs, start saving the plastic for a hammock like the one described by Jean Ray Laury and Joyce Aiken in *The Pantyhose Craft Book* (Taplinger, 1978). To make the hammock, cut old pantyhose in half and tie the legs together until you have eighteen 6-foot lengths. Lay out sets of rings with their long sides touching until you have a row 5½ feet long. Lay a second row of rings over the first, staggering them so each set of six overlaps four of the original rings. Tie two pantyhose legs to a metal ring and twist them into a rope. Weave the rope in and out of the first row of rings, and when you get to the other end, tie a second ring to the rope. Repeat the process for the second row of rings. Then lay down another row of plastic overlapping the empty row of rings and weave stockings through it. Continue the process until you have nine strands of nylon woven through the hammock. Tie a strong rope through the rings at the end of the hammock and hang the hammock about 5 feet above the ground. Get in. It will stretch a lot but it's comfortable—and cheap.

SLACKS

See PANTS

SOAP BITS

Even the fanciest soaps end up as soap bits—scraps and slivers too little to lather. Our thrifty ancestors solved this problem with "soap savers," little cages that held odd bits of soap. When she needed suds, Grandma swished the soap saver through the water. Today, soap savers can be ordered from the Cumberland General Store, Crossville, TN 38555, for about $3.95. If that seems like an extravagant way to recycle soap, you can get similar results by tying your soap bits in an old nylon stocking. Let the stocking dangle in the water for a moment before you swish for suds.

Here are other uses for old soap:

SQUEEZE-UM SOAP. To make liquid soap, break soap scraps into even smaller bits and put them in an empty detergent bottle. Fill the bottle with warm water and let it sit for a day or so. Then set the bottle by the bathroom sink and squeeze out soft soap for washing.

BARGAIN BAR. To make new bars of soap from bits, save all the scraps in a can with the label removed. When it is three quarters full, set it on the stove and turn the heat on low. When the soap melts, stir it gently and pour into Styrofoam cups. Let the new soap harden and peel away the molds.

NEATER NAILS. Keep several small bits of soap in a box next to the sink. Before doing a greasy, dirty job, run your nails across the soap bits. Later when you wash, the dirt will come easily out from under your nails.

SLIPPERY SOAP. Soap is an effective lubricant that won't stain what it touches. Rub soap on the runners of a drawer that won't slide. Stick pins and needles through soap scraps to make them pierce fabric more easily. Or rub soap over the threads of a stubborn screw or onto the base of a light bulb going into a sticky socket.

See also SPONGES.

••••••••••••••••••••••••••••••••

SOCKS

No one knows what happens to the partners of the mateless socks at the bottom of the laundry basket. Fortunately, there are plenty of things to do with single socks. Think of the toe of the sock as a little sack and the cuff as a warm ring of stretchy fabric. Then it will seem natural to use the socks for these and other jobs:

BLANKET PROTECTION. If you have a lot of odd socks, try making them

into a comfy, curious afghan. Cut the cuffs off the socks and whipstitch around three sides of each cuff with contrasting-color yarn. Stuff the resulting pockets with old stockings and whipstitch them closed. Make one hundred of these puffs and stitch them together into an afghan.

★ THOSE DARN ★ SOCKS

Many a worn sock could be salvaged by reviving the respectable art of darning. Darning, an ideal television-watching job, requires only rudimentary needle skills. Instead of regular thread, use darning cotton (available at notions counters), because it will make the darned spot softer and easier to walk on. For the same reason, don't tie a knot in the thread. Instead, take three tiny stitches, one on top of another, to secure the end. Put a darning egg—a burned-out light bulb is a good substitute—into the sock and stretch the hole over it.

Now make one row of small horizontal stitches directly above the hole. Move down 1/16 inch and take several small stitches on one side of the hole, run your thread over the gap, and take several more stitches on the other side. Continue this pattern until the entire hole is covered with parallel threads about 1/16 inch apart. Now repeat the sequence vertically, but instead of leaping over the hole, weave the vertical threads over and under the horizontal threads. When you're finished, the hole should be filled with a flat, rewoven patch. Obviously, darning is easier when the hole is little, so catch holes before they devour the sock!

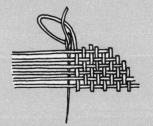

★ GETTING THE ★ MOST FROM YOUR SOCKS

One way to eliminate the aggravation of mateless socks is to buy all your socks in one color. If one gets lost or wears out you can match its mate with any of the others.

SOCKS FOR TOTS. Use old socks to make cheap but endearing toys for children. To make a sock puppet, pull a sock over your hand and stitch on buttons and bits of felt for eyes, nose, and tongue. If you want your puppet to have a proper mouth, poke the toe of the sock in and take a few quick stitches along the side to hold it in place. Sock dolls are almost as easy as puppets. Make a 3-inch cut in the cuff of a sock. Then stuff the toe and tie it with yarn to make a neck and waist. Sew up the inseam of the legs and stuff them, too. Add arms made from a second sock and sew on buttons for the face. Still another sock toy is a hobbyhorse, made by stuffing a sock and inserting a broomstick into one arm of the L. Tie a stout string around the horse's neck and leave a loop for reins. Sew on appropriate features, including a mane made from yarn.

A SOCK AND A PROMISE. When you want to make a quick job of dusting, pull an old sock on your hand and run it over the furniture. Use the old sock-on-the-hand trick for polishing metal, too.

SOCKS FOR YOUR HEAD. A warm ski band is easily made by cutting the foot off a knee sock and sewing the ends of the long portion together. Making a stocking cap is not much more difficult. Start with a pair of large socks and cut off an 8-inch section from each cuff. Cut the sections down one side and sew them, right sides together, to make one large tube. Now make small stitches around the cut edge of the tube and pull the thread tightly to gather the material. Turn the cap right side out and add a pompom made from scrap yarn (see YARN).

NO-SCUFF SOCK. When you have to move heavy furniture, slip old socks over the legs to keep them from marring your floors. Similarly, slip socks on the upper ends of the ladder so it won't scratch the siding when you lean it against the house.

WINDBREAK. Cut the cuffs out of old socks and sew them into the sleeves of coats and jackets to keep the wind from rushing up your arms. If it seems like too much trouble to sew the cuffs in place, you can get a similar result by leaving the socks intact and cutting finger holes in the toes. Pull the socks over your hands so your fingers stick out through the holes and the cuffs reach up to your elbows. When you put your coat and gloves on over the socks, there won't be any gaps for the wind to find.

SOCK COZIES. If you want a cute little cover to keep a mug or a baby bottle warm, cut the cuff off the sock, turn under the raw edge, and stitch it with elastic thread. Pull the thread so the sock end is gathered and tie it off. Slip the jacket over the glass or bottle. For mugs, add a slit for the handle.

TURN ABOUT. Shoes usually go over socks, but there's no reason not to slip old socks over shoes before packing them in a suitcase or simply to protect them in the closet.

IT'S A DIRTY JOB. Keep two socks in the back of the car and pull them over your hands when you have to change a tire or brush snow off the windshield. Indoors, keep old socks to cover your shoes when you do messy jobs like painting.

CANDLE CANS. The lightweight metal in aluminum soda cans is easy to cut and shape, and the size is just right for making old-fashioned candle-holders. Use tin snips to trim the can into the shape shown. Cut a 1 × 5-inch strip of metal from the discarded section of the can and bend ½-inch tabs at either end. Make slits in the back of the holder, insert the tabs, and glue them in place with epoxy. To hide the tabs and brighten the reflection, cut a liner for the back panel from a piece of foil and glue it in place. Add a bottle cap to hold the candle and you've made a new lamp for romance or emergencies.

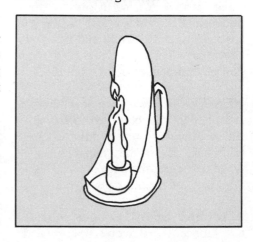

FLOWERS THAT BLOOM IN SPRING. To plant spring bulbs the required depth underground, turn a steel soda can into a tool that cuts through the earth and pulls out a plug of sod. Use tin snips to cut off the bottom rim of the can, leaving the sharp edge sharp. If you dent the can in the process, straighten it with pliers. To plant a bulb, press the open edge into the ground, twisting slightly as you go. Plant the bulb and cover with the soil in the can.

SODA AND BEER CANS

Whenever possible, buy beverages in returnable bottles. When you do buy cans, remember the aluminum ones are a good source for lightweight metal that can be easily cut. The Chinese noticed that right away. When Coca-Cola first became available in China, the thrifty Chinese immediately started splitting the cans to make mudguards for bicycle fenders. If your beverages come in steel instead of aluminum cans, don't despair. The steel cans have sharp edges when they're cut open, so they can be used in cutters, choppers, and scrapers.

Never in Your Wildest Dreams

It's a bird! It's a plane! It's a Toobee! That's what they've been saying in California ever since a couple of entrepreneurs invented what they hope will be the outdoor fad of the decade. Their product is a small aluminum cylinder made—you guessed it—from beer and soda cans. Lest you try to duck their $3 price tag by cutting your own can in half, the inventors are quick to point out that their Toobee is aerodynamically designed and carefully filed to eliminate sharp edges.

RECYCLE→RECYCLE→RECYCLE

More and more beverage cans are made of aluminum, a relative newcomer in the world of cans. Although there is some doubt about whether cans are the best containers for beverages, there is no doubt about the value of recycling aluminum. Last year community groups and individuals earned $45 million recycling cans. Aluminum companies also appreciate the economic advantages; using recycled aluminum instead of aluminum ore saves 95 percent of the usual energy costs.

For that reason, all major aluminum companies have sponsored recycling programs since the early 1970s, and one can in four is recycled. The companies pay about 23 cents a pound for clean beverage cans as well as other aluminum scrap, such as pie plates, foil, frozen food containers, aluminum siding, lawn furniture, gutters, and so on. It takes about twenty-four 12-ounce cans to make a pound.

How can you tell an aluminum can from a steel can? Aluminum cans are softer and lighter and have no side seams. The foolproof test is magnetic—a magnet will not stick to the sides or top of an all-aluminum can.

Twenty-one hundred recycling centers across the country take aluminum. To find out about the one near you, call the Aluminum Association. To get their toll-free number, call 800-555-1212.

The major aluminum companies sponsor regular programs to collect and recycle aluminum soda and beer cans.

SODA CAN CAPS. A few years ago the craze was beach caps made from soda and beer cans. To make one of these caps, cut the name panels from eight cans and punch holes in their edges, ½ inch apart. Lace or crochet the panels together. For more detailed instructions, order "Aluminum Can Apparel" (HA 34) from Craft Course Publishers, 260 South Paseo, Tesoro, P.O. Box 74, Walnut, CA 91789.

Beer drinkers who are loyal to one brand of brew can wear matching accessories.

SODA CAN SNAKE. Turn half a dozen soda cans into a lovable toy. Find a piece of scrap fabric 2 feet longer than all the cans stacked end to end and wide enough to encircle a single can. Fold the fabric in half and make a running stitch up the long side. Turn the tube right side out and tie off the bottom with yarn or string. Insert one can and tie a second piece of yarn right above it. Keep adding cans and tying yarn between them. Stuff the last section of the tube with nylon stockings, sew it shut, and decorate the face with buttons. If you think you can stand the racket, put pebbles or dried beans in the cans before sewing them in.

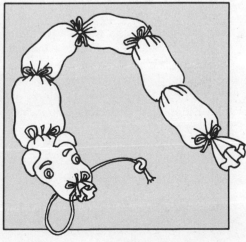

To "canstruct" a single house, architect Mike Reynolds uses thousands of aluminum cans.

SOLAR CANS. Aluminum cans are being taken seriously as a building material. Mike Reynolds, a New Mexico architect, builds walls by cementing cans side by side and covering the exterior with adobe. With 75,000 cans, he can construct a one-bedroom house, at a cost of about $17 per square foot. More important, when the cans are filled with water and sealed, they become thermal collectors. Other inventors have extended the idea, building Trombe walls and other solar collectors from water-filled cans. One Illinois school district modified the idea a little by building a solar collector from 24,000 beer cans, cut in half and riveted to secondhand litho plates. The collector worked just fine, saving the school thousands of dollars in heating costs.

THAT'S A POINT. Once a pull tab can has been opened, the lid of the can has a V-shaped hole that's perfect for sharpening large crayons and other soft writing instruments. If you want a really sharp point, file the edges of the can.

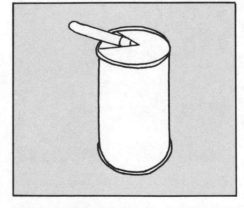

SODA BOTTLES

Ever since the soft drink industry introduced plastic liter bottles, craftspeople have been busy slicing, snipping, and otherwise mutilating these bottles. The soda bottles are unique among plastic containers because they are transparent and they have nifty black snap-on bottoms. Those two properties inspire uses like these:

MINI TERRARIUM. The bottles practically beg to be turned into terrariums. Pry off the black bottom and cut off the clear bottle to be 6 inches tall. Fill the black dish with potting soil—it already has drainage holes—plant some little plants, and invert the clear bottle bottom over it.

TRUNK PROTECTOR. The trunks of young trees often need winter protection from rodents and summer protection from lawn mowers and weed trimmers. To provide both, cut the top and bottom off a plastic soda bottle. Slit the bottle up one side and lap it around the tree trunk. Secure with twine if necessary.

GROW BOTTLE. The liter bottles can easily be converted into hot caps by cutting them off about 4 inches from the top. Invert over tender young plants on nippy spring nights.

BUG TRAP. To make a trap for Japanese beetles or other garden pests, cut three 4 × 4-inch openings in a plastic soda bottle just above the black base. Punch a one-inch hole in the lid of a large jar and screw the neck of the bottle into the lid. Make a narrow bag from a nylon stocking or mesh bag and stuff it with beetle lure, available in any garden supply store. Hang the bag of bait inside the cut-out soda bottle and hang the entire contraption from a tree.

BOTTLED LIGHT. If you need inexpensive lanterns for your next outdoor party, make them from liter bottles. Cut off the bottle at the rim of the black bottom. Drill a hole through the center of the black dish and through the bottom of a juice can. Run a long bolt through the hole in the black bottom, the neck of the other half of the bottle, and the hole in the can. Tighten down and set a votive candle in the open end of the can.

See also PLASTIC CONTAINERS.

SOFAS

See FURNITURE

SPICE CONTAINERS

Spices and herbs are packaged in appealing containers, so it's hard to throw them away. To prevent uncontrolled accumulation of little jars and tins, consider buying spices in quantity and refilling old containers. Remember, too, that the metal tins with pry-off lids make fine waterproof containers for stamps, matches, and other small objects. Shaker containers with screw-on caps can be refilled with lemon pepper, cinnamon and sugar for toast, and other homemade seasonings. Keep extra shakers refilled with salt in your desk drawer at work, in the glove compartment, and in the picnic basket. Fill a larger container with seasoned flour and sprinkle it on meats that need to be browned. Keep toothpicks in a large-hole shaker so you can shake out just one when you need it. Fill a shaker with seeds when you're planting wide rows.

See also CANS.

SPONGES

Cellulose sponges generally disintegrate, so you don't have to throw them out. If a sponge does outlive its original purpose, you can take advantage of its obvious ability to soak up water, as well as its interesting texture, with uses like these:

STICKER LICKER. Next time you need to seal a lot of envelopes or put stamps on all the Christmas cards, spare your tongue by cutting a chunk from an old sponge and glueing it to a jar lid. Fill the lid with water and run each envelope's edge over the sponge.

SPACKLE SPONGES. Extra sponges are ideal for texturing paint on walls, furniture, and other projects. Just press the sponge into the wet paint and pull it up. Press and pull. For that matter, when painting difficult things like wrought iron railings or curlicued furniture, cut a sponge into little pieces, put on rubber gloves, and then use the sponge to do the painting. When a piece gets sticky, toss it out and pick up another.

SILENT SPONGE. Cut a badly worn sponge into little squares. Glue the squares to the bases of appliances that are noisy and the frames of doors that slam.

GERMINATION TEST. Want to use last year's seeds in this year's garden? Before going to the effort of planting, test the germination rate by cutting a sponge in half and putting half a dozen seeds between the halves. Keep the sponge moist but not soggy. Check the seeds at the end of the germination period listed on the label. If less than half have sprouted, buy new packets.

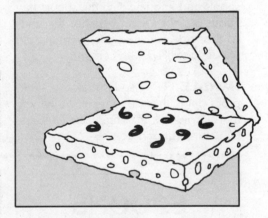

SNORE NO MORE. To cure the snorer in the family, sew a chunk of old sponge into the back of his pajamas so it will touch the sleeper between the shoulder blades. When the snorer rolls onto his back—snoring position for most people—the sponge will produce just enough discomfort to make him flip onto his side.

SOAPED UP. When a sponge is wearing at the corners, trim them off with a heavy pair of scissors. Then slit the sponge with a knife and slip soap scraps into the pocket. Use the soaped-up sponge for cleaning sinks, walls, countertops, and so on.

SPOOLS

Empty spools have a way of vanishing from the sewing kit and reappearing in the toy box. That's not such a bad fate. Kids use spools as beads, blocks, and wheels for homemade vehicles, and they don't seem to care whether the spools are made of wood or styrofoam. If you don't have children to confiscate your spools, find adult uses for these shapely cylinders and their predrilled holes. Spools can be rollers, pegs, and spacers as well as all the things listed below.

POOL SPOOLS. Spools float, so you can use them as bobbers on fishing lines. Try jamming pencils and the handles of other waterside tools through spools so they'll float if they're dropped into the water. If you have a lot of spools, make a float rope to mark the boundary of a swimming area by threading a nylon cord through the spools and knotting it so the spools stay about 6 inches apart. Anchor the ends of the rope with weights, perhaps old plastic jugs filled with cement.

HANDLE IT. A spool makes a heat-proof pot lid handle to replace a handle that's broken or missing. Fasten it to the lid with a nut and bolt.

NIFTY KNIFE RACK. Make a neat and easy knife rack by nailing two rows of spools to a wall or the inside of a cupboard door. Arrange the spools so their rims touch—the space between their cores will still be large enough for the blade of a knife.

BEADS AND BAUBLES. Spools have always been used as beads by small children, but wooden ones can also be adapted to adult crafts like macramé. Carve and cut the spools into interesting shapes and stain them dark colors.

PULL IT. Spools, used whole or cut in half, make quick handles, knobs, and drawer pulls. Use them to replace original hardware in an emergency or to finish off homemade designs. Simply screw them down, inserting a screw ½ inch longer than the spool through the center hole.

KNIT WIT. Even people who have no patience for needlework can make braided straps, belts, and "macramé" with a spool knitter. Pound five brads into the top of a large spool, equidistant from each other. Thread the end of a ball of yarn through the spool and make a slipknot around one brad. Loop the yarn around the other brads. When you come to the first brad, use a crochet hook to pull the lower loop up and over the brad. Move on to the next brad and pull the lower loop up and over. As you continue this process, a cord of knitted yarn will form inside the spool. Pull the "tail" so it emerges at the other end of the spool. Make it as long as you like and tie off the ends when finished. Long tails can be coiled into coasters and hot pads. Slip-stitch the coils together.

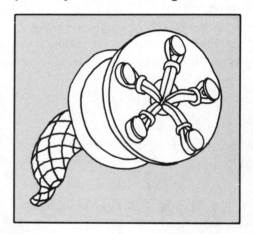

See also STYROFOAM; WOOD SCRAPS.

SPOONS

Extra spoons can be used for all the ideas listed under SILVERWARE and for special projects like these that take advantage of their sensuous shape:

SPOONDANT. A spoon makes a smooth, seductive base for a pendant. Cut off the handle of the spoon where it joins the bowl and drill a hole through the bowl near its upper edge. Use a ring to hang the spoon from a silver chain, and glue a three-dimensional treasure—perhaps a polished stone or a piece of coral—in the bowl.

SKIMMER. Often a slotted spoon is

Odd pieces of sterling silverware can become the basis for distinctive jewelry.

more useful than an ordinary tablespoon. To convert the latter to the former, hold the spoon in a vise and cut slots in the bowl with a hacksaw.

Smooth off rough edges with steel wool and use the spoon for skimming foam off jelly, retrieving bay leaves from sauces, and so on.

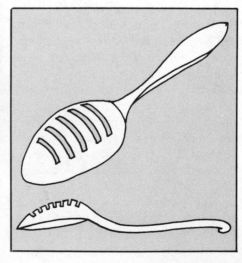

BURNISHING BOWL. The smooth bowl of a spoon makes a handy tool for smoothing out aluminum foil or papers that have been glued together.

PINNED. To keep pins at your fingertips when you sew, make yourself a tiny pincushion that will fit into the bowl of a spoon. Bend the handle of the spoon to fit over the arm of your chair or your wrist and glue the pincushion into the bowl with superglue.

See also METAL SCRAP; SILVERWARE.

STOCKINGS

Of all the things people buy, few wear out as quickly as nylon stockings. Most women complain about their fragility and wear them anyway. Until someone invents an indestructible pair of pantyhose, most women will need an inexhaustible supply of ideas about what to do with snagged, ripped, and "runned" stockings.

Fortunately nylon is a loosely woven, easily washed fabric with a somewhat rough texture. Further, a stocking is constructed as a long, narrow bag that can be stretched, filled, or twisted into a rope. If those characteristics don't suggest dozens of household uses for old stockings, use these starter ideas to jog your imagination:

HANDY WIPE. Stuff a sponge inside an old stocking and use it for washing windows, dishes, the car—anything. The rough texture of the stocking helps with difficult dirt.

MOTH ALERT. Fill the toe of an old stocking with mothballs and tie a knot at the top. Throw the stocking over the bar in the closet.

STOCKING STUFFER. Use cut-up stockings to stuff homemade pillows, quilts, and toys. The nylon stuffing is tough, lightweight, and—best of all—washable.

BACK SCRATCHER. Take advantage of the rough texture of nylon to make an after-bath buffer that will remove dry skin. Simply tie each end of a nylon leg to a plastic ring, cut perhaps from six-pack plastic or saved from cellophane tape. Throw the nylon over your shoulder and pull it vigorously back and forth.

FIT TO BE TIED. Stockings are stronger than string but just as flexible, so you can use them to tie up bundles of newspapers for recycling, boxes that need to be moved, and almost anything else.

THE STRAIN OF IT ALL. Old stockings can be used to strain lumpy paint or filter gasoline. Just stretch a panel of nylon over the mouth of the container.

TIEBACKS. Stockings are soft but strong, so they make good ties for holding up plants. And while we're in the garden, make a plant duster by filling a nylon stocking with powdered insecticide and jiggling it over infested plants.

MOP TOP. To make a lightweight mop that's washable and easy to wring out, cut the tops and feet off eight or nine stockings. Knot the stockings together in the middle and use an extra stocking to tie the entire bunch to the wire contraption on the end of your mop.

GONE FISHING. Make a free fishnet for your home aquarium by cutting the toe out of a stocking, making a loop in a piece of hanger wire, and whipstitching the stocking to the loop.

HAIR TODAY. If you need to hold your hair in place while you run, swim, or clean house, make a lightweight hair net out of a stocking. Cut a 6-inch section from one leg and tie off one end with a piece of yarn. Turn the stocking inside out and slip it over your hair.

LOST AND FOUND. Next time someone loses a contact lens, stretch an old stocking over the nozzle of the vacuum cleaner and move it gently over the rug. The suction will locate the missing lens and hold it against the stocking. Obviously, this trick works equally well with stray needles, screws, and other small objects.

★ PANTYHOSE ★ CRAFTS

If you go through a lot of stockings, get *The Pantyhose Craft Book* by Jean Ray Laury and Joyce Aiken (Taplinger, 1978). Even people who don't wear stockings will be amused by their playful and practical suggestions. The authors start sensibly with basic techniques like dyeing, cutting, and braiding and then apply the techniques to dozens of projects. Believe it or not, stockings can be turned into sandals, curtains, handbags, hats, halters, rugs, placemats, and fantasy figures.

Directions for making soft sculpture like Margaret Trembley's "Sister" can be found in The Pantyhose Craft Book.

STRING

Saving string is a classic sign of thrift. It also makes good sense, because bits of string can solve so many irksome problems. Many of the best ideas about reusing string apply to highly individual problems—using string to tie back the curtain that's flapping over the stove or to hold together the rungs of a chair while you glue it. The quick ideas that follow are more general. If you don't have a string long enough to try one of them, tie two or more pieces together with square knots. If your string doesn't seem strong enough for the job you have in mind, twist several pieces together. Then use the string as a

- Clothesline
- Tieback for a climbing plant
- Shoelace (dip the ends in nail polish)
- Cord for ceiling light
- Plumb line (tie a weight to the end)
- Fishing line
- Candle wick (*see* CANDLE STUBS)
- Package tie
- Drawstring (*see* FABRIC SCRAPS)
- Tie for recycled newspapers
- Dishcloth (crochet string into a loose square)
- Patch for volleyball and other kinds of nets
- Poultry truss
- Door quieter (loop one piece of string around both doorknobs so the door won't slam shut)

Never in Your Wildest Dreams

Francis Johnson started saving string because he hated to throw it away. Now, hundreds of miles of string later, he can't throw it away because the ball of string weighs five tons and is eleven feet tall. The Johnson ball of string is reportedly the largest in the world and has to be rolled with a special hydraulic roller.

★ STRUNG OUT ★ ON MACRAMÉ

Those who take the time to learn macramé can turn leftover bits of string into belts, necklaces, plant hangers, table runners, handbags, vests, hammocks, and placemats. Wash the string if it looks dingy. Use warm, sudsy water and hang it up with a weight, perhaps an old key, tied to the end so it will dry straight. String can also be dyed for special effects. To learn about macramé, consult any of the following books:

Macramé Accessories: Patterns and Ideas for Knotting by Dona Z. Meilach (Crown Publishers, 1972).

Creative Macramé Projects by Charles Barnes (Dover, 1976).

Craft of Macramé by Helene Bress (Scribner's, 1977).

STYROFOAM

Styrofoam, Dow Chemical's brand of plastic foam, is a popular form of packaging because it's lightweight, shock-resistant, and doesn't absorb water. Thin sheets show up as meat trays, produce containers, and egg cartons; fat chunks come packed around stereos; and little pellets are often used to cushion packages. Styrofoam can't be recycled on a large scale, so it's up to each household to reuse as much of the stuff as possible. Fortunately, Styrofoam is easily cut, carved and reshaped into models, mobiles, and projects like these:

STYROFLOAT. Styrofoam floats, so it's a natural material for homemade tub toys. Add a toothpick mast and a paper sail to make a clipper ship from a chunk of foam. In the pool or at the beach, string pieces of Styrofoam on nylon rope to mark the edge of a swimming area. Knot the rope around each piece of foam to keep it in place.

STUCK UP. Use flat pieces of Styrofoam as inexpensive bulletin boards. Attach the board to the wall with two-sided tape and replace it when it gets full of holes. Chunks of Styrofoam also make good catchalls for pins, tacks, and other sharpies. Glue one in the corner of your miscellany drawer and save yourself a lot of pricked fingers.

SHREDDED FOAM. Styrofoam of all sizes can be shredded by cutting it with a knife or putting small chunks in the blender. Use the pellets to pack fragile objects that must be mailed. Or mix them into heavy soil to texturize it. Or, use Styrofoam as artificial snow at Christmas.

PLANT PELLETS. Styrofoam pellets make an excellent drainage material for planters, especially the large tubs so popular on city terraces and suburban patios. A 4- to 6-inch layer of Styrofoam doesn't add extra weight to the planter but protects the roots of the plants from excessive moisture.

THRIFTY CRAFTS. Styrofoam cubes, spheres, and cones are the basis of many craft projects. Instead of buying these shapes, carve them yourself from leftover Styrofoam. Remember too that Styrofoam is a good rainy-day craft material for kids. Use flat pieces to make gliders and "paper" dolls. Use chunks for quiet blocks.

FOAM FURNITURE. Families that accumulate a lot of Styrofoam should try stuffing it into free-form furniture, like bean bag chairs. Break up and save all the Styrofoam that comes into the house until you have several boxes full. Stitch up a casing and stuff it with foam.

This furniture is lightweight, comfy, and inexpensive, especially if you use recycled fabric. For design suggestions, see *The Craft of Soft Furniture* by Anne Wyke (Hutchinson, 1978).

POINT PROTECTION. Chunks of Styrofoam can be used to keep knives, scissors, and other sharp instruments clean, dry, and out of harm's way. Just plunge the blade into the plastic.

See also COFFEE CUPS, STYROFOAM; EGG CARTONS; MEAT TRAYS; SPOOLS.

★ STYROFOAM ★ STRATEGIES

Styrofoam is easy to cut and carve, so you can use leftover pieces to make toys, models, decorations, and craft forms. Although the "official" tool for Styrofoam cutting is a hot-wire cutter, you can get good results with a sharp knife lubricated with a bar of soap. Razor blades and utility knives also make clean cuts. If a cut edge shows signs of crumbling, seal it by heating the bottom of an old can and pressing the Styrofoam against the hot metal. To make holes in Styrofoam, heat a sharp instrument and poke it through the foam. To join two pieces, use ordinary white glue.

SWEATERS

Be careful about reusing sweater material. All fabrics ravel, but sweaters are woven more loosely so they ravel quicker. One false move and you're left with a tangle of yarn. To prevent such mishaps, whenever possible make new seams before you cut into the fabric, and bind all seams and cut edges with purchased seam binding or strips of fabric cut from old sheets.

WINTER WEAR. Need a ski mask, a pair of mittens, a set of heavy socks?

Make them from old sweaters. Turn a sweater inside out and lay it flat on the table. Use the ribbed edge of the sweater as the cuffs of the mittens or socks or the neck of the ski mask. To make mittens, trace around your hands with chalk, allowing a generous length of fabric at the wrist. For socks, draw two sets of parallel lines 4 inches apart and join them with a curve at the top. For the ski mask, draw parallel lines 17 inches long and 10 inches apart and join them with a curve. Stitch along the lines you've

made and cut ½ inch outside the seam. Bind the seam. Turn the mittens and socks right side out—they are ready to wear. Reverse the ski mask and pull it over your head. Use the chalk to indicate where your eyes and mouth are, stitch around the lines, cut out the holes inside the stitching, and bind the edges.

LOOK FOR THE SWEATER LINING. A cardigan too disreputable to appear by itself can function as the lining of a not-so-warm winter coat. Put on the sweater, slip the coat over it, and take them off together. Tack the sweater into the coat at the cuffs, neckline, and lower edge.

LONG JOHNS. It's no secret that an old sweater can be concealed under almost any top for extra warmth. What's not as widely known is that a sweater can warm your other half too, with a little modification. Turn an old sweater inside out, pin the neckline closed, and stitch an arc around it. Trim off the excess material. Cut cuffs and waist from a second sweater and use them to extend the legs and top of the first sweater. Taper the sides of the underwear and trim off excess fabric. Sew a thick piece of elastic around the waist and pull on your drawers. There's no denying this underwear looks weird, but it's warm and cheap.

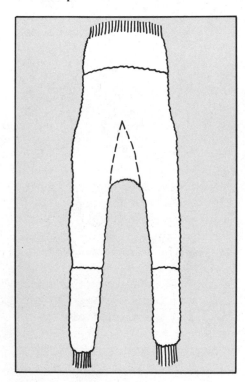

ELBOW HOLES. Sweaters always wear out first at the elbows. To stall the process patch the sleeves with squares of leather salvaged from a boot or handbag. Or make a vest by cutting off the sleeves just above the armhole and hemming the raw edge.

FOOT WARMERS. If your feet are always cold, make a set of foot warmers from your old sweater. Cut two 10 × 10-inch pieces of fabric from the sweater. Fold each piece in half and stitch up the short ends. Turn the top down 1 inch and stitch around it to make a casing. Cut the seam just enough to get into the casing and thread elastic through it.

Tighten the elastic until the opening is about 4 inches long and tie it off, concealing the knot in the casing. If you want to shuffle around in these slippers, stitch on a sole cut from a hot water bottle or an old handbag.

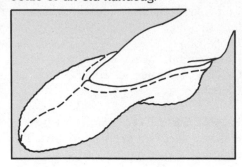

TOASTY TUBES. To make knee, elbow, or ankle warmers from an old sweater, simply cut off the sleeves, hem the cut edges, and pull the tubes of fabric over the cold joints.

Americans discard 200 million tires every year. Since tires aren't biodegradable, they are one of our most exasperating disposal problems. They can't be thrown into the ocean, because they float; they can't be used in landfill, because they make the ground mushy; and they can't be burned, because they pollute the air. As a result, 2 billion tires are sitting around in unsightly heaps waiting for someone to discover a use for them. If you have a new idea, contact the Rubber Manufacturers Association, 1901 Pennsylvania Avenue NW, Washington, DC 20006, a group that functions as a clearinghouse for information about scrap tire reuse.

Meanwhile, use the available tech-

★ COMING ★ UNDONE

A bulky sweater with a hole here and there can be unraveled and the yarn salvaged for other projects (*see* YARN). Carefully cut through the stitching joining different sections of the sweater. Then cut straight across a row of stitching just above a hole. Find a loose thread and start unraveling. As you free the yarn, wrap it around an old hanger stretched out to form a square. When all the yarn is wrapped on the hanger, suspend it over a pot of boiling water so the steam will smooth out kinks.

TABLES
See FURNITURE

TIES
See NECKTIES

TIRES

nology by retreading tires whenever you can. Ordinarily, the tread of a tire wears out first, because it's in constant contact with the road. If the rest of the tire is sound, the tread can be replaced, extending the life of the tire and delaying the cost of replacing it. About 25 percent of all discarded tires could be salvaged as retreads. To decide whether your tire qualifes, examine the carcass for cuts or tears in the bead, holes or exposed tire cords in the casing, and deep surface cracks in the sidewalls. If your tire is free from those defects, find someone to restore it by looking in the Yellow Pages under "Tires, Retreads and Repairs." Even if you don't want to use the retread yourself, these shops will usually trade in the old tire toward a new one.

Even if you can't retread your tire, you can probably still reuse it. Tires are flexible but tough enough to be used as a construction material. One man built a durable stairway from tires by embedding them in the side of a hill and filling them with earth. Another designed a swinging fence that can't be washed away when his creek floods. A few companies are still making tough rubber doormats out of old tires, and one man claims he can make canoes by bolting strips of tread together and sealing the joints with a plastic waterproofing compound.

The number of things you can do with your old tires increases significantly if you know how to cut them up. Before cutting, remove the rim from the tire and take out the inner tube, if there is one. If you are cutting only one tire, do the job with a sharp kitchen knife or a utility knife, but if you are cutting several use a saber saw. To separate the tread of the tire from the sidewalls, plunge the knife into the tire at the edge of the tread and saw up and down, making the cut as smooth as possible. If you are cutting a steel-belted tire, have wire clippers on hand to snip the cables.

Having mastered cutting, you are ready to move on to specific projects. Here are suggestions:

KID STUFF. Kids have been swinging on tires for years. More recently, innovative designers have created more ambitious playground equipment by stacking and bolting tires into bridges, tunnels, steps, walls, climbers, and barricades. Remember that tire constructions should always be anchored securely. Paint the tires white so they won't get hot in summer, and drill holes in them so rainwater can escape. *Playgrounds for Free,* a book about constructing playgrounds out of all kinds of used materials, including tires, is available from Playground Clearing House, Inc., 26 Buckwalter Road, Phoenixville, PA 19460.

TREAD ON ME. Pieces of tire tread can be glued or nailed to outdoor ramps, docks, garage floors, and stairways to improve your footing.

Old tires are an ideal material for playgrounds because they are cheap, durable, and versatile.

★ THE SOLAR ★ TIRE

Kurt J. Wasserman, publisher of *Solar Age,* has patented a solar collector made from worn-out tires. His invention, called the Solartorus, involves stacking the tires so their black surfaces absorb heat. The heat collects in the central hole of the stack and can be used to warm air or water.

BUOY OH BUOY. Because they float, tires can be used as buoys, channel markers, or indicators at the edge of a swimming area. Drill holes in the tires so they won't fill with water and sink. To make them more visible, paint the tires with white waterproof paint. Then anchor them with a weight—perhaps an old bleach bottle filled with cement and tied to a rope—so they don't float away with the tide.

★ HOW TO GET ★ MORE MILES FROM YOUR TIRES

Experts estimate that you can get 30 to 40 percent more miles from your tires—and be faced with disposal less often—if you follow two simple rules. First, keep the proper air pressure in your tires at all times. The recommended pressure for the tire is printed on its sidewall, and you should check once a month to see that the pressure in the tire is the same as what's recommended. To get an accurate reading, check a cool tire that has been driven no more than a mile. In other words, if you live more than a mile from your service station, get yourself a pressure tester—they cost about $1.50. Second, rotate your tires. All tires except radials wear more evenly if you switch their position once every 5,000 miles.

RUBBER PLANTER. Tires are often converted into functional, all-weather planters for the lawn. For this reuse, leave the rim in the tire and lay it on its side. Planters are usually cut into a zig-zag pattern, though you can try other variations. Cut through the sidewall of the tire so the tip of each zig touchs the rim and each zag meets the tread. Next, have a strong friend help you turn the tire inside out, exposing the smooth inner side, which can be painted if you like. The rim of the tire forms the bottom of the planter and has drainage holes.

HEAVY STORAGE. If you need storage bins instead of planters, follow the procedure described above, making a smooth cut around the tread of the tire. Cover the container with a second tire and use it for gravel, outdoor equipment, tools, and so on.

TIRES IN THE GARDEN. Inventive gardeners have figured out lots of ways to use tires to grow more vegetables. First, convert a tire into a solar greenhouse by laying it on its side. Fill the lower rim with water and cover the top with plastic. Set the greenhouse over young seedlings or transplants and they won't be damaged by chilly weather. A tire buried halfway makes a raised garden for vegetables that like to wander and keeps them more compact. Tires can also be used as supports for tomatoes—just slip the tires over them as they grow.

Never in Your Wildest Dreams

Cecil Heidelberger started collecting tires during World War II, when the government paid a penny a pound for the rubber. When the war ended, Heidelberger kept collecting. People often paid him to haul away used tires. After twenty-five years, he'd accumulated 20 million on his twenty-three acres in Minnesota and made a nice living doing it. The living turned even nicer when the International Tire Recycling Company offered Heidelberger over a million dollars for 12 million of his tires. The company will shred the tires and use the fragments to make pressed rubber products; Heidelberger will use the newly freed space for his next collection—junked cars.

RECYCLE ➞ RECYCLE ➞ RECYCLE

On average, each American discards one tire every year. Tires are tough to recycle because most are made of metal *and* rubber, so they're heavy and expensive to ship.

Still, tires have been converted into fishing reefs, crash barriers, floating pipelines, artificial turf, road-surfacing material, adhesives for plastic tiles, and more. Another alternative—destructive distillation—reduces tires to their chemical components so they can be reused to make new tires. Under controlled conditions, tires can even be used as fuel. Pound for pound, they produce more BTUs than coal, but the conversion process is still too expensive to be practical.

Unfortunately, none of these processes are profitable yet, so only a handful of companies are working with them. If you live near a Goodyear, Firestone, or other rubber plant, you might contact them to see if they collect secondhand tires.

BUMPERS AND BARRIERS. Boaters have always used sections of tire to keep their boats from scraping against the dock. Do the same thing in a narrow driveway or a snug garage by cutting the tire into curved pieces. Nail the pieces to the wall at the level of your bumper. Cabdrivers and others who have to drive in heavy traffic sometimes reverse this procedure and bolt the pieces of tire directly to the car.

On a larger scale, tires have been used as crash barriers around bridge abutments, highway signs, road dividers, and so on. The tires, which are bound together with steel cables, absorb the force of the crash and bring the car to a gradual stop. In communities where people can be persuaded to donate their tires, these barriers are a cheap way to save lives. For more information about constructing highway impact barriers from scrap tires, write to the Research Division of the Goodyear Tire Company, 142 Goodyear Boulevard, Akron, OH 44316.

ON THE FENCE. If you need a cheap fencing and don't care too much what it looks like, use the strips of tread from old tires as the crosspieces between posts. Position the posts as far apart as the diameter of the tires and nail the tread in place.

UP ON THE ROOF. If you have a lot of old tires, consider using them as roofing material. Some people nail long strips of tread to the roof in an overlapping pattern, adding roofing tar to fill the cracks. Others turn tires into roofing tiles by cutting them into 8-inch sections and nailing them in a one-up, one-down pattern.

★ THERE'S MONEY ★ IN THEM THAR TIRES

A few entrepreneurs have turned old tires into good businesses. One business involves picking up old tires at service and auto repair stations—some will even pay to have them carted away—and selling the good ones to retread shops for about a dollar apiece.

For a second business, people collect old tires, split them with a special machine, and use the rubber to make things like gaskets and doormats. In 1945, one hundred and twenty-five small companies were splitting tires and turning them into new products. Today, only five or so are in operation. The raw materials for this business are abundant, so if you can find a market for the product, you've got it made.

FISH STORY. Fish love to spawn in the cavities of old tires, so throwing a tire or two into the pond will probably encourage game fish. To be sure the tires stay on the pond bottom, weight them with rocks or cement. Waterfront communities may also want to collect large numbers of tires for artificial reefs. The Rotary Club in Marathon, Florida, for instance, recruited volunteers to build an underwater reef from 5,000 junk tires, and the fish population exploded.

Fish congregate in reefs made of old tires fastened together.

WOOD SPLITTER'S PAL. If you need to split wood for kindling but aren't awfully accurate with an axe, stand the pieces of wood on end inside a tire, packing them just tight enough so they won't fall over.

FOOT TREADS. The tread on an old tire can be used to repair worn soles on shoes (see SHOES). You can also make a tough pair of sandals entirely from an old tire. Use a linoleum knife to cut a 2-foot piece of tread. Trace the shape of each foot on the tread and cut them out. Cut two Y-shaped strips of inner tube and insert them into slits you've made in the foot-shaped pieces of tread. Staple

the ends of the inner tube strips to the bottoms of the sandals.

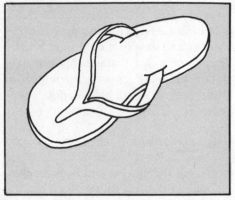

See also INNER TUBES.

TOOLS

Good tools are expensive, so it's worthwhile to use old tools, either those you have on hand or those that invariably show up at garage sales and auctions. To recondition a rusty old tool, start by soaking the metal part overnight in a bucket of used motor oil. Then sand off the rust with a wire-wheel attachment and an electric drill. Finally, take the tool apart so you can clean under nuts and around handles. While the tool is apart, refinish wooden handles and resharpen cutting edges with a flat file. (For complex cutting tools like saws, you may want to get a professional sharpening—check the Yellow Pages under "Sharpening Service.")

Broken tools that cannot be repaired can sometimes be reclaimed for parts. Power tools, for example, yield the same assortment of screws, switches, cords, and motors found in other appliances (*see* ELECTRICAL APPLIANCES). Hacksaw blade fragments can be bolted to short handles and used to cut, file, or clean otherwise inaccessible places. For the most part, the uses of broken tools are highly individual, depending upon the parts you have and the jobs you need to do. For additional suggestions, consult *The Recycling, Use and Repair of Tools* by Alexander Weygers (Van Nostrand Reinhold, 1979), and *Handmade Tools* by Keith Daniels (Lost Data Press, 4410 Burnet Road, Austin, TX 78756).

TOOTHBRUSHES

Lots of annoying cleaning jobs can be done in a flash with an old toothbrush. You need a for instance? Here are eleven cleaning chores for which a toothbrush is invaluable if not indispensable.

- Typewriter keys—use a little alcohol to dissolve the dirt
- Around the faucets and between the tiles in the bathroom
- Telephone dials
- Elaborate carving on wood furniture—spray a little polish on the brush

- Blender and food processor blades, cheese graters, and food grinders
- Costume jewelry—try a bit of baking soda to get out the dirt between the stones and their settings
- The crack on shoes where sole meets leather
- Battery terminals in your car
- Around the burners on the stove
- Your fingernails
- Between the blades on double-edge razors—if you brush out the stubble, you'll get extra shaves

See also PLASTIC HANDLES.

TOOTHPASTE TUBES

Most toothpaste tubes are now made of plastic so they can be reused rather easily. The first step is to open the tube by cutting off one end with a pair of scissors and rinsing out the inside with warm water. If you cut off the nozzle end, you're left with a plastic sheath that can be used as a protective covering for a knife, a pair of scissors, or even a toothbrush when you go traveling. If you cut off the other end, you have an empty squeeze tube that can be refilled with anything—grease for lube jobs, putty for repairing cracks, caulk for weatherstripping windows, even frosting for decorating cakes. Clean the tube carefully, using an old toothbrush, if necessary, to clean out the nozzle. Fill the tube two thirds full, roll down the open end, and squeeze gently.

★ SOLDER ★ SUBSTITUTE

Toothpaste tubes that are made from metal can be used as a solder substitute. Cut off the end of the tube, rinse out the paste, and scrape off the printed coating on the outside. Then heat the tube with a blowtorch and use the molten metal as you would any other kind of solder.

TOWELS

Towels are, of course, flat fabric, but their absorbency makes them specially suited for reuses like those described here.

CLEAN UP. The nap in terry cloth makes it ideal for scrubbing and dusting. To get rid of cobwebs, for example, make a cover for your broom from an old towel and sweep out those hard-to-reach ceiling corners.

ETERNAL TOWEL. Tired of picking up towels after the kids (or grownups) have used them? Solve the problem by piecing together a patchwork of scraps from old towels until you have a strip 6 feet long and 2 feet wide. Sew the ends of the strip together. Install brackets in the bathroom so you can have a removable towel rack—perhaps the roller from an old window shade. Slip the towel loop over the rod.

OLD TOWEL ROBE. A serviceable robe can be made from worn-out towels. Start with a simple kimono pattern. To make the pattern fit your body, measure your arm length and the length from neck to ankle. Trace a full-size pattern on newspaper. Cut out the good sections from old towels and arrange them on the newspaper until you have covered the pattern. Stitch together the pieces of terry cloth. Now fold the pieces at the shoulder, right side to right side, and make two long seams, from the hem of the robe up the side and under the arm. Hem all rough edges, turn the robe right side out, and belt with a cord.

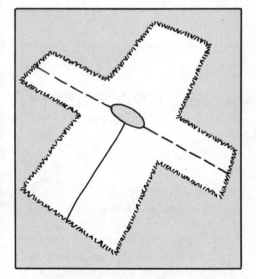

SWEAT MOP. Make a quick sweatband from an old towel by cutting off a 6-inch strip from the long edge and folding it in half lengthwise. Fold the strip in half again to conceal the cut edges and stitch the open edge shut. Tie the band around your head or cut it to fit and sew it shut with a piece of elastic.

FACE SCRUBBER. Towels tend to wear out in the center, leaving plenty of good material around the edges. Trim off that material and cut it into squares for washcloths. Turn the edges under and hem. If washcloths seem dull, make a bath mitt by folding a rectangle of fabric in half, sewing up the sides, and rounding off the top corners. Trim the seams and turn right side out.

BATH MAT. Make an inexpensive rug to drip on when you get out of the shower by piecing together the good sections from two or three old towels. Arrange the patchwork so it is the same size and shape as another old bath towel. Sew together the patchwork and press open the seams. Hold the patchwork right side to right side with the bath towel and stitch around three sides. Turn right side out and hem the fourth side by hand. Tack the back panel to the front at half a dozen places to keep them from slipping around.

SILENT SHELVES. Line shelves in your kitchen, bathroom, or bedroom with old towels. It cuts down on clatter when you remove objects and provides a nice soft storage surface.

••••••••••••••••••••••••••••••

TOYS

Really good toys—those sturdy enough to survive a childhood—should be recycled by passing them on to a new child. If you don't know children of the appropriate age, donate the toys to community groups that distribute gifts to needy kids at Christmas.

Unfortunately, most of today's toys

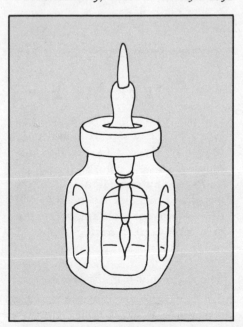

★ NEVER TOO YOUNG ★ TO LEARN

Making toys from "trash" is a good way to teach kids about recycling and the problems of solid waste. Another good way is to take advantage of special educational materials. You can order single copies of the materials described below to use with your own kids, or talk to their school about incorporating them in a science or social studies curriculum.

"Don't Waste Waste" is a packet of materials about solid waste problems and solutions. It's aimed at grades 4–6 and costs $3. Environmental Action Coalition, 417 Lafayette Street, New York, NY 10003.

"The Importance of Being a Garbologist" is a twelve-page pamphlet that intersperses activities with its information. Aimed at grades 4–6, it costs 25 cents. Group for Recycling in Pennsylvania, P.O. Box 7391, Pittsburgh, PA 15213.

"Reduction, Re-use and Recycling: The Three R's to the Best Use of Earth's Finite Resources" is a twenty-five-page book describing a long-range plan for teaching resource conservation to grades K–12. Cost is $2.50. Department of Education, Environmental Education Section, 942 Lancaster Drive NE, Salem, OR 97310.

"Connections: A Curriculum in Appropriate Technology," for grades 5–6, is available for $5 from the National Center for Appropriate Technology, Box 3838, Butte, MT 59701.

break easily and can't be repaired or recycled. You can salvage parts here and there—wheels from toy trucks, markers from games, and clothes from dolls—but otherwise there isn't much to do with broken toys. Still whenever possible, it's important to show children that their own possessions can be recycled as they outgrow them. For example, the swing set your son loved at seven can be turned into a backstop when he's ten if you remove all the swings and stretch a netting across the back of the set's skeleton. The bottle your child used as a toddler can become a paint pot when she's a preschooler. And so on.

Many child-development experts also recommend letting children create their own toys from household discards. The open-endedness of empty boxes, bits of string, spools, and other found materials encourages resourcefulness in children. When their efforts are rewarded with parental enthusiasm, children will find it perfectly natural to make their own playthings. The suggestions in the box are classics, but don't limit yourself to them. Here are a few of many ideas:

ABACUS DABACUS. A simple abacus to teach counting can be made from small spools, coat hangers, and a wooden frame, perhaps an old picture frame made from thick wood. Drill two sets of $1/16$-inch holes on opposite sides of the frame, leaving a little more than a spool's width between the holes. Cut pieces of wire half an inch longer than the frame is wide. String spools or half spools onto the wire and insert its ends into the holes you drilled.

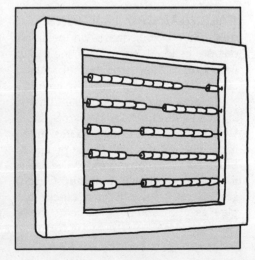

★ TOY BOX ★

Kids can make toys out of almost anything that isn't sharp or coated with toxic paint. The discards listed below have time-tested appeal.

- Oatmeal boxes for drums
- Thread spools for wheels on homemade vehicles
- Old magazines for scrapbook pictures
- Shoe boxes for saving things
- Old clothes for dress-up
- Socks for puppets
- Buttons for necklaces
- Window shades for pull-down blackboards
- Egg cartons for saving things
- Milk cartons for blocks
- Clothespins for dolls
- Cardboard boxes for looms
- Fabric scraps for doll clothes
- Old pots and pans for banging
- Plastic squeeze bottles for squirt guns
- Margarine tubs for saving things
- Old sheets for tents
- And so on and so on . . .

CARDBOARD COMMUNITY. Big appliance boxes make natural playhouses for kids. Turn the box on its side for an instant residence or be more civilized and cut doors and windows into the box with a kitchen knife. With a little poster paint, a box becomes a post office, a store, or a stage for puppet shows.

CALENDAR CALCULATIONS: Cut up the numbered squares on the calendar so children can make their own flashcards. Older children can turn a calendar into a bingo game by cutting 4 × 4 blocks out of six months and marking the squares randomly with S, M, T, W, Th, or F. Mark the squares in the remaining months with the same letters, but make them correspond to the day of the week they really represent. Cut the second set of months into blocks and play as you would an ordinary bingo game.

BIG FOOT. Turn cast-off tennis rackets into snowshoes for your kids. Cut off the handles from two wooden rackets and use leather thongs to lace them to your child's feet, tying one thong around his toes and a second around his ankles. These shoes won't carry a kid down the Yukon but they're fun to tramp around in, and the neighbors will be flabbergasted by the footprints in your yard.

PUZZLED. For an older child, use two 6-inch nails to create a classic puzzle. Hold each nail in a vise and bend it into the shape shown by hammering it around a quarter-inch pipe. Leave a gap that is too small for the nails to slip through. The object of the puzzle is to free the two nails. In case the ten-year-old asks for help, here's how you do it: Bring the points of the nails together, pass one behind the other, and pull it around so the heads and loops of the nails are aligned. Slip the heads of the nails through the loops and they should be free.

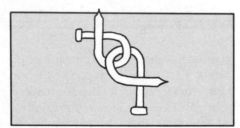

DEXTERITY. Anyone with a decent hardware collection can rig up a dexterity board for a small child. Start with a piece of plywood, sanded and painted with bright lead-free paint. Drill holes in the board and thread bolts of various sizes through them so the shaft of the bolt protrudes through the front of the board. Add nuts of corresponding sizes for the child to screw on and off the bolts. Screw on a hinged door with a funny picture under it, a hook and latch, an old doorknob that turns, a chain lock, and anything else you can think of.

If you need still more ideas, consult any of the following books:

Making Things: The Handbook of Creative Discovery by Ann Wisemen (Little, Brown, 1973).

"Toys, Fun in the Making," a free booklet available from the Government Printing Office, Washington DC 20402.

reSTORE Booklet, available for $2.50 from the Maryland Committee for Children, The Chocolate Factory, 608 Water Street, Baltimore, MD 21202.

Teachables from Trashables by Emma Linderman, Gryphon House, P.O. Box 217C, Mount Rainier, WA 20822.

T-SHIRTS

T-shirts do, of course, make wonderful dust rags—they are soft, easy to wash, and dust clings to them. But there are other alternatives. If you're handy with a needle, try alterations like those suggested below. Also, a T-shirt that is no longer a suitable body covering can be used for covering something else. Here are suggestions:

FANCY T. Cover little holes and other minor imperfections in a favorite T-shirt with embroidery.

LOOK MA, NO SLEEVES. When your T gets tatty around the armholes, snip off the sleeves, making a curve that goes from under the arm to a point 3 inches from the neck hole. Trim the armholes and perhaps the lower edge of the shirt with bias tape so they won't ravel.

★ COLOR ME T ★

T-shirts tend to fade, spot, and bleed in the wash. If that's your reason for discarding one, dye, dye again. Choose a color that's a little darker than the original and follow the directions on the package. If the original color complements the dyed color, try batiking the shirt (see CANDLE STUBS). Or make patterns by tying the shirt into knots before you put it in the dye.

PILLOW TALK. If your favorite T-shirt shrinks in the wash, stuff it. Turn the T-shirt inside out and stitch up the bottom. Stitch the sleeves shut just below the armholes. Turn the T-shirt right side out and stuff it through the neck hole with old stockings or polyester fill. Whipstitch the neck closed and toss your new pillow on the sofa.

PILLOW TALK II. If your T-shirt isn't fancy enough for a throw pillow, use it as a liner under a pillowcase. This time, turn the shirt inside out and stitch the arm and neck holes closed. Trim off excess fabric and insert the pillow through the open end.

HALT. Is your T-shirt ratty at its lower edge? Turn it into a halter top. Put the T-shirt on and make a mark 1½ inches below your bust. Measure from the bottom edge and cut the T-shirt off evenly all the way around. Turn up a ½-inch hem and stitch in place. Make a tiny slit in the hem in the front of the top, and work a ribbon through it. Slip on the halter and tie the ribbon in front.

FIT TO BE TIED. A narrow strip of T-shirt fabric will curl at either edge, making a sort of natural hem. You can exploit this property by turning otherwise unusable T's into a sort of squishy rope that can be used for tying packages, weaving rugs, or crocheting whatever. Cut the hem off the T-shirt. Now cut into the shirt at an angle and cut a continuous 1-inch strip around and around the shirt until you get to the sleeves. Pull gently on the strip and its edges will curl under. Roll your new "rope" into a ball.

See also CLOTHES; FABRIC SCRAPS.

TUBES, CARDBOARD

See CARDBOARD TUBES

TUNA CANS

Tuna is one of America's favorite sandwich fillings, so there are lots of tuna cans out there waiting to be recycled. Fortunately, the shallow shape suggests several possibilities:

TINY PANS. A clean tuna can (remove the label) is just right for heating single servings of meat loaf, potatoes, and other foods in the oven. Or use a tuna tin to bake individual tarts and pot pies. If you wrap a coat hanger around the can to make a handle, you can even use a tuna fish pan for melting butter, heating paraffin, and other odd jobs.

ASH CAN. If you need a disposable ashtray for a workshop, use an empty tuna tin. To make a rest for your cigarette, leave the lid attached to the can on one side and use pliers to fold it down so its edge rests on the bottom of the can.

DISH IT OUT. Use an empty tuna fish can as a dish for your kitten, gerbil, or parakeet. You can also assure fair distribution of snacks like peanuts, raisins, and jelly beans if you give each child an individual, unbreakable tuna fish dish.

JINGLE JANGLE. To make a wide bangle from a tuna can, remove both lids, file down any rough edges, and wrap the metal ring with denim, cord, yarn, or raffia.

A lidless tuna can, covered with denim and studs, becomes a cuff bracelet.

EGG RING. Make a ring for a poached egg by removing both lids from a tuna can. Set the ring in a skillet of simmering water and pour the egg into it.

See also CANS.

TV SET

If you have an old television that doesn't get good reception, don't get rid of it. Sooner or later you're going to want a home computer or video game and an old television makes a fine display terminal as long as the picture tube is functional.

If the picture tube is kaput, you can still cannibalize the television for parts. You need to know something about electronics to make much use of the circuitry, but anyone can salvage the cabinet. Leave the picture tube unplugged for a week or two so any residual charge will dissipate. When you take the back off the set, notice the rubber cap attached to the picture tube. It's called the anode cap, and any remaining charge will be centered on it. If the set is unplugged, the shock you get won't be more than a tingle. But to be safe, use a piece of wood to knock the cap free from the picture tube. Then remove the electrical components from inside the television. Tack a velvet curtain over the back of the set and use it to store liquor. Or add a shelf and store your favorite books or albums in the set, spines facing screenside. Or use the television cabinet as your own private museum case, displaying your favorite collectibles. Aside from protecting your treasures, the television turns them into a "media event."

Treat the picture tube with care because there's a vacuum inside and it can implode if handled roughly. If you want to reuse the tube, tap the narrow end gently with a mallet to crack it slightly to relieve the vacuum. Television repairmen say even this can be hazardous, so wear safety goggles or turn the job over to a pro who will also have a hot wire cutter to slice smoothly through the tube.

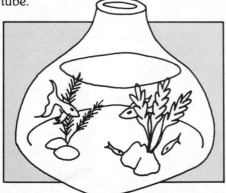

Once the pressure is normal inside the picture tube, it's a glass container with an interesting shape. Black and white tubes made 25 years ago have gray paint on the inside which can be cleaned off by soaking it in diluted paint thinner overnight. Turn the clear picture tube into an eye-catching aquarium or terrarium. Newer tubes have a thin coat of aluminum inside which is virtually impossible to remove.

It should be clear that cannibalizing a television is more difficult and potentially dangerous than cannibalizing other appliances. Unless you know about electronics you're probably better off giving an old set away or trading it in on a newer model.

TV TABLES

If you find that you don't use your television tables very much anymore, reeducate them. The trays can, of course, be removed and used as serving trays for lemonade or hors d'oeuvres. As for the legs, add a brace if they don't already have one and use them to support a bag for laundry, leaves, or trash during the spring cleanup.

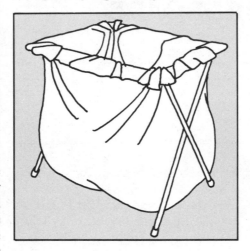

See also METAL SCRAP.

UMBRELLAS

An umbrella consists of a handle, several spokes, and the fabric that covers them. What you do with an old umbrella will depend upon which of these parts is still intact. Here are a few possibilities:

DRYING RACK. Cover the ribs of the umbrella with tape so things won't catch on them and hang it upside down as a rack for drying clothes. When your clothes are dry, fold up your rack and store it for the next wash day.

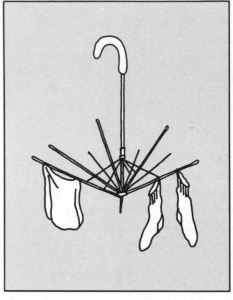

RIB TICKLERS. The metal ribs of an umbrella can be sawed off and used as engraving tools, crochet hooks, knitting needles, probes for loosening things stuck in drains, and other tools.

SHOWER FLOWERS. Plant an umbrella frame, handle down, in a flower bed and train ivy or some crawling cousin to wrap itself all over the top.

HANDLE WITH A HOOK. The typical umbrella handle has a deep curve, making it ideal as a hook for clothes in the closet, the hose in the garage, or electrical cords in the kitchen. Remove the handle from the umbrella, drill two holes straight through it, and screw it onto the wall.

See also FABRIC SCRAPS; PLASTIC HANDLES.

UNDERWEAR

See LINGERIE; SOCKS; T-SHIRTS

WASHERS

Throughout this book I've suggested dismantling appliances to salvage bits of hardware. Of all those bits of hardware, washers are perhaps the most reuseable. With the addition of a washer, a screw that's just a smidgeon too long becomes the right length. A washer's convenient center hole makes it easy to tie on a string so it can serve as just the extra weight you need on a fishing line or just the right thing to reach for at the end of a light pull. Here are other ideas:

WILD ABOUT WASHERS. Flat washers of all sizes add flash to jewelry, belts, and clothing. Work the washers into crochet or macramé designs. Sew them into vests and jackets, using bright embroidery thread and taking several stitches over the washer, top and bottom, right and left.

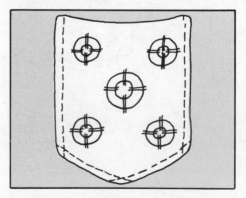

HANGING WASHERS. If you like to hang plants from the ceiling, use monofilament fishing line to suspend a large washer at the height where you want the plant. Hanging the plant from the washer makes it easier to take it down for watering and maintenance.

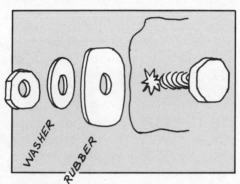

WASHER
RUBBER

PATCH IN TIME. Every handy person has a favorite idea for using found hardware and mine is this simple nut/bolt/washer combination that can be used to patch small holes in buckets, tea kettles, and other metal containers. Insert a bolt through the hole from the outside. Select a washer large enough to cover the hole and slip it over the bolt. Tighten down the nut. If the container still leaks, take a patch cut from an inner tube, punch a small hole in it, and sandwich it between the washer and the wall of the container and tighten again.

can also be removed and used wherever you need a little extra protection from the weather.

DRUMMING UP COMPOST. One way to speed up the composting process (*see* GARBAGE) is to put the organic matter in a drum that is rotated every day. Although you can buy a drum composter, it's just as effective to make your own from an old hot water heater. Remove the hardware from the tank and cut a rectangular door in the side of the tank with an acetylene cutting torch. Attach the door with a set of heavy hinges and a hasp latch. Drill a ¾-inch hole through each end of the tank and insert a length of ½-inch pipe that protrudes at least 9 inches on each end. Support the composter on fence posts or 2 × 4s that you've pounded into the ground. Drill ¾-inch holes in both posts so you can slip the pipe through one hole, the composter, and the other hole. Screw fittings around the pipe to hold it in place. Then load up the composter and give it a whirl every day. Your compost should be ready in two weeks.

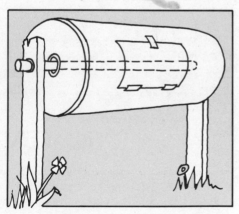

PERSONAL PIPELINE. An old water tank can be converted into a heavy-duty culvert, just the thing for channeling a drainage ditch under the driveway. Remove all the hardware from the tank and pry off top and bottom. Weld two or three tanks together if necessary and bury them in a ditch under the drive.

WATER HEATERS

A hot water heater is nothing more than an insulated water tank with a heating element. You won't get to throw away many in your lifetime, so when your chance comes, be ready to use it. The large projects described below all make use of the tank itself. In addition, you may be able to salvage other parts. Re-

move copper pipe, electrical wires, and thermostats from electric heaters, or gas burners from gas heaters. Remember too that the outer shell of the tank is made of sheet metal, which can be cut with tin snips and used for shingles, flashing, patches, and other projects. The insulation between the two shells

BRINGING IN THE RAIN. An old hot water tank makes a dandy rain-barrel, something that has won new popularity during the recent droughts in many parts of the country. Pry off the top of the tank and remove the heating elements. Plug or patch any holes with resin glue. Set the tank on a platform under a downspout and cover it with a piece of screen to filter out debris. Draw off the pure rainwater through the spigot at the bottom of the tank.

A TROUGH FOR TWO (OR MORE). If you have animals to feed, make a sturdy but inexpensive trough for water or grain out of a hot water tank. Cut the tank in half lengthwise with an acetylene cutting torch and weld or bolt angle irons to the ends so it won't tip over.

WOOD HEATER. Heating a house with wood seems like a cheap solution to the energy crisis—until you price wood stoves. Try making your own stove from an old hot water heater. The job requires a knowledge of welding, and detailed plans are available from *Mother Earth News.* Send $10 to Mother's Plans, Dept. W, P.O. Box A, East Flat Rock, NC 28726.

★ **WHERE TO GET** ★
HELP WITH
YOUR HEATER

Many of the projects for hot water heaters require cutting through the metal tank, a job best done with an acetylene torch. If you don't have a torch, call a local welder (under "Welding" in the Yellow Pages) and ask if he'll do the job.

WINDOWS

Many homeowners have an old window or two stashed at the back of the garage. Pull it out, dust it off, and put it to use. At the very least, you can dismantle the window and use the wood for scrap (*see* WOOD SCRAPS). Flat glass also has dozens of uses. Trimmed to the right size, sheet glass can be used in picture frames, to cover tables, to protect collectibles in boxes, and to make appealing glass shelves. You can cut glass yourself with a Red Devil glass cutter and a drop of oil, but I find the job gets done faster, with less frustration, if I take it to the local hardware store, where they'll cut the glass with a professional cutter.

Of course, before you take the window apart, you might try to figure out some way to use it intact. It is, after all, a preframed piece of glass that might be useful in building a solar collector or adding a skylight to the studio. Here are other ideas:

LIGHT TABLE. To make a simple light table for sorting slides or doing layout work, glue translucent paper—Eskimo Freezer Paper works fine—to one side of the window. Turn the window over and set it on two sawhorses or some other support. Position an ordinary lamp under the table and work on top of the glass.

HOT HOUSE. Old windows make the perfect top for cold frames. Build a slanted box with a top the size of the window. Make the front of the box 2 feet tall, the back 30 inches, and position it on a southern slope with good drainage. Bury the frame 1 foot in the ground and fill with good rich soil. Hinge the old window on top of the box so it can be opened on sunny days and closed on cold nights.

WINDOW SCREENS

Changes in window construction are making down-in-winter, up-in-summer screens obsolete. Happily, old screens have plenty of secondary uses. When thinking about ways to reuse screens, remember that their primary purpose is to allow ventilation. Screens can also be reduced to their component parts—sturdy wooden frames and hardware cloth. Whatever their condition, old screens are a find. And here are a few suggestions about reusing them:

HOME-DRIED FOOD. Dried foods consume less space and energy than other preserved foods. Although commercial food dryers are available, you can build a reasonable facsimile from old screens. Build a two-sided box with slats to support the screens, or support them with bricks. Either way, drape the dryer with cheesecloth to keep bugs off the food. For information about drying food, consult *How to Dry Fruits and Vegetables at Home* by the editors of Farm Journal (Countryside Press, 1975) or *Food Drying at Home the Natural Way* by Bee Beyer (J. P. Tarcher, 1976).

★ A Patch in Time ★

Use pieces of old screening to patch holes in new screens. Cut a square of screening 2 inches larger than the hole. Remove four strands of wire from each edge of the square, and use pliers to bend the loose wires at a right angle. Position the patch over the hole, stick the loose wires through the screen holes, and bend them over on the other side.

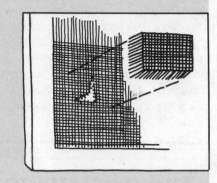

ENERGY SAVER. To convert a screen into a storm window, cover the inside of the screen with heavy sheet plastic and staple it to the wooden frame.

SEED SAVER. When you sow fine seeds for patches of grass, rows of vegetables, or beds of flowers, lay a screen over the seeds so they won't blow away or get eaten by birds.

COLLAPSIBLE COMPOSTER. Four old screens can be used to make a portable compost bin that collapses for easy storage (*see* GARBAGE for instructions).

FRAMED. The wooden frames from old screens can be salvaged as scrap wood or they can be used as the skeleton for all kinds of projects ranging from doghouses to cold frames.

DRY AGAIN. Use an old screen to dry hand washables like sweaters, which must be laid flat. Cover the screen with an old sheet and support it on the backs of two chairs so air can circulate underneath.

THE STRAIN OF IT ALL. Keep pieces of screen handy for straining all kinds of things. Fasten one over the end of the gutter to keep debris out of the downspout. Cut another to fit in the lid of a mason jar and use it as a convenient strainer when you grow sprouts. Put another square over the drain to catch hairs when you shampoo.

BRUSH OFF. To make a very stiff brush, cut a strip of screen about 7 inches wide and 2 feet long. Unravel 1 inch of the screen's long edge by pulling out the crosswires with needle-nose pliers. Roll the screen and stick it into a soup can so the loose ends stick out. Use the brush for tough scrubbing and scraping jobs.

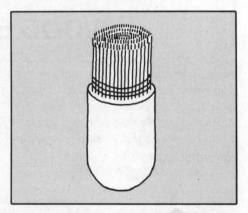

WINDOW SHADES

Finding new uses for an old window shade is no problem if you remember that its essential function is concealing things and protecting them from sunlight. In addition, the shade itself is made of a durable material which can be refashioned into covers or mats; and the roller/bracket combination can be used to hang almost anything from a fresh window shade—just staple to the roller—to a bath towel. Here are some starter suggestions:

SUN SCREEN. If you need to shelter delicate plants from the scorching sun, use an old window shade as a temporary sunscreen. Leave the shade attached to its roller and find a second roller to staple to the lower end. Find four brackets and screw them into four 5-foot poles. Measure the length and width of the shade and pound poles into the dirt at that distance apart from each other. Slip the rollers into their brackets so the shade casts its shadow on the plants you are trying to protect.

FLAT MAT. Keep a rolled-up window shade in the trunk of your car. Next time you have to change a flat, unroll the shade beside the car so you won't dirty your knees or snag your stockings. This same roll-up mat can be an impromptu tablecloth for a picnic, a drop cloth for small paint jobs, or a waterproof ground cover for gardeners to kneel on.

HANG IN THERE. Even when it's separated from its shade, a roller has uses. Hang it from its original brackets and use it as a rod for café curtains or a support for hanging plants. Or use a roller as a towel bar in the bathroom. Find brackets that extend out 2 inches from the wall. Mount them and slip the roller into place. Try installing similar brackets with rollers in the linen closet so you can hang sheets over the bars instead of piling them on shelves.

★ SHADES OF ★ DIFFERENCE

A window shade needn't be a dingy white piece of vinyl-coated fabric. Replace the original material with linen or upholstery fabric. Or cover it with wallpaper. Paint a country scene on the old shade with acrylic paints. Or glue on a map or travel poster. Finally, try painting an old window shade with blackboard paint and using it as a pull-down message board.

HIDEAWAY. There's no reason why a window shade has to hang in front of a window. Cut a torn shade off evenly above the tear and finish the cut edge with decorative tape. Remove the brackets that held the roller and reinstall them in the pantry, in front of an open closet, or above a messy bookshelf. Next time you need to conceal your everyday clutter, just pull down the shade.

WOOD ASHES

See ASHES

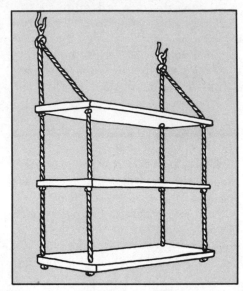

suspended shelves like those shown, or buy L-brackets and mount the shelf by screwing one leg of the L to the shelf and the other to the wall. Match the size of the shelf and its bracket to the weight you want it to support, and be sure to fasten it to a stud.

WOOD SCRAPS

Any carpenter worth his nails knows you never throw away a scrap of wood. Someday, somehow, you'll need it to finish a whammy doodle or a doghouse. For more occasional woodworkers, here are some suggestions about what to do with odd bits of wood.

SAWHORSE. Every carpenter needs a sawhorse, and you can knock one together from pieces of scrap wood. Use a 2 × 4 for the top and plane the long edges to make a 60-degree angle with the bottom of the board. Add 1 × 6 pieces, braced at each end, and attach 1 × 4 legs that are at least 2 feet high.

GAME BOARDS. To make durable game boards, cut out 15-inch squares of

hardwood. Drill holes in one and raise it on legs to make a Chinese checkers set. Make a chessboard by glueing on parquet-size squares from other scraps of wood.

SHELVES. Any piece of wood longer than it is wide and wider than it is thick can be a shelf. Use brackets to put up a system of movable shelves, make rope-

CUT-UP BOARDS. Turn clean chunks of hardwood into bread, cheese, and pastry boards. Cut the wood into interesting shapes or simple geometrics. Add handles, and perhaps peg legs. Then sand the board satin smooth and rub with linseed oil.

★ BUILDING FROM SCRAP ★

There are hundred of books describing projects that can be made of wood, and all those projects can be made from scrap wood. The danger is that you'll start a project believing it can be made from the scrap on hand and find that you need half a 2 × 4 to finish it. So you buy the 2 × 4 and have half of it left as scrap, which inspires you to do another project, for which you need an extra piece of plywood. And on it goes. If the escalation of your commitment to carpentry doesn't worry you, the following books contain plenty of good project ideas.

Build It Better Yourself by the editors of Organic Gardening (Rodale Press, 1979).

Woodworking with Scraps by Percy Blanford (Arco, 1978).

Homemade, 101 Easy-to-Make Things for Your Garden, House or Farm by Ken Braren and Roger Griffith (Garden Way, 1978).

Fifty Handy Things to Make with Wood by Jack Kramer (Butterick, 1978).

Working Wood: A Guide for the Country Carpenter by Mike and Nancy Bubel (Rodale, 1977).

ROVING WORKBENCH. If you don't have room for a workshop, make yourself a portable workbench so you can set up shop in any room of the house. Simply lay a rectangle of plywood over two chunks of 2 × 4 and nail in place. Drill holes at the top of the board to accommodate your favorite tools.

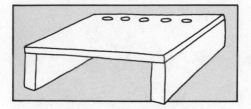

TOOLBOX. If you are a now-and-then carpenter, treat yourself to a toolbox made from the scrap from your last project. Cut three pieces of wood 2 feet by 8 inches. Now cut two trapezoidal end pieces. They should measure 8 inches at the narrow end, 10 inches at the wide end, and 12 inches on the sides. Drill holes in the end pieces for a broomstick or a dowel and put the box together with glue and nails.

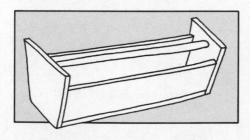

See also BROOMSTICKS AND OTHER TOOL HANDLES; FURNITURE; PICTURE FRAMES.

WRAPPING PAPER

Much of the pleasure of presents is in the anticipation, so take your time in opening them. Slit through the tape, unfold the paper gently, and set it aside. Later, retrieve it and iron out the creases with a warm iron and a damp pressing cloth. Use your recycled paper to wrap new presents or to dress up recycled cans and boxes.

See also PAPER.

YARN

Scrap yarn can, of course, be used in knitting, crocheting, and macramé. If you don't have the ambition for long projects, use your scrap yarn on quickies like these:

TIE ME. Use scraps of yarn instead of ribbon when tying up gift packages. If the yarn seems thin, twist several strands together, mixing colors for a festive effect.

FRINGE ON TOP. Scraps of yarn can be used to fringe a poncho, blanket, or pillow. Thread both ends of a 5-inch piece of yarn through a large needle and pull it through the fabric so a small loop remains on the back of the garment. Pull the two ends of the yarn through the loop and tighten it down. Repeat the process all the way around the item to be fringed. This is a handy method for concealing worn edges.

OFF-LOOM WEAVING. If you know how to do off-loom weaving, scraps of yarn can be woven into unusual belts, ponchos, purses, and other items. The essential techniques are clearly described in *Weaving Off Loom* by Dona Meilach (Contemporary Books, 1978) and *Weaving Off Loom—A Basic Manual* by Elflida Russell (Little, Brown, 1975).

ALL WRAPPED UP. Use yarn to add color and texture to recycled containers. Simply spread glue over a can, box, or cardboard tube and wrap the yarn around it, pressing each strand close to the last.

POM-POMS. Pom-poms can be used as decorations on packages, tails on stuffed animals, and tassels on drawstrings. To make a pom-pom, cut a 1 × 4-inch strip of cardboard. Lay a short piece of yarn along the cardboard and wrap a second yarn piece around it. When you've made about sixty loops, tie the single piece of yarn in a knot, gathering together the loops. Remove the cardboard and cut through the loops at the top. Fluff out the ends of the yarn and use the original tie to attach the pom-pom.

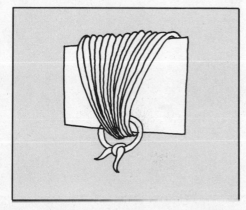

ZIPPERS

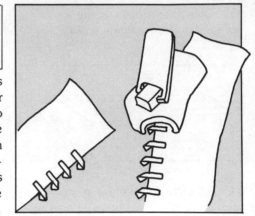

Never consign a garment to the ragbag without ripping out its zipper. Even if you don't make your own clothes, you can use zippers in duffle bags and tote bags. To make a zipper stiff and easier to install, spray it with starch and press with an iron. To make a zipper slide after it's been installed, lubricate it with the point of a pencil stub.

To repair a zipper that's come off its track, unfasten the stop at the lower end. Remove the pull and rethread it so the two zipper tracks are aligned in the holes at the top. When the pull has been threaded onto both tracks, pull it halfway up and run a dozen stitches across the track just above the point where the zipper derailed in the first place.

Part II.
THE NEXT STEP:
What to Do with What's Left

Group Approaches to Garbage

Try as we may, most of us can't possibly use up our trash as fast as we produce it. No matter how many rag rugs and tin can camp kits we make, some things remain to be thrown away. Traditionally, in this country that means packaging up the trash, setting it on the curb, and waiting for it to go away. Of course, we all know the garbage has to go somewhere, but most of us really don't care to know the grubby details.

Today, that's changing. Many people make money on things they don't want by having garage sales. Others barter their unwanted belongings or simply give them away to someone who can use them. Some communities have set up material exchanges where they collect reusable items ranging from appliances and lumber to arts and crafts material. And many communities are reevaluating garbage disposal to take advantage of new technologies.

In other words, even when you don't have a right-this-minute use for a discard, there are alternatives to dumping it. This section of Re/Uses explores ideas for coping with larger quantities of garbage—not one or two egg cartons but a year's accumulation, not a single old dresser but a roomful of furniture, not one family's newspapers but those of an entire neighborhood. Some of the ideas can be carried out by individuals, but most require the cooperation of neighborhoods, organizations, or even cities.

Just as no one could carry out all the projects described in the A–Z Encyclopedia so no individual can get involved in all these activities. Still, because each of us produces more garbage than we can reuse by ourselves, we have an obligation to think about what should become of it. We also have an incentive, since people who think creatively about trash often profit from its reuse. The profit may be personal if you sort and sell cast-off belongings. It may accrue to social institutions such as schools if they stretch tight budgets by using trash in arts and other programs. The profit may go to entrepreneurs who set up recycling operations that make money; or it may be used by local governments to defray the cost of garbage disposal and keep down taxes. Finally, we may all profit from the tantalizing new technology that turns trash into energy.

So even when you have no personal use for your discards, they still have value. And it's up to you to see that their value is exploited—by you or by someone else in your community. What follows are suggestions about how that can be done.

Trash for Sale:

Garage Sales and Flea Markets

Call them tag sales, attic sales, porch sales, or lawn sales. In many communities people have found that the quickest way to get rid of what they don't want is to sell it to someone else.

Of course garage sales have proliferated because they are a fun way to turn lots of unwanted possessions into quick cash. They can still work that magic—if you remember there's heavy competition for the customers who wander from sale to sale in search of the "ultimate bargain." To capture those customers, you'll have to distinguish your sale from all the others by being organized, courteous, and very visible. Here are some pointers:

Choices. If you have a lot of stuff, you may want to have a one-family sale. Many people find, however, that they get better turnout if they pool their inventory with that of a few neighbors. To be sure your feelings toward one another will be neighborly after the sale, decide in advance how you will divide the work and the money. In some communities garage sales have been institutionalized, and professional organizers take over the arrangements for a whole group of sellers. In other places an auction barn holds a regular swap meet where sellers can rent a booth for $10 to $20 for an afternoon. The most famous of these meets is the Rose Bowl Swap Meet in Pasadena, California, whick attracts as many as a million customers to its monthly sales.

What's the Law? If you decide to have your own sale, be sure to find out about local regulations. Many communities now require a small licensing fee on garage sales, and others prohibit the sale of certain items like food, medicine and firearms. Also, remember that your profits are taxable income and that the IRS has a right to ask you about them.

What's for Sale. Selecting items for a sale can be tricky. To you, most of your inventory will be worthless—after all, you're getting rid of it. But you'll have to recognize that some of it—the real trash—will be worthless to everyone. Start by collecting everything you don't want. Check in the back of cupboards; the neglected corners of the attic, basement, and garage; even under the beds. Now discard the real dogs and make the other things as presentable as possible. It's worth taking time to repair damaged items, wash clothes, shine up tools, and dust the glassware. The better things look, the better they'll sell.

In addition, try to gather at least two-dozen items that have genuine and general sales appeal. The hot items vary from place to place, but working appliances are usually strong sellers along with furniture, tools, sporting goods, antique clothes, garden equipment, toys, baby items, records, and kitchen utensils.

Setting the Date. Most people hold their sales during warm weather so at least part of the action can take place outdoors. The best seasons are undoubtedly spring, when people are looking for any excuse to be outside, and late fall when the frantic search for Christmas presents has begun. If you're simply trying to clear things out, choose a long weekend for the sale. Start on Thursday or Friday and run right through to Sunday evening. Announce a discount policy—starting Sunday at noon, prices will be reduced 10 percent every hour until everything is gone. Select your date at least six weeks in advance to give yourself plenty of time to get organized and spread the word. Also, if the sale will be held outdoors, make rain plans or announce a rain date.

Spreading the Word. More people mean more sales, so you'll want everyone within ten miles to know about your sale and why it's special. Start by telling friends and relations. Next decide whether you can afford to invest in a small ad in the local paper or the advertising weekly. Mention date, time, place, your big items, and end with the teaser about "items too numerous to mention." For a weekend sale, start the ad on the preceding Monday. If you decide on a one-day ad, see that it appears on Thursday, the traditional day for announcing sales and auctions.

For free advertising, tack up colorful 3 × 5 cards announcing your sale on every bulletin board within reach. Before the sale, letter a giant sign—a banner made from an old sheet is effective—for the front of the house and smaller ones for lampposts at key intersections. Remember to remove the signs when the sale is over. All posters should announce address, dates, and time of the sale.

Setting Up. There's no question about it—you'll have more walk-in traffic if your house or apartment is on a main street. If your home is very inaccessible, consider moving the merchandise to a friend's garage (for a percentage of the take) or even to a parking lot (be sure to get permits for selling in a public place if they are needed).

On location, make the physical arrangement of your sale as attractive as possible. Borrow long tables to display the items or lay planks over sawhorses. Set up racks to hang the clothes and keep small or valuable items in display cases. (For the purposes of a garage sale, a display case is a clear bottle or plastic container inverted over the item.) Leave plenty of room between tables to accommodate the crowd you hope to have, and place advertised items at the back so customers have to pass other merchandise to get to them.

If possible arrange the sale so there's only one way in and out. Set up a cashier's station at the entrance and have it manned at all times. Remember that you'll need some change at the beginning of the sale. Also, collect bags, boxes, and wrapping paper for packaging the merchandise.

Pricing. Deciding how much things should cost is tough. Visit other sales and auctions to get an idea about prevailing prices and then use common sense. If your object is to get rid of things, price a little under what you think is "fair"; if you want to make more money, price a little high and give discounts as it seems appropriate. One rule of thumb is that most things should be priced about one quarter their store value. To find out store value, look up something comparable in a Sears catalogue. Naturally, there are exceptions. Working appliances can often be sold for about half their original price, while clothing is worth, perhaps, a tenth.

If you suspect that some items may be antiques or collectibles, find out about their value before the sale. If a dealer visits your sale and spots a rare piece of carnival glass priced for a quarter, you can be sure he won't mention it—at least not until he paid for it. Many people price their merchandise 10 percent higher than they hope to get to allow room for haggling. It does make buyers feel good to think you knocked the price down just for them. On the other hand, every item should be tagged with a basic price. Use little stick-um labels or mark with chalk. Finally, give the cashier a break by rounding prices to the nearest quarter. No $3.98 specials, please.

Gimmicks. So far we've covered the basics. There's still that nagging question about how to make your sale stand out from the fourteen others planned for the same weekend. Here are suggestions:

- Feature really special items no one else has, such as handcrafts or homemade preserves. Or advertise a few collectibles like quilts, crocks, or rocking chairs.
- Offer free refreshments like coffee and cookies.
- Plan something to attract kids. Offer free balloons to every child accompanied by an adult. Or have carnival games to occupy kids while parents browse.
- Create a carnival atmosphere by decorating with streamers and balloons. Persuade a neighborhood kid to juggle or clown or do magic tricks on the front lawn to draw in strangers.
- Have a lottery or raffle for one of the most appealing items. Everyone who comes to the sale registers to win the prize.

★ **MORE TIPS** ★ **AND HINTS**

Several books and pamphlets have been written about garage sales. All are full of practical advice and you might skim one or two of them before your own sale.

Garage Sale Handbook by Bette Harrison (Ace, 1979).

Great Trash by Jim and Jean Young (Harper & Row, 1979) has a good chapter on garage sale mechanics.

How to Hold a Garage Sale by James Michael Ullman (Rand McNally & Co., 1980).

How to Make More Money with Your Garage Sale by Ryan Petty (St. Martin's, 1981).

Garage Sale Succe$$: Every Tip in the Book by Kate O'Malley Elfstrom (ELF Ink, 728 West Country Road C, Saint Paul MN 55113. $4.50).

- Advertise a grab box full of freebies. Wrap up some "worthless" items—paperback books, interesting little bottles, candy or cookies—in paper bags or newspaper.

All these ideas reward people just for coming to your sale. And chances are that they'll return the favor by carting away some of your unwanted possessions.

★ SPOTTING COLLECTIBLES ★

Though the collectible craze seems to have peaked, there are still plenty of people who will pay top dollar for an item that's rare to them though worthless to you. The trick, of course, is to identify the collectibles before you sell them or, worse yet, haul them to the dump.

For a while collectibles were being "discovered" at such a rapid rate that no one could keep up. Some were old (quilts and weathervanes), some were new (comic books and Mickey Mouse memorabilia), and some were simply bizarre (barbed wire and beer cans). Today, most collectibles can be quickly identified through reference books like the *Encyclopedia of Collectibles* (Time-Life Books, 1979). As a quick reference, check the list below. Finding one of your possessions on the list doesn't mean it's valuable, just that it might be if you can get it to the right collector.

Advertising giveaways	Fishing tackle	Posters
Arrowheads	Guns	Puppets
Autographs	Handbags	Quilts
Auto-hood ornaments	Hats	Radios
Banks	Hooked rugs	Railroad
Barbed wire	Hubcaps	memorabilia
Baseball cards	Ice-cream molds	Razors
Baskets	Inkwells	Records
Beer cans	Insulators	Rock 'n' roll
Bells	Jazz memorabilia	memorabilia
Bibles	Jewelry	Samplers
Buttons	Kids books	Scissors
Cameras	Kitchen utensils	Scrimshaw
Candle holders	Lace	Shaving mugs
Canes	Lanterns	Shawls
Carnival glass	Locks	Sheet music
Cash registers	Magazines	Sleds
Chess sets	Marbles	Snuff containers
Christmas ornaments	Medals	Spoons
Circus memorabilia	Music boxes	Stamps
Clocks	Musical instruments	Teddy bears
Coins	Napkin rings	Thimbles
Combs	Neckties	Tin soldiers
Cookbooks	Neon signs	Tinware
Corkware	Nutcrackers	Toasters
Crèches	Oak furniture	Toleware
Cut glass	Optical toys	Trivets
Dance memorabilia	Paperweights	Typewriters
Decoys	Patent molds	Umbrellas
Depression glass	Perfume bottles	Valentines
Dollhouses	Phonographs	Watches
Doorstops	Pipes	Weathervanes
Embroidery	Playing cards	Wicker
Eyeglasses	Political mementos	World's Fair
Fiestaware	Postcards	memorabilia

Giving Away What You Can't Sell:

Swap Boxes, Rummage Sales, and Other Good Causes

If you can't use them yourself and you can't sell them, try giving your discards away. In our affluent culture, lots of us want to get rid of things before they're worn out. Many of these objects could and would be reused if we could just match them with people who wanted them. Here are suggestions:

Swap Box. Setting up a swap box or table is simple. Pick a well-traveled place—perhaps a table in an apartment laundry room, a corner of a community center, a box at the back of a food co-op, even a shed at the entrance of the town dump. Put up a sign explaining that people can bring and leave usable objects they no longer want such as books, records, dishes, clothes, toys. Anyone who wants something in the box takes it and leaves a discard of his or her own. Before long, you'll have a lively exchange going, with everyone finding things they want and getting rid of what they don't want. Check the swap box periodically and remove things that have gone unclaimed for a week or two.

★ THE CRAFTY RECYCLER ★

All of the materials on this list are commonly used in crafts projects, so you might want to save them for your local school, day-care center, scout troop, senior-citizen center, or freebie exchange.

Aerosol-can tops	Dixie-cup spoons	Paper-towel rolls
Aluminum food containers	Egg cartons	Pie tins
	Fabric	Plastic bags
Beads	Feathers	Plastic containers
Beans	Felt	Ribbon rolls
Bottle caps	Fur	Rope and string
Boxes	Fruit cartons	Rug samples
Brushes	Gift wrap	Seeds
Buttons	Gloves	Sewing trim
Burlap	Ice-cream containers	Shells
Calendars	Jar lids	Shopping bags
Candles	Lace	Socks
Cardboard	Leather	Spools
Carpet scraps	Linoleum scraps	Straws
Chalk pencils	Magazines	Styrofoam meat trays (clean)
Christmas cards	Milk cartons (wash them out!)	Toilet-paper rolls
Cloth scraps		Tongue depressors
Clothespins	Mirrors	Toothpicks
Coat hangers	Nails, tacks, screws	Wallpaper samples
Coffee cans	Oatmeal boxes	Wood scraps
Cookie cutters	Onion skins (for natural dyes)	Yarn
Corks		Yogurt containers
Cotton	Paper bags	
Crayon stubs	Paper of all kinds	

★ SWAPPING ★ GOOD TIMES

Whether you have a garageful of things to get rid of or just an item or two, you may get more value for them if you're willing to swap for goods and services. The ancient art of barter has achieved new respectability among people who would like to be less dependent upon money. Many people now exchange things they no longer want—appliances, cars, bicycles, clothes, sporting equipment, and other things—for someone else's discards or for services—carpentry, typing, massage, photography, and much more.

Every barter transaction is unique. The only rule is that both parties be satisfied. In fact, many people go away more than satisfied because they've gotten something they wanted but might not have been able to afford if they'd had to pay cash. Sometimes you can advertise for swaps, but they are usually a word-of-mouth activity. Start talking about something you want to get rid of and see what develops.

Local Needs. Before throwing out a working appliance, a usable piece of furniture, or an unbroken set of dishes, contact local centers for teen-agers, toddlers, or senior citizens. These organizations often have kitchens to equip and rooms to furnish but no budgets. Also, check with schools, summer recreation programs, scout troops, and other groups to see if they can use empty packages in their arts and crafts programs.

Thrift Stores. Everyone knows that the Salvation Army and Goodwill Industries accept reusable clothing, furniture, and household items. Between them, these two organizations have the country pretty well covered, so you should be able to find one of them in the phone book. The centers usually have collection boxes, and may send out a truck to pick up your items. Both organizations sell reclaimed items cheap, and the money they make goes for adult rehabilitation centers, family counseling, work with the handicapped, and emergency assistance. Though you won't be paid for your discards, you can ask for a receipt and claim the probable resale value of your "gift" as a tax deduction. To obtain further information about either of these organizations, contact their national headquarters: Goodwill Industries of America, Inc., 9200 Wisconsin Avenue, Washington, DC 20014; The Salvation Army, 50 West 23rd Street, New York, NY 10010.

Rummaging Around. Churches, schools, and other social service organizations often have rummage sales to raise funds for worthy causes. They'll be glad to accept your reusable discards. Just call your favorite group to find out when their next sale is scheduled.

Freebie Exchange. An Oregon county with some extra public space set up a storage place for common discards which could be used as crafts supplies. People in the community donate their scrap materials and the Freebie Exchange makes them available to community groups—schools, scouts, senior citizen centers, and even grandmothers who needed to entertain their grandchildren. For more information on the project, write to Freebie Exchange, 1085 S.E. Seventh Avenue, West Linn, OR 97068. A variation on the same theme is reSTORE, a "store" which stocks "useful junk" and makes it available to teachers. For information, write to the Maryland Committee for Children, The Chocolate Factory, 608 Water Street, Baltimore, MD 21202.

★ ARTS, CRAFTS, AND TRASH ★

It's often been said that one person's art is another person's trash. The converse is also true. One person's trash may become art in the hands of another. At one end of the spectrum, highly respected artists use cast-off objects to create collages, assemblages, and sculptures. At the other, den mothers, church bazaar organizers, and summer camp counselors seize upon discards as inexpensive crafts materials. Between these two extremes are the countless people who turn Perrier bottles into vases.

Are decorative objects made from trash witty or tacky? The answer is largely a matter of style, but boldness is essential. If you want to make a wall hanging out of six-pack plastic and you feel that you have a good eye, don't apologize for it. Treat your discards as seriously as an artist treats more traditional materials. The transfiguration of trash requires a leap of imagination. Instead of perceiving discards as things to be hustled out of sight, focus on their colors, shapes, and textures. If you need inspiration, consult *Found Objects* by Joseph Ruggiero (Crown Publishers, 1981). This "source and style book" is filled with photographs of everyday objects elevated into sculpture, tableware, and objets d'art.

Recycle, Recycle, Recycle:
How to Make Recycling Work

Many materials that are ordinarily thrown away should instead be recycled. Glass, metal, and paper are obvious candidates for recycling, but other materials such as fabric, motor oil, fats, and even plastic can also be reprocessed. In the past recycling may have seemed altruistic, but now that many resources are becoming scarce, it's foolish not to recycle whatever we can.

The best way to recycle basic materials is to keep them separate from other trash. The process is known as "source separation," and it means simply that you bundle newspapers, keep empty bottles in a special container, and set aside scrap metal. What happens next depends upon the facilities available in your community.

In many communities you can earn money for your scrap. If there's a paper plant nearby, you can probably haul in your newspapers and receive a fixed amount per pound. Aluminum, too, is worth good money—about 23 cents per pound—if you take it to a center sponsored by one of the aluminum companies. Other kinds of metal scrap can often be sold to local salvage companies (see METAL SCRAP).

Other recyclables should go to a nonprofit recycling center. Although many of the centers that sprouted in the sixties withered in the seventies, plenty of centers still exist. Some sponsor one or two collection drives a year—the Boy Scout paper drive is a classic example. Others are open every week to collect bottles, papers, and cans. If your community has a nonprofit center, support it, not only by taking in your materials but also, perhaps, by volunteering some time.

With clearly labeled bins like these, source separation is so easy even a child can do it.

★ GARBAGE GRAPHICS ★

If you need a lively reminder to re-cycle, order one of the Garbage Day posters by Diane Schatz. Created to celebrate Oregon's first Garbage Day in 1979, the posters are colorful cartoons filled with elaborate and often hilarious de-tail. Titles include "Technology!," "Why Recycle!," "Buyer Be- Aware!," "Recycling Is for Everyone!," "Running Out/ Running Over!," "Garbage Is What You Throw Away!" and "Great Garbage Machine." Posters cost $3.50 apiece plus postage. For more information, write Transition Graphics, P.O. Box 30007, Eugene OR 97403.

★ How to Sell Your Scrap ★

Many of the recycling centers born in the sixties died because their organizers couldn't sell the bottles, cans, and papers they collected. Take their experience as a lesson and support your source separation program with reliable markets. In most communities you *can* sell scrap if you are tough about negotiating a contract and consistent about supplying high-quality material.

The scrap market has always been volatile, so for a recycling center to survive it needs a realistic marketing plan. One approach is to take bids from local scrap dealers and sign a contract with the company making the best offer. Other centers hold materials in storage when prices are low and release them when they rise. Still others work with a range of recyclable materials so a drop in the price of a single commodity won't wipe them out.

However you proceed, be sure to get answers to all these questions:

• What are the maximum and minimum amounts the buyer will accept?
• What are the requirements for preparation?
• What hours does the buyer accept materials?
• Will the buyer provide shipping and/or hauling?
• What base price can the buyer guarantee?

• Will the buyer supply containers?

If your program accepts several different materials, you may have to make arrangements with several different buyers. Each buyer will have its own specifications for material, but the guidelines listed below are widely used.

Glass. Most buyers want crushed glass (cullet) sorted according to color. Those who accept whole bottles will insist that all metal bands be removed. The price of glass is around $35 per ton and doesn't fluctuate very much. It takes about two hundred 55-gallon drums of whole bottles or sixty drums of cullet to make one ton. To find a buyer, check the Yellow Pages under "Glass, Scrap." You can also obtain help from the Glass Manufacturers Institute, 330 Madison Avenue, New York, NY 10017, or the Glass Packaging Institute, 1800 K Street NW, Washington, DC 20006.

Aluminum. Aluminum companies are eager to buy all the aluminum scrap they can find—cans (check to see that a magnet is *not* attracted), lawn furniture, household siding, frozen food trays, and so on. The price is 23 cents a pound, so aluminum is a good money-maker for most centers. To locate a buyer, contact the Aluminum Association, 750 Third Avenue, New York, NY 10017.

Iron and Steel. Most buyers want crushed cans, but some will accept other forms of metal scrap such as old appliances. To find a buyer, check the Yellow Pages under "Metal, Scrap" or contact the National Institute of Iron and Steel, 1729 H Street NW, Washington, DC 20006. The price of steel scrap is usually around $20 per ton.

Paper. Scrap paper buyers may accept a wide range of papers, including newspapers, corrugated cartons, and high-grade scrap such as stationery, mixed scrap, magazines, and computer cards. Prices fluctuate drastically and range from $10 per ton for mixed scrap to $35 per ton for newspaper to $150 per ton for computer cards. To locate a market, check the Yellow Pages under "Paper, Scrap" or write to the American Paper Institute, 260 Madison Avenue, New York, NY 10016.

General. For general information on markets for recycled material, get a copy of "Market Locations for Recovered Materials, A Current Report on Solid Waste Management" from the Environmental Protection Agency, Washington, DC 20460. Useful information can also be obtained from the National Association of Recycling Industries, 330 Madison Avenue, New York, NY 10017.

Some recycling centers offer curbside service, because they can't collect enough material if they wait for people to bring stuff in. Eco-Cycle in Boulder, Colorado, uses recycled school buses to pick up materials every Saturday morning. In addition to the usual newspapers, cans, and bottles, the program accepts and recycles motor oil, appliances, tires, and egg cartons.

In some communities the city government offers curbside pickup of recyclable materials. Since the city is already paying for trucks and people to collect the trash, they simply add special racks or bins to the trucks. Homeowners put papers, cans, and bottles in specially marked containers, so they can be put in the appropriate bins. Over two hundred communities have such programs. Although many collect only newspaper, the money earned from selling the paper helps defray the cost of trash collection.

Finally, in at least one city residents have started a recycling cooperative. Garbagio in Eugene, Oregon, handles all the wastes from the homes of member-owners. The members pay an annual fee and agree to sort their trash into special containers provided by Garbagio. At the end of the year, co-op members are eligible for a dividend if the money received for materials is greater than the cost of collection. In addition to glass, metal, and paper, Garbagio also collects and composts organic materials.

In all of these programs, individuals take responsibility for presorting their trash. The effort isn't much, especially if you use a trash container with several compartments. Still, many local officials are convinced most people won't do source separation. As a result, some are investigating "resource recovery" systems which extract recyclable materials like glass, paper, and metal from unsorted garbage.

If your community has a resource recovery center, you throw all trash into the same container. A truck collects the trash and takes it to a processing plant, which may be owned by the city or by an independent contractor. In the plant, the trash is chopped into uniform pieces. Ferrous metals are extracted with a magnet, and glass, aluminum, and other materials are removed by special machines.

Resource recovery is a convenience for people who are too lazy to sort their trash, but it has several problems. First, the plants are very expensive to build. To get a return on the investment, the plant must be guaranteed a certain amount of trash with a certain percentage of metals, glass, and other materials. This obviously discourages efforts such as bottle bills and paper drives, which reduce the amount of trash produced. In fact, in some communities government officials have signed contracts agreeing to deliver a certain amount of trash per capita and to pay penalties if the city doesn't meet its trash quota.

The composition of garbage varies greatly, so it's difficult to design machines that can reliably extract recycleable materials.

A second problem is that the complicated machinery in resource recovery plants often doesn't work. Of the plants which have been built in the U.S., many have been closed because they pollute or because their equipment just can't handle the volume of trash. Perhaps technology to make these plants reliable will eventually be perfected, but at the moment cities that depend on them for trash disposal are taking an unnecessary gamble. Instead of paying for complex resource recovery plants, most communities would be better served by a good source separation program.

If your community already has such a program, support it. If it doesn't, consider starting one. Unlike resource recovery, a source separation program can be started by one person and a pickup truck. Or you and your neighbors can adapt one of the more sophisticated models described above. However you proceed, you'll need to consider several important factors:

- Goals—does the program have objectives beyond recycling? Do you want to produce a profit by manufacturing something from the waste materials—perhaps insulation from newspaper? Do you want to raise money for local organizations or cut the cost of waste disposal?
- Competition—are there already recycling programs in the community? Is there a private collection service that has prior claim to the trash? Could the city itself be persuaded to add source separation to its trash collection program?
- Quantity—how many potential participants do you have for your program? What kind of trash do they generate? (Garbagio did a painstaking five-month study to find out!) Are they responsive to the idea of recycling? Will local media help you publicize the center?
- Laws—will the program need a license? Will fire, safety, health, or zoning ordinances effect your center?
- Budget—will you need full-time employees (most centers do)? What equipment will be required? Who will pay for transportation to the scrap buyer?
- Markets—the most important question of all since most recycling programs fail because they haven't nailed down a market for their materials (see BOX).

Obviously, these guidelines are sketchy. If you are serious about developing a source separation program in your community, the following publications can help:

"Operating a Recycling Center: A Citizen's Guide." Office of Solid Waste, United States Environmental Protection Agency, Washington, DC 20460. Free.

"Community-Based Waste Recycling: A Neighborhood Action Guide." Civic Action Institute, 1010 16th Street NW, Washington, DC 20036. $1.00.

"A Guide to Recycling the Source Separation Way." Indiana State Board of Health, 1330 Michigan Street, Indianapolis, IN 46202. Free.

"Curbing Trash." League of Women Voters, 1730 M Street NW, Washington, DC 20036. 40 cents.

"A Guide to Running a Recycling Project." Oregon Department of Environmental Quality, 1234 S.W. Morrison Street, Portland, OR 97205. $1.55.

"Recycling, Establishing a Citizen-Sponsored Reclamation Center." Keep America Beautiful, 99 Park Avenue, New York, NY 10016. $1.50.

> *Once is not enough—Recycle!*
> —Bumper sticker in Oregon

Beyond the Trash Can:

Seeing That Your Government Does Right by Your Garbage

Okay, by now you've used, stored, sold, bartered, given away, or recycled as much of your trash as you possibly can. And you still have a sack—albeit a smaller sack—of stuff you don't want. At this point, most people expect the local government to step in and take the stuff away. And that seems to be the end of it. But it's not. What your community does with its garbage can have big effects on your pocketbook, your health, and your future access to important resources such as energy. How? Let's look at the facts.

First, garbage disposal costs money, and guess who pays. Since 1950 the cost of waste disposal has doubled in most cities, and today garbage is the second largest expense, surpassed only by education. Simple collection costs an average of $35 per ton in most places, and that figure may rise to $50 per ton by 1985. You might shrug and say such costs are inevitable, but they're not. In some communities, garbage disposal breaks even or makes money because governments treat trash like the resource it is.

Second, trash disposal can seriously affect the quality of your air, water, and landscape. Everybody knows about Love Canal and the dangers of hazardous wastes being dumped indiscriminately. Not so many people know that ordinary dumps can produce similar results when water trickles through them, picking up chemicals that eventually show up in drinking water. In communities that are running out of landfill sites, the question boils down to whose backyard will be sacrificed to a future garbage disposal site.

Third, the usual ways of getting rid of garbage result in the irreversible loss of all the raw materials in it. Every year, prices of consumer products go up, in part because this country pays billions to import many of the same resources that are going to waste in our landfills. We make expensive fertilizers to replenish croplands when we could nourish them with compost made from garbage; we buy fuel from foreign countries at ever-increasing prices when we could be making some of it from trash. We pay more for almost everything we consume because local governments waste the resources in our trash.

Today, many communities are rethinking what they do with their trash, motivated partly by a desire to trim municipal budgets and partly by alarm at the dangers of hazardous waste. Most of all, shortages of energy and resources have made many officials turn a covetous eye on trash as a "mine above ground." Whatever the reasons, chances are good that at this very moment some task force or commission in your community is looking into the future of your trash. If you are going to understand, much less influence, their recommendations and decisions, you need to know a little about the available alternatives for trash.

In the old days, communities simply dumped the trash in an out-of-the-way place. Thanks to the Resource Recovery and Conservation Act, such dumps will be illegal in 1983, and local officials have been busy creating "sanitary landfills." In a landfill, all the trash is dumped into a depression in the land and then covered each day with several inches of dirt. The system is better than an old-fashioned dump because it minimizes rats, odors, and disease organisms.

On the other hand, landfills can also cause problems. For one thing, the land they create is unstable and can't be used for construction for at least fifteen years. For another, if landfill sites are carelessly placed or managed, water drains through them, picking up chemicals. Although ground water moves slowly, eventually the polluted water may show up in wells and streams.

The worst part about landfill is that so much material is wasted. The problem is minimized to some extent by source separation programs like those described in the previous section. Yet, even in the most trash-conscious communities, some people can't or won't separate their trash and some potentially recyclable materials aren't handled by the source separation program.

One solution is to salvage materials on the landfill site before they are dumped and covered. In Lane County, Oregon, the Office of Appropriate Technology hires "high-graders" who work at the landfill site. Their job is to spot and salvage recyclable materials, particularly metal. During one experimental period, the high-grading operation actually made a profit. For additional information on high grading request "Gone Today, Here Tomorrow!" from the Institute for Local Self-Reliance, 1717 18th Street NW, Washington, DC 20009.

Properly managed, landfill can also produce energy. As the organic garbage in a landfill decomposes, it creates methane gas. Left unmanaged, the methane can cause dangerous explosions. Engineers, however, have come up with a way of extracting the methane so it can be used as fuel. A report called "Recovering Gas from Landfills" is available from the American Gas Association, 1515 Wilson Boulevard, Arlington, VA 22209.

There are, however, more efficient ways to make energy from trash. In fact, many communities see trash-to-energy plants as the magic solution to all the problems related to garbage disposal. Though the idea still seems novel in America, Europeans have been turning trash into energy for years. Paris has burned garbage to produce electricity since 1902, and today 7 percent of the city's houses are heated with steam produced by a garbage-fueled power plant. In Denmark, 60 percent of the municipal waste is converted into energy; in Switzerland, 40 percent. By contrast, the U.S. uses only 1 percent of its 160 million tons of trash to make energy. That figure should increase if the more than one hundred cities that are now

In the future dumps like this may become mines above the ground, providing energy and raw materials.

CHOPPED PAPER

CLEAN SHREDDED LIGHT IRON

CHOPPED PLASTICS

HEAVY IRON

HEAVY NONFERROUS METAL

ORGANIC WASTES

GREEN GLASS

CHOPPED ALUMINUM

COLORLESS GLASS

AMBER GLASS

Resource recovery plants take in mixed trash and extract reusable materials like these.

planning garbage-to-energy plants go through with their plans. Essentially, there are five approaches.

• Water wall incineration is widely used in Europe. In this system, waste is deposited on movable grates which circulate through a furnace. Noncombustible material falls through the grates, and ferrous metals are recovered from the residue. The furnaces are surrounded by tubes filled with water, which absorbs the heat, making steam that can be sold to power companies. The technology for water wall incineration is most thoroughly developed, and plants are operating successfully in several U.S. communities, including Saugus, Massachusetts, Chicago, Nashville, and Harrisburg, Pennsylvania.

• Modular incineration means converting incinerators used by apartments, cities, and industries into energy-producing systems. In the past, these incinerators burned trash simply to reduce its volume. Now, with heat recovery equipment added to the old-fashioned incinerators, they can also produce steam, hot water, or heated air. About two dozen such systems are in operation from Grovetown, New Hampshire, to Blytheville, Arkansas.

• Refuse Derived Fuel (RDF) consists of the paper and plastics in trash. It is produced by shredding the waste into 4-inch fragments and then separating out heavy materials like metal and glass. The remaining material, further shredded, is mixed with coal and burned in specially designed boilers. RDF has caused the most excitement among resource recovery enthusiasts, yet the plants which have been built with this technology have faced serious technical problems. A pilot plant built in Saint Louis had to be closed, and a model plant built by Americology in Milwaukee has had trouble with the RDF fouling its boilers. Nonetheless, many cities are considering RDF plants.

• Pyrolosis is still an experimental possibility. In this system garbage is heated to extremely high temperatures in an oxygen-free system. Without oxygen the waste can't burn, so it decomposes into gaseous or liquid fuel. Small pyrolysis plants have been built and tested in San Diego, Baltimore, and other cities. Although the process may hold promise for the future, it is not yet commercially feasible.

• Biological processes can be used to produce energy if organic materials are separated from the rest of the trash. They can then be converted into alcohol or methane (see GARBAGE).

Turning garbage into energy is such a tantalizing prospect that many communities are rushing headlong into building such plants. Unfortunately, of the thirty-eight plants built so far in this country, many have encountered serious problems ranging from air pollution (one plant emitted highly toxic dioxin) to equipment malfunction. Experts are uncertain about why a technology which has been so successful in Europe should be so problematic in America, but some blame the composition of American trash, which is more varied and contains more plastics.

Whatever the reason, the watchword for taxpayers should be caution since, as one expert put it, these plants could end up as "tax burdens, like convention centers and astrodomes." Finding out what happens to your trash may be tedious

Before trash can be converted into energy heavy metals and other noncombustible material must be removed by machines like this.

★ FUTURE SHOCK ★ FOR TRASH

Stardust 80, a resource recovery plant in Japan, may be a portent of things to come in trash technology. The plant, which claims to be the most modern in the world, recycles 70 percent of the materials collected from Yokohama's hundred thousand citizens. From 100 tons of trash, the machinery in the plant can extract 28 tons of compost, 25 tons of paper pulp, 3 tons of iron, and assorted plastics that are converted into methane gas. The plant cost $18 million to build, but it now operates at a profit.

and time-consuming, but it's simply an extension of household recycling. If you encourage your kids to make beads out of spools and airplanes out of fast food boxes, it makes sense to encourage local officials to make energy, raw materials, and even money out of trash. So where do you start?

First, find out what happens to your garbage. Call your sanitation department or local councilperson and ask where the garbage goes after it leaves the curb. Does your community send its trash to a dump, incinerator, sanitary landfill, or resource recovery plant? Does the community have a functioning source separation program? Are there plans to change the current system for trash disposal?

Second, familiarize yourself with all the alternatives for trash disposal. In addition to the overview presented here, useful information is available from the following organizations:

Solid Waste Management Information, U.S. Environmental Protection Agency, Cincinnati, OH 45268. Ask for the Resource Recovery Plant Implementation Series and the National Survey of Separate Collection Programs.

Environmental Action Foundation, Suite 724, Dupont Circle Building, Washington, DC 20036. Ask for the Garbage Guides on "Resource Recovery" and "Source Separation." $1 apiece.

Institute for Local Self-Reliance, 1717 Eighteenth Street NW, Washington, DC 20009. Ask for "Garbage in America." $2.

National Center for Resource Recovery, 1211 Connecticut Avenue NW, Washington, DC 20036. Ask for the Information Kit. $2.

League of Women Voters, 1730 M Street NW, Washington, DC 20036. Ask for pamphlets called "Reduce, Recycle" and "Is There Enough Trash for Everyone."

Third, compare what your community is doing or plans to do with what's being done elsewhere. If the comparison doesn't make you proud, get involved in the decision-making process. At the very least, write letters to the editor of the local paper and vote on relevant referendums and bond issues. Join your local environmental organization. Consider participating in more sophisticated strategies such as lobbying legislators, testifying at public hearings, and building coalitions between like-minded organizations. For more information about political strategies, consult the following sources:

"Don't Leave It All to the Experts: The Citizen's Role in Environmental Decision Making." Environmental Protection Agency, Washington, DC 20460.

"Solid Waste—It Won't Go Away Unless . . . A Sampling of What Citizen Leaders Can Do." League of Women Voters, 1730 M Street NW, Washington, DC 20036.

"The Waste Watchers: A Citizen's Handbook for Conserving Energy and Resources" by Arthur Purcell (Anchor Books, 1980).

Changing the way your community handles trash may be more difficult than changing the way your household handles trash. Yet the rewards are similar. Just as changing a bag of rags into a quilt produces the satisfaction of making something useless into something useful, so monitoring local solid waste policies may turn a problem into a community resource. It's worth a try since in your home and in your community, this is no time to waste.

Where to Stash the Trash:

How to Throw Away Less Without Having Your Home Look Like a Dump

Just because you can't use something at the moment doesn't mean it should be thrown away. Still, lots of people throw away things they might be able to reuse simply because it keeps the house tidy. It is true that saving bottles to be cut, appliances to be repaired, and newspapers to be recycled can soon make a house, much less an apartment, look cluttered and unkempt. The only way around this problem is a storage system specially designed to hold your recycleable valuables.

A recycling storage space must be tailored to you, the waste you make, and the things you are likely to do with it. No one can save everything, so set your own priorities. Find out about the local recycling center and save what they accept. Then think about your own habits. Are you likely to make a braided rug from old clothes? Do you like the idea of cannibalizing appliances for parts? Will you actually reuse the parts? If you are short on space, save only the things that have a realistic chance of being reused.

After making a list (yep, write it down) of what you want to save for yourself and your local recycling center, budget space for each item. If you drink wine every night, reserve extra space for tall bottles. If you consume six-packs, save space for crushed cans. If possible, the space for newspapers should be large enough so the papers can lie flat and the space for cans and bottles should allow them to stand up.

When you have a general idea about the things you want to save and the space you'll need for saving them, look around your home for potential storage spots. Don't get stuck on conventional ideas about closets and cupboards. American homes are not built with recycling storage in mind, so you'll probably have to steal whatever space you can. Here are thirteen suggestions:

Under the Sink. This is the classic place for "trash," so you may want to modify it as your recycling storage space. Find two corrugated cartons or build two wooden boxes as deep as the space behind the doors and half as wide. Subdivide one box for cans and bottles and put newspapers in the other. Cut handles into the sides of the boxes or add casters to the bottoms to make them easier to handle. Install shallow shelves along the walls of the space for small jars and cans of hardware.

In a Closet. If you have an underutilized closet, create a recycling workshop in it. Build shallow shelves for crushed cans and bottles on the door or install a prebuilt system like Dor Wall. Inside the closet, install a large shelf, waist high, hang a light over it, and use it as a workbench. Store newspapers in boxes on the floor and small recyclables on U-shaped shelves hung on the closet walls.

In an Old Bureau. If you have one of those squat, three-drawer dressers, turn it into a recycling station by replacing the bottom two drawers with tip-out bins for cans and bottles and a cupboard for newspapers. Install dividers in the space where the drawers were and build the bins from quarter-inch plywood. To curve the sides of the bins, cut out panels as tall and deep as the space. Set the point of a compass on the bottom front corner of a panel and open the compass until the pencil touches the top corner. Move the pencil across the top of the panel to make a curve and cut it out. Hinge the bins' front panels to the front of the dresser and put a door on the cupboard. Refinish to match the dresser.

Under the Stairs. The space under the staircase in most homes is wasted. If you can get to it, build a closet under the stairs and equip it with shelves and bins on casters. If you can't gain access to the space, make small storage areas by removing the top panel of the first several stairs and cutting off strips two inches wide from the

Systems like Dor-Wall were designed to hold full containers, but there's no reason recyclers can't use them for empties.

back. Replace the narrow strip on the stair and hinge the front part to it. Build partitions between the stair areas and use the first one for small objects, the second for crushed cans, the third for bottles, and the fourth for newspapers.

Inside a Kitchen Cabinet. If you have extra space along a kitchen wall, perhaps beside the door, purchase or build a cabinet that matches your others and build removable bins to fit inside it. Make one large bin to fit across the bottom for newspapers and four small bins to fit into the top. Cut a curved notch in the front panel of each bin so you can grab hold of it. One advantage to this system is that you can pull out entire bins and carry them to the recycling center to be dumped.

In a Bookcase. If you have an extra bookcase with deep shelves, it can be converted into a recycling station. Tack strips of two-inch furring to the front of each shelf to keep things from falling off and add partitions if you wish. Then use the bottom shelf for newspapers and magazines, the middle shelf for cans and bottles. Attach a curtain rod to the top of the case and hand a simple gathered curtain made perhaps from an old sheet dyed a bright color.

In Front of the Sofa. If you don't already have a coffee table, make one from four modular units with doors on one side. You can build or buy the units, but be sure they are large enough to accommodate flat newspapers. Paint the cubes, cover them with a collage of photos cut from magazines, arrange them so you have access to all the doors, and set a piece of Lucite or glass on top. This unit is so attractive that no one will suspect you of storing your old bottles, cans, and newspapers in it.

In a Corner. Instead of arranging your four modular units under a coffee table, stack them in an unused corner. This unit would be most convenient in the kitchen, but it could also go in the bedroom, bathroom, or living room if that's where you have the space.

Above the Kitchen Cabinets. Most kitchens have a foot or two of unused space above the cabinets. Storing your recyclables there will not be very convenient, but it can be done. Add a sliding-door track above the cabinet or hang a short café curtain from the ceiling and store your empty cans and bottles behind it. Don't store newspapers or magazines in this space unless you reinforce the cabinets so they will accept the extra weight. And do get yourself a step stool so you can reach your recycling hideaway without much difficulty.

Under the Window. If you aren't using the space under one of your windows, build or buy a window seat with three large drawers. Cover a foam-rubber cushion to make the seat more comfortable and keep your crushed cans, bottles, and papers in the drawers. These storage seats are often handsome enough to be used against walls where there are no windows.

Over the Car. If you are lucky enough to have a garage, build a storage unit in the unused space above the hood of your car. Attach the unit to the studs in the back wall of the garage at least three and a half feet above the floor so the car's nose will fit under it. Build in shelves as you need them and add hinged doors. This unit is especially convenient because when you want to take your collection to the recycling center, you simply back the car up to the unit and load everything into the trunk.

Under the Rafters. If you have a basement, you probably won't have any trouble saving whatever you want. But if you do find yourself pressed for space, build small shelves under the rafters for cans and bottles. Just nail pieces of 1 × 8's directly to the joists.

Anywhere. If you still haven't found a spot for your recycling center, build yourself several plywood cubes, about three feet in every direction, with hinged lids. Put cushions on their tops and casters on their bottoms. Paint the cubes bright colors and fill them with cans, bottles, papers, and anything else. The cubes can double as movable seats.

★ MAKING THE SYSTEM WORK ★

No matter how clever you are in designing your recycling storage area, it will become a nuisance if you don't follow a few rules:

1. Wash out all cans and bottles. The quickest way to become disillusioned with recycling is to find bugs setting up colonies in old soup cans. To prevent that event, rinse, and, if necessary, soak all containers you want to save, especially soda bottles and cans.

2. Make everything as compact as possible. No matter how much storage space you've set aside for recycling, it won't be enough. Use it wisely by crushing cans and smoothing out newspapers so they will stack neatly. Put small bottles inside large ones and stack some bottles upside down in the box so their necks fill the spaces between the other bottles.

3. Make regular trips to your recycling center. Decide on a schedule for taking things to the recycling center—every fourth Saturday is good—and stick to it. If you ac-

cumulate materials for much longer than a month, hauling them to the center will seem like a terrible burden. Making regular trips, on the other hand, will seem no worse than schlepping the garbage can to the curb.

4. Concentrate on what you are able to save. One of the most persistent problems for household recyclers is a feeling of futility. The little box of cans accumulating in the corner of the kitchen seems insignificant compared to the mountains of trash being thrown out every day. Recyclers often get discouraged because although they save cans, bottles, and papers, an awful lot of stuff still goes into the garbage. When those doubts strike, remember that this country has spent years developing an economy in which everyone has to consume as much as possible. Changing that trend is long, slow work and much of it must be done one can, one bottle, and one newspaper at a time.

Your Own RE/USES

If this book has done its job, you will now be seeing RE/USES all around you. Some will become such an automatic part of your daily routine that you'll wonder what you did before you discovered them. Others will be happy inspirations—on the spot solutions for pesky problems with a resource you might once have thrown away.

Since the best RE/USES are highly individual, we've left the next several pages blank so you can jot down RE/USES as you come across them. Try using the pages to:

- Inventory your trash for a week to find out what you actually throw away

- Make a brainstorming list of RE/USES for your most common discards

- Make note of RE/USES you see, read, or hear about

- Sketch plans for some of your more complicated RE/USES

- List things you intend to save for the kitchen, the garden, the workshop, or the kids

★ BETTER IDEA ★ DEPARTMENT

I can hear it now—readers crying out in surprise and disbelief because this book doesn't contain their favorite reuse for bird cages or beer bottles. Well, gentle reader, if you should find your pet project for recycling whatever has been overlooked, let us know about it. Better yet, if this book inspires you to invent a new use for something you used to throw away, tell me. Send ideas that were missed, omitted, or not invented at time of publication to Carolyn Jabs, c/o Crown Publishers, Inc., One Park Avenue, New York, NY 10016.

Name of local recycling center:

_____

Address: _____

_____

Phone number: _____

Collection days: _____

Hours: _____

What do they accept?

____ newspaper ____ other metals

____ glass ____ motor oil

____ aluminum ____ organic materials